SOUNDMAN

A Journey Through Rock 'n' Roll Sound

Happy Birthday
Wilkie

John Wilford.

SOUNDMAN

A Journey Through Rock 'n' Roll Sound

John 'Wilf' Wilford

The Book Guild Ltd

First published in Great Britain in 2018 by
The Book Guild Ltd
9 Priory Business Park
Wistow Road, Kibworth
Leicestershire, LE8 0RX
Freephone: 0800 999 2982
www.bookguild.co.uk
Email: info@bookguild.co.uk
Twitter: @bookguild

Typeset in Adobe Garamond Pro

Printed and bound in Great Britain by CPI Group (UK) Ltd, Croydon, CR0 4YY

ISBN 978 1912362 691

British Library Cataloguing in Publication Data.
A catalogue record for this book is available from the British Library.

MIX
Paper from
responsible sources
FSC® C013604

To the Band members, Road crews, Stage crews, Managers, Promoters, Organisations and Staff who helped along the way.

ACKNOWLEDGEMENTS

MUSICIANS AND BANDS

AC/DC, Al DeMiola, Alan Price, Barry White, Billy Bragg, Billy Connelly, Black Sabbath, Canned Heat, Chas & Dave, Chris de Burgh, Chris Rea, Cockney Rebel, Commodores, Cozy Powell, Damned, David Gates & Bread, David Sanborn, Def Leppard, Del Amitre, Dennis Brown, Denny Laine, Desmond Decker, Dexy's Midnight Runners, Dr Hook, Elkie Brooks, Eric Clapton, Faith No More, Gary Moore, George Harrison, Graham Bond, Graham Parker & the Rumour, Hank Wangford, Huey Lewis, Ike & Tina Turner, Joan Baez, Joan Jett, Joe Cocker, John Denver, John Martyn, John McLaughlin, Johnny Cash, Journey, Kris Kristofferson, Labi Siffre, Level 42, Lindisfarne, Love Unlimited Orchestra, Mahavishnu Orchestra, Mary Hopkins, Mary J Blige, Meat Loaf, Michael Ball, Michael Crawford, Mud, Nashville Teens, Paco DeLucia, Pat Metheny, Pat Travers Band, Paul Young, Pearl Jam, Ralph McTell, Ravi Shankar, Ramones, Ray Charles, Renaissance, Robert Palmer, Rose Royce, Roy Harper, Runaways, Shirley Bassey, Soft Machine, Spandau Ballet, Spirit, Status Quo, Steeleye Span, Steve Hackett, Steve Marriott, Stiff Little Fingers, Style Council, Thin Lizzy, Three Degrees, Tina Turner, Tom Jones, Tom Robinson Band, Tony Joe White, UFO, Van Halen, Van Morrison, Vinegar Joe, Waylon Jennings, Wham, Willy Nelson, ZZ Top.

BUSINESSES AND ORGANISATIONS

Adrian Hopkins, Asktam, Atkinson Sanders Trucking, Barry Clayman Concerts, Barry McKay, BBC, Britannia Row, Clair Brothers, Colosseum Acoustics, Concert Sound, Edwin Shirley Trucking, Electrosound, Entec, HiWatt Amplification, Kennedy Street Enterprise, Limey Sound Inc, Limit Audio, Marshall Arts, Marshall Amplification, Martin Audio, Maurice Plaquet Hire, Midas Audio, Nitelites Sound & Light, Olympic Studios, Radio Geronimo, Stage Audio Services, Showlites, SSE, Showco, Tasco, TFA Sound, TransAm Trucking, Tubosound, Tyne Tees Television, WEM Audio, Zenith Lighting.

INTRODUCTION

For many years my friends have been telling me I should write a book about my life on the road, I wasn't sure about doing it because I've never worked with The Beatles, The Rolling Stones or Pink Floyd, so why me? My friends told me that not many people had been there right from the start during the 1960s, or worked with so many different types of bands and artistes from different genres. I said "OK, I will start to write and see what comes out," what I found was that memories came flooding back and this book is the result.

This book is an autobiography of my life on the road and with the bands, musicians and celebrities, the road crews, stage crews and people I've met along the way and the liggers I wish I hadn't. It traces my 30 plus years working as a roadie, a sound engineer, tour manager and production manager. It tells what happens on stage, off stage, backstage, and what happens on those live television shows and in the recording studios, at sound checks and rehearsals, on the tour bus and in the hotels.

The events and problems that happen on tours, the good, bad and the disastrous. Events like me perforating Ozzy Osbourne's eardrum, watching a lighting truss crash onto the stage just before a show, being stopped at gunpoint by German police, wrecking a tour truck, having a festival blown out by a cyclone and flying in your own private jet. Did you ever wonder where the real Spinal Tap stories came from? I've been there and seen it all in real life.

From The Marquee Club to Wembley Stadium, from The Newport Jazz Festival to The Hollywood Bowl, the pubs, clubs, ballrooms, theatres, concert halls, arenas, festivals and stadiums, they are all here. What it's like to work for a band versus working for a sound rental company, working in a television studio versus owning my own sound company.

This is also the history and evolution of the Rock'n'Roll sound system as it came to be used in the entertainment industry and by many performers around the world. How the sound system started out as a public address system for a vocalist, evolving into a sound reinforcement system for the band to what is now a totally sophisticated digital sound mix.

It's about the technology and how it has changed over the years, where it started and where it's going, from microphones to loudspeakers, from mixers to digital processors, and the special effects that are used. The mistakes sound engineers make and what we had to put up with in the early years.

No matter what you're listening to, whether it's a folk singer in a pub, a disco in a nightclub, an arena rock concert, an orchestra or just your own personal hi-fi at home, the sound system is an important part in the overall experience. A bad sound system can ruin your entertainment and a good one can make your entertainment experience great and you probably won't even notice the sound.

The 'Sex, Drugs and Rock'n'Roll', I know it went on and I was exposed to a lot of it but this book is not about that, there are plenty of books telling the stories of life in the music business, just read any autobiography of a rock or pop star.

I've called this book *Soundman* because that is what people called me, I've been given a number of different titles over the years including sound engineer, audio engineer, sound mixer, sound tech, and I've even been called the noise boys. Some professions associate the inclusion of the word 'engineer' with a university degree or college diploma, no such qualifications existed in 1965 and the only sound engineers as such that existed in those days worked in radio, television or recording studios, wore white coats and were mostly self-taught on the job or by their colleagues. Live sound engineers for pop groups didn't even exist when I started out because there was no actual sound 'engineering' to do as such, so I've just gone by the name I was usually called and that is simply 'Soundman'.

I make no apologies for what seems like name dropping, but I did work with a lot of people and they are all part of my story, there may be people reading this book that didn't realise that a musician who is in band B, once played with band A and then later went on to play with band C.

I have oversimplified some of the technical terms for those not familiar with the music or sound business. I apologise to any soundmen or musicians who may feel that the technical explanations are oversimplified or stating the obvious.

All the information contained in this book is from memory, my gig diary, tour itineraries or notes. I've changed some of the names to protect the innocent and sometimes the guilty but everything in this book is true. It's not a complete history of the music business but it's my history and what happened to me on my journey.

So climb about the tour bus and click on your seat belt. It's going to be a bumpy ride.

No matter what nationality you are or what your religion is, your culture, your politics or the language you speak.
Whatever conflicts divide us, the one thing that unites people around the world is music.
Despite our differences, listening to live music is the only time people unite and agree to enjoy something together.

John Wilford.

CONTENTS

1

MEET THE TEAM

Listed below are the people you might expect to meet on a music tour, no two tours are ever the same, so this is a guide only but fairly typical.

ACCOUNTANT collects the ticket money and pays all the bills on tour including trashed hotel rooms.

BACKLINE CREW is anyone who looks after the backline, consisting of guitar amplifiers, drums, keyboards etc.

BUS DRIVER drives the band or crew to each venue.

CATERERS cook the crew's breakfast, lunch, and evening meal, organises food and drink for the dressing rooms.

DRUM TECHNICIAN looks after the drums and percussion.

ELECTRICIAN will wire in the power and takes care of electrics.

FOLLOW SPOT OPERATOR operates the follow spots.

GOFER will 'Gofer this' or 'Gofer that' at the request of the stage crew, road crew, band or promoter. May be part of the stage crew.

GUITAR TECHNICIAN looks after the guitars, changes strings, tunes and ensures the artiste has the correct guitar for each song.

KEYBOARD TECHNICIAN looks after the keyboards, may also be a computer programmer or software engineer.

LIGHTING TECHNICIAN (or LAMPIE) assists the lighting designer in building the lighting rig, will set up and wire the lights.

LIGHTING DESIGNER (LD) is in charge of the overall lighting, from design to the position and colour of lamps.

MAKE-UP & HAIRSTYLISTS takes care of make-up and / or hair.

MANAGER is there to manage the artiste and take care of business affairs and make loads of money for their client and for themselves.

MERCHANDISING sells the band's merchandise, i.e. T-shirts, sweaters, programmes, CDs and anything else they think they can sell to make money.

MONITOR ENGINEER does the on-stage monitor mix, so those on stage can hear what they are playing and singing through their monitor speakers or in-ear plugs.

PRODUCTION MANAGER is in charge of the whole production. Organises the sound, lights, trucks, buses, road crew, stage crew and security.

PROMOTER does everything to promote the show, books the artiste, the venue, and sells the tickets.

PROMOTER'S REP represents the promoter on tour. Travels with the band and looks after the band on behalf of the promoter.

PYRO TECHNICIAN is responsible for all the pyrotechnics, fireworks and special effects that are let off.

RIGGER will rig the flying positions for the sound and lighting rigs. They hang from the roof to fix the points just where you want them.

ROADIE generally means someone who sets up and maintains backline equipment, (i.e. guitars, drums, keyboards etc.)

ROAD CREW refers to anyone on the crew who is actually on the road with the artiste.

ROAD MANAGER stands in for the business manager and takes care of business 'on the road'.

RUNNER is sent out to pick up supplies or run an errand to the shops.

SOUND ENGINEER or SOUNDMAN will mix the sound for a live show.

SOUND TECHNICIAN assists the sound engineer and systems engineer in rigging the sound system.

STAGE CREW are local crew members supplied by the local venue or promoter to help the road crew, unloading and reloading the trucks.

STAGE MANAGER is responsible for what happens on stage, organises what goes where.

SYSTEMS ENGINEER is responsible for the entire sound system and assists the sound engineer.

TOUR MANAGER organises the daily routine for the band and crew, takes care of hotels and travel arrangements.

TRUCK DRIVER hauls the equipment from one venue to the next and is responsible for the safe loading and stacking of the equipment inside the truck or trailer.

WARDROBE takes care of the artiste's on-stage costumes, washes and irons or dry cleans the clothes ready for the show.

2

THE WAY IT WAS

A soundman died and was met at the gates of heaven by an angel.
He was told "The good news is you get to do the sound with the very best equipment. You'll get to work in a room with perfect acoustics, with the best musicians that have ever passed through these gates and no one will ever ask you to turn the volume down.
The bad news is St. Peter has a girlfriend and she thinks she can sing."

A lot has happened in the last 50 years since the Beatles played at Shea Stadium in 1965. The band couldn't hear themselves on stage and the 55,000 screaming girls in the audience couldn't hear the band either. The Shea Stadium show was considered to be the first major stadium pop concert at the time and the sound system provided was woefully inadequate. There were no such stadium concerts ever held in Britain at that time, not even for the Beatles, the closest I recall was a New Musical Express poll winner's pop concert the same year at Wembley Empire Pool, (now known as Wembley Arena), featuring The Beatles, The Rolling Stones, The Animals, The Kinks and others. It was a venue where promoters actually expected the bands to use the house Tannoy PA system, which was only designed for vocal announcements and was the same sound system used for sporting events such as the Horse of the Year Show. It just shows that the promoters back then had no real concept of sound quality. The only microphones used were for vocals and very few were used for instruments. In big halls the band just turned up their amps and played louder.

The first outdoor festival that I went to took place in a field at Woburn Abbey, on 26th to 28th August 1967. Apart from the Reading Jazz Festival which had been running for 7 years Woburn was regarded at the time as the first ever rock festival in the UK. It featured The Small Faces, The Move, Eric Burdon and the Animals, Jeff Beck Group, Marmalade, The Alan Price Set, and a few others.

I remember Jeff Dexter was the DJ there although I admit to only staying for the Saturday night when The Small Faces headlined. What I remember about that weekend was that the sound system was very basic but it didn't sound too bad for its time and The Small Faces even used a Phaser in their show, this was a sound effect featured on the Itchycoo Park record.

The first concert held at a major outdoor stadium in Britain was for Status Quo, The Nice and Yes at Wembley Stadium in 1969, probably the only stadium capable of putting on a live music event. From that point audio technology improved at a snail's pace until the 1980s when monster PA systems were built that became so big they cut off huge swathes of the seating and prevented seats on the sides being sold because of poor sight lines, but at least you could hear.

Today's music concerts are a lot more advanced using digital technology, total instrument mixes, sampled sounds and improved speaker technology, with pencil-thin line array speakers hanging from the sky. High-tech audio equipment means the audience hears a show that sounds more like the original record or CD. Today's line array speakers flown above the crowd create a visually clean stage and unrestricted views from all angles. The promoters are happy as they can sell more seats, the audience can see more of the stage and they enable the artistes to see more of the audience.

Today's digital mixers are more compact than the old analogue mixers as all the channels are controlled by one single set of controls, which are switched to the channel you are selecting. But as I'm what they call 'old school' or 'old-fashioned' I prefer an analogue mixer over a digital mixer any day.

Although digital mixers are constantly improving I don't feel they have that natural sound, just like those who prefer vinyl to CDs or Betamax to VHS and guitarists who prefer valve amps to transistor amps, it's what you prefer and what you instinctively feel is superior. Having high-tech equipment doesn't necessarily mean you get a better sound or that you need less crew. For the Rolling Stones 2016 tour the sound company used a staggering 24 sound crew.

Not only has concert sound technology improved but so has domestic hi-fi. How we got from valve radios to mp3 players in just 50 years is remarkable. Every generation has its own format of music. My parents listened to 10 inch shellac records playing at 78 rpm known as seventy-eights, on a wind-up gramophone with a horn on top just like the HMV (His Master's Voice) dog picture. The problem with shellac records is that they only played for 3½ minutes, they would break if you dropped one and they didn't have very good quality sound, with hardly any bass at all. These 78s died out in the mid-1950s when vinyl came along and my parents exchanged their wind-up gramophone for a Dansette record player. Dansette record players with a built-in speaker were the latest gadget to have, even though they were the size of a small suitcase they were portable and you could stack ten records one on top of the other to play in sequence which was part of the novelty.

When the 12" vinyl record was introduced, it played at 33 rpm and had a playing time of 50 minutes. Although they didn't break when dropped they could still get scratched. Later the 7" single, which played at the faster 45 rpm arrived, so-called because it just had a single track on each side and could play for up to 5 minutes. Singles were more popular with the younger generation as they could buy the latest pop song relatively cheaply, the shorter the track the more likely it would get played on national radio. Some songs were only two minutes long. Bob Dylan was the first to release a 6-minute single 'Like a Rolling Stone'. The first British band to exceed the normal 3-minute rule with a 4-minute single were the Animals with 'House of The Rising Sun'. Record companies thought that radio stations wouldn't play a record if it was more than 3 minutes long but they misjudged the market and they both became huge hits.

The Wurlitzer jukebox was an amazing machine, found in coffee bars and pubs, just watching it work was fascinating. After putting your coin in, you saw it select the record at the touch of a button and mechanically placing the disc on the turntable, then after playing the track, it replaced the disc back in the rack. It also had a half decent sound to it which you didn't have at home with your Dansette record player. For 6d (2.5p) a play or 3 for a shilling (5p) you could listen to your favourite tracks in what we considered a decent sound quality. Rockola and Wurlitzer made the jukeboxes and they came in bright colours with flashing lights which made them all the more attractive to look at.

When the transistor radio was invented in the mid 1950s it changed everything. The transistor radio was as groundbreaking to our generation as the iPod is to the current generation which meant you could listen to music on the go.

The only way to copy music in those days was with a reel-to-reel tape recorder using a ¼ inch tape and placing a microphone in front of the loud speaker on your radio or record player. I started experimenting with connecting wires direct to the back of the speaker and bypassing the microphone. It worked quite well and by adjusting the volume controls I managed to record music from the radio or record player without distortion or background noise.

In 1962 new magnetic tapes came along in the form of a cassette released by Philips, allowing you to record your own tapes at home by plugging into phono sockets. I would select tracks from different albums or singles, which I did all the time, even making up music cassettes as presents for my girlfriends.

In 1980 the Sony Walkman changed everything again and was the most iconic product of the 1980s. For the first time you could carry your music around with you on a bus or train and listen to your favourite tracks via headphones.

In 1982 the 4.7 inch compact disk (CD) came along using a laser beam instead of a stylus and very quickly made the vinyl record redundant. With its cleaner sound it could play 80 minutes of audio and it quickly took over. When shops stopped selling vinyl, that spelt the death of the vinyl record except for die-hard collectors. The CD was launched as a revolutionary new invention that was supposed to be indestructible. It was claimed you could cover them in jam, even scratch them and they would play forever, however we know that is far from the truth. If you're lucky the CD won't stick in a loop or go silent halfway through a track, even the laser will wear out eventually just like a record stylus but they didn't tell you that at the time.

The main advantage for the CD over vinyl and tape was you didn't get the pop and crackle like you did from vinyl records or the background noise and hiss from the magnetic tapes. CDs very soon made vinyl obsolete for most people, some even re-bought or replaced their entire vinyl record collection with a CD collection, great for the record companies as they managed to sell the same product with no recording costs making themselves a massive profit. Rereleased old albums were allegedly remastered but in effect they were just the original analogue recordings transferred to digital format, a real con. So-called remastering is nothing more than transferring the original analogue recording into a digital format, at a fraction of the price. There's no guarantee that a remastered CD was even remixed from the original recording. The problem came when the record companies got greedy and released compilation albums and new albums with only one or two decent tracks on them. I stopped buying albums as they rarely had more than one or two tracks out of 20 worth listening to. I got fed up paying £12 for one track. CDs were then used to store digital information in the form of compressed audio (mp3) so you could store around 1000 tracks on one CD.

Quite often record companies were not promoting their artistes' albums, they were not putting them into record shops and sometimes not even pressing enough copies. They claimed the record wasn't selling because it wasn't good enough. No, stupid, of course it's not selling, the people don't realise it has been released, if they did they can't buy a copy because you haven't supplied the record shops with the records and even if the shops ask for them you can't deliver the records because you haven't pressed enough copies. So why are they surprised that the record isn't in the charts? Sometimes I think record companies are run by idiots.

The Walkman made music portable but the iPod made it possible to carry your whole collection. When mp3 was invented the thought of carrying 10,000 songs around in your pocket was a total game changer. Then came the online music stores, iTunes, Napster and others offering a single track for less than £1.00 that you could download onto your mp3 player or mobile phone, without having to buy the whole album.

Streaming was the next thing to catch on, with people just listening to an unlimited selection of songs through the internet, but you never actually own the songs, no more than listening to a radio station. I dare say a new format will probably be around the corner in a few years making CDs and mp3 old technology. Where the technology goes from here is anyone's guess. My guess is studio quality tracks that sound like you're actually in the recording studio, it has to come.

The music business has changed over the years. In the early sixties the business was dominated by a few big record companies, then independent record labels began to emerge throughout the seventies to challenge the big labels both in the music that was recorded and the way it was being recorded.

By the time we get to the nineties, the independents have been bought up, swallowed up or taken over by the original big record companies, again going full circle. The business has changed in another way; in the sixties singles were the big sellers with albums only being made by successful singles artistes, then albums took over and singles were released to promote the album. Record companies would also help finance tours to promote the album. Philips bankrolled the entire Dire Straits world tour just to promote the new CD format and their new CD player. It worked. Dire Straits *Brothers in Arms* CD did more to sell CD players than any other event, each member of the Dire Straits crew got a free portable CD player. It took a few years before CDs overtook vinyl but eventually they did. CDs were then overtaken by mp3 downloads but with a loss of quality.

Bands weren't getting the advance payments they used to or the royalties and had to rely on concerts to supplement their income. Record companies realising this are now taking a slice of live shows as well.

In the early days of live albums the record companies would mix out any mistakes, choose the best tracks from each evening and clean up the vocals and guitar tracks in a studio. Also a common practice was to add some audience noise to the recording, not necessarily from the same show, some were adding pre-recorded applause and crowd noise between tracks to add atmosphere. One of the most popular live audiences used on live albums was of a Motorhead audience, which has been used on a few live albums because it was felt it had the best crowd atmosphere. I don't know where this will lead but I'm sure the industry will survive in one form or another and another generation will make it evolve into something else.

Most kids of today who grow up listening to mp3s on their tinny headphones haven't experienced the sound of vinyl coming from a pair of Tannoy studio speakers driven by a valve amplifier or listened to a studio track on a reel-to-reel tape machine spinning 15 inches a second. I wish everyone could hear music as it should be heard.

ALL ABOARD THE GRAVY TRAIN.

A track from Pink Floyd's 1975 album *Wish You Were Here*, 'Have a Cigar', is about the band having a go at record company executives who have no consideration for the music. To them the band is just a 'product' to sell and make money. To them selling music is no different to selling washing powder, they thought Pink was the name of a band member.

Going on tour with a big rock band, you realise what excesses, corruption and fiddling goes on. Tour managers and road crews are wasting money like there's no end to it. Hauling a 'spare' truck and trailer around just in case one breaks down might seem like a precaution but is an expensive insurance premium to pay. Building flight cases with the drum kit already assembled so the drum tech doesn't have to screw them together each day is taking the mick and means you're going to need more truck space or more trucks. That's just plain lazy and wastes money.

But you don't need to work for Pink Floyd or Led Zeppelin to ride the gravy train. Managers have been ripping off artistes since the beginning of time. Bands were ripped off by everyone; managers, agents, publishers, producers, record companies, promoters, and of course lawyers. Most bands earnt a lot of money but ended up making money for everyone except themselves. The manager is only as good as the artiste they are managing, full stop. If the band succeeds, the band takes the credit, if the band fails, it's the manager's fault. It's always the manager's fault, but at the end of the day just like a football team, a manager is only as good as the team he is managing.

In the early days, a band's manager would sign up a band and put them on a weekly wage with the manager making all the money without the band having any idea how much they were earning. The bands who were just young kids straight out of school or college were so glad to be 'in a band' and doing what they always wanted to do, playing music and making records, they were grateful they actually had a recording contract, something every band strives for in their early days of stardom.

Some managers, but not all, were crooks. The best known managers were Larry Palms, Andrew Loog Oldham, Brian Epstein and Robert Stigwood, Peter Grant and allegedly the most ruthless gangster of them all, Don Arden. There are good managers and there are not-so-good managers. I wouldn't tar all managers with the same brush, but let's just say some have a 'reputation', some like to live up to their reputation and some are just good managers.

When I toured as a road manager and collected the band's fee at the end of the night, some venue managers would tell me about the bands that Don Arden owned. Don Arden is one whose reputation travels ahead of him. Arden would walk into the box office, sit down and place a loaded revolver on the table whilst he counted the ticket money from the box office. He claimed it was for protection against being robbed, but others claim it was to intimidate the venue manager into not short changing him out of the ticket money. Don Arden had a reputation for being a bit of a gangster, everyone knew it and he wanted everyone to know it.

My friend the Nashville Teens piano player John Hawken told me, after the band had split up he went to Don Arden's office in Carnaby Street to ask where all the band's money had disappeared to. Don Arden swiftly grabbed hold of John by the throat and attempted to push him over the railings of his first floor balcony. The Small Faces who had a number of chart hits had to ask Arden if they could 'borrow' some cash to buy their families Christmas presents. When you're on the road and everything is supplied for you, food, drink and accommodation, you don't have much need to spend cash, you're told.

Young bands who spent their days having a good time, enjoying the limelight, making the most of being stars could be forgiven for thinking that they were earning big money with their hit records, appearances on television and performing lots of shows. At the end of their high life when the band eventually had their day, they would ask how much money they had only to be told they didn't have any money which would of course surprise the innocent beginners.

But the answer they got was always the same. "Who do think has been paying for all the five star hotels you've been staying in? Who has been paying for the after-show parties, the limousines, the backstage champagne and food? Not the record company, not the manager, you of course. Remember that record advance you had before you started recording in the studio? Well that comes out of your royalties and has to be paid back, if you don't sell any records, it still has to be paid back."

Managers will negotiate a deal with a record company with an advance which is repaid out of record sales. If the record doesn't sell, the money has to be repaid, something bands forget when they splash out on flash cars and 5-bedroom mansions. These facts come as a shock to the new fledglings who think that life is a ball and the life they have been living is being paid for by someone else. When bands say that the record company picked up the bill for the hotel they wrecked, it comes out of their royalties. What they also don't tell you is that the money you're spending is against future earnings. The money you're spending on tour for restaurants, bar bills, drugs and frivolous spending is against future earnings and is an 'advance', it's not actually your money you're spending.

The managers percentage would vary between 15% to 50% and that would be straight off the top of everything they earn before any expenses were paid. Once everything was paid, the band would get the balance. The manager usually charges the band his expenses as well, that's after he takes his cut, not before. It's a double whammy. If anything is left, you pay income tax on that. It would also be common for managers to want a slice of the action for the expenses they pay out. The manager may have a stake in the sound and lighting company they hire or take a cut from the limo driver for putting work his way and then there's the catering businesses who supply all the food and drink for the backstage dressing rooms and after show parties.

Hotels give nice discounts too for booking lots of rooms. Some tours will book maybe twenty rooms or more and who collects the bonus points and free rooms on return visits? The manager or road manager of course. He will collect bonus points and use them the next time he takes his family on holiday, and collects the air miles on the flights he books. Can't say I blame him though for grabbing what is a freebie but it's at the artiste's expense.

When the manager strikes a deal with the record company it's for his benefit, not the artiste. The manager will make sure he has a percentage of the royalties on record sales and on music publishing rights. Those usually last for life so even if you change managers, change record companies or move to a different band the songs you wrote don't actually belong to you.

Many songwriters have been shocked and outraged to find that the songs they had written don't even belong to them. Somewhere along the way, in the small print, they signed away the rights to someone else. One young inexperienced band I knew was told they would be getting 75% of everything they earned on record royalties. That sounds good except the contract they signed said 0.75%, not 75%, that's just three quarters of one percent, quite a difference. Col Tom Parker, manager of Elvis Presley, took 50% of everything Elvis made, so did Ron Haffkine, manager of Dr Hook.

The only way to make money in the music business is to write your own songs, retain ownership of those songs and don't sign any publishing deals. This gives you credit on the record and royalties for publishing, airplays, cover versions and record sales. On record sales most of the money first goes to the record label, then the manager, then the agency, the artiste comes last and gets whatever is left. They then pay tax on that.

Years ago an artiste would tour to promote their latest album, but things have turned around and the artiste now has to tour to supplement their income by selling tickets and merchandise, (more on merchandise later). The manager also made money from promoters. In the early days it was normal for bands to ask for 70% or 80% of the tickets sold at the gate but Led Zeppelin's manager Peter Grant asked for and got 90% because he knew he could demand that fee and the promoter had to accept it or lose the show to another promoter. Something that set a precedent.

Some musicians would call up their manager and say, "I've bought a car can you pay for it?" or "I want to buy this house, can I afford it?" It has been known that managers would buy these items and put it them their own names so the artiste doesn't even own the house they are living in. Not mentioning any names but it makes you wonder how low they will go to rip off their artistes.

Then one day I discovered live bands playing in a nearby pub and my life changed.

3

IN THE BEGINNING

In 1961 at the age of thirteen I was taking the backs off radios and televisions just to see how they worked and see what they looked like inside. All those wires, odd looking components and glowing valves fascinated me. Valves were hot and attracted a lot of dust, not like todays printed circuit boards (PCBs) and integrated circuits (ICs). One day when my dad's radio stopped working, I took the back off and poked and prodded around hoping to find a 'loose wire' and fix it. I found the waveband switch was full of fluff and dirt and just needed cleaning, so with the help of some white spirit I cleaned the contacts and the radio was working again. That was the moment I picked up the bug; the bug to explore, tinker about and fiddle with electrical devices and try to fix them. Some of it was rewarding and some of it became a learning experience. Sometimes I learnt the hard way by making mistakes but I had discovered the world of electronics and I was hooked.

My interest in music was like most children at that time, we listened to our parent's music, which for me wasn't very inspirational. They listened to musicals like *The Sound of Music*, *The King and I*, and *South Pacific*. I was more interested in listening to Eddie Cochran, Gene Vincent, Chuck Berry and those rockers of the day.

My access to music was by listening to the radio. This generation of course takes online radio, digital and FM radio for granted, but it wasn't always like that. In 1961 radios were still mono and broadcast only on medium wave

(MW), stereo records had only just been issued but you could only benefit from the stereo experience if you had a stereo record player and my parents didn't have one. Radiograms were normally huge pieces of furniture and were often the size of a small coffin. Typically inside would be a turntable that played records at 78rpm, later models had the 33rpm and 45rpm turntable speeds which played the newer vinyl records. Radiograms also had a mono valve radio and a single mono speaker. The only radio stations that transmitted from the UK were three BBC stations.

The only pop music we heard on the radio was either on the BBC Light Programme, 'Saturday Club' for a couple of hours on a Saturday morning, which had live performances by all the latest pop groups. Bands were queuing up to perform on the programme, even The Beatles did some live shows and 'The Chart Show' on a Sunday afternoon where we eagerly waited to see who had made it to the No 1 spot.

There was also Radio Luxembourg on 208 metres medium wave. The quality on Radio Luxembourg was terrible. As the name implies, it was transmitted from Luxembourg in Europe and broadcast in mono. It started at 6pm so that when it got dark the signal disappeared or phased in and out with the weather and atmospherics, but it was all we had and we got used to it; we knew no different. Many a night I would sit in the car with my girlfriend listening to the latest pop songs from Luxembourg by the light of the radio dial.

On television in the 1960s there were shows like *6.5 Special*, *Oh Boy* and *Juke Box Jury* featuring new artistes like Cliff Richard, Marty Wilde, Billy Fury, Tommy Steele etc. We'd watch them on a 12-inch screen in black and white with a grainy picture and poor quality sound, and there was only one channel.

The 1950s introduced us to American Rock'n'Roll, by the early 1960s it all changed, London became the music and fashion capital of the world in what was called 'The Swinging Sixties' and life was never the same again. It became a more liberal society with abortion and divorce made easier, women's liberation, an end to capital punishment and homosexual acts decriminalised.

Then one day came a cultural earthquake, something that had never happened before or has ever happened since and the effect of it would change the world forever, both musically and culturally. That was the day in 1963 I heard 'Please Please Me' on the radio by The Beatles. Then a few weeks later 'From Me to You' hit the charts followed by 'She Loves You' and 'I Want To Hold Your

Hand'. The effect was phenomenal and you had to be there to experience and appreciate it. Four No 1's in one year and it was the only time an artiste had three songs at numbers one, two and three in the singles charts all at the same time and a number one in the album charts. The album *Please Please Me* stayed in the charts for 30 weeks.

The Beatles' music was influenced by American rock and soul music and there were of course copycat bands who came out of Liverpool jumping on the Merseybeat bandwagon. Around 300 bands were estimated to be working out of Liverpool. The best known were Gerry and the Pacemakers, The Merseybeats, Billy J Kramer and The Dakotas, The Searchers, The Fourmost, Swinging Blue Jeans, Billy Fury and Cilla Black.

As well as the Merseybeat sound from Liverpool other areas of Britain were producing bands; from Birmingham The Spencer Davis Group, The Move and The Moody Blues. From Manchester Herman's Hermits, The Hollies, Wayne Fontana and The Mindbenders and Freddie and The Dreamers. Newcastle had The Animals and from London we had bands influenced by rhythm and blues like Alexis Korner, The Steam Packet, The Rolling Stones, The Who, The Yardbirds, The Pretty Things, The Kinks, The Dave Clark Five and others.

In 1963 I left school at the age of fourteen and got a job at a company which built emergency lighting systems where I learnt to wire up electrical circuits and understand circuit diagrams. A year later I decided to leave when I was offered a job as an apprentice service engineer in a radio and television shop at Cambridge Corner Electrical, an old-fashioned electrical shop where I started off learning how to repair domestic appliances like vacuum cleaners, irons, kettles, toasters etc. In those days people actually had these items repaired, now you just bin them and buy another as new products are so cheap and labour so expensive. It's not worth getting them repaired even if you could find someone to do it. At sixteen I went to Southgate Technical College one day a week on a City and Guilds course to learn Radio and Television servicing and Electronics. At work I moved on to repairing record players, tape recorders, radios and televisions. Then in 1965 on my seventeenth birthday I started driving lessons and soon passed my driving test. The first day I got my licence I was immediately given the firm's van to go out and repair televisions in people's homes. I loved it, driving around with a box of valves and spare parts in the back of the van. Some customers would ask for "that nice young man with the long hair." Unfortunately I also had some complaints from some grumpy old customers about my long hair saying that "it was not suitable for a TV repair man." I was, after all, a fan of The Beatles, Rolling Stones and Yardbirds and that was the fashion then. Most of my friends at college had long hair so I couldn't see what the problem was.

The BBC was run by stiff shirts and men in suits who played mostly middle-of-the-road orchestral tunes and big band jazz. The highlight of the week was 'Saturday Club' and 'The Chart Show'. This was before the days of 24-hour pop music radio stations and all-day TV music channels.

Then in 1964 came the pirates. Radio Caroline, Radio North Sea and Radio London. They set up pirate radio stations in ships in the North Sea just outside British territorial waters and beamed non-stop pop music to England, sometimes broadcasting 24 hours a day. The most popular was Radio Caroline which transmitted from 1964 to 1968. I also listened to Radio London which broadcast from 1964 to 1967. A lot of bands then and some still around today owe their success to the pirates and the DJs who promoted their new kind of music.

The BBC, who had a monopoly over the three radio stations broadcasting in the UK, didn't like the pirate ships and tried to get the government to close them down; the BBC's campaign did nothing to dent the success of the pirates which, by 1966, had audiences in excess of 20 million listeners. The campaign to close down the ships ended in 1967 with the introduction of the Marine Broadcasting Offences Act, passed by the Labour government of Harold Wilson which made it illegal to work for, advertise on or supply any goods to pirate stations. Despite a fight, the pirate radio stations eventually had to close, but as a concession to the public the BBC reorganised their own three channels, The Light Programme, The Home Service and The Third Programme and added a fourth station, changing to the new format of Radio One, Two, Three and Four. Most of the DJs from the pirate stations were employed by the BBC on Radio One to carry on the music in a legal framework, playing pop music for a youth audience. Although better than the old BBC stations it didn't have the style or character of the pirates.

In 1973, the first commercial radio station, Capital Radio, started broadcasting from London, but the BBC, still wishing to hold on to their monopoly, tried to prevent commercial radio stations from happening at all.

In January 1965 I went with my school friend Steve to see The Beatles at the Hammersmith Odeon, an old cinema with a big stage converted for live shows which years later would be rebranded Hammersmith Apollo, a venue where later in life I'd spend many nights working with various bands.

As we approached the venue, the place was surrounded by a ring of police with police vans parked in nearby streets. Hundreds of people my own age were queuing up for the second show as we waited for the audience from the first show to leave. As we entered the foyer it was like a casualty clearing station with St John's Ambulance and Red Cross nurses attending to young girls clearly in a state of distress. I wondered what the hell had gone on during the first show at 6.15. My friend and I were waiting for the second show at 8.45 and we took our seats in the balcony.

Also on the bill that night was Elkie Brookes who I later got to know very well whilst doing the sound for her band. She also came to my wedding. Also the Yardbirds with Eric Clapton on guitar, three of whose members I also got to work with in different bands and an awful joke band called Freddie and The Dreamers who I'm glad to say I never got to work with.

This wasn't a concert, it was an event. When The Beatles came on it was total hysteria, girls screaming and jumping up and down on all sides, girls fainting in the front rows and when the band played 'She Loves You', the screams went into overdrive. There was no let-up, it was continuous all through the show.

What I did notice that night was that the sound was terrible, even though the room had good acoustics. It was the first time I'd been to a pop concert in a theatre and I couldn't hear a thing. Not only were the tiny speakers insufficient for the large venue but we were surrounded by hundreds of screaming girls who were drowning out the PA.

I enjoyed the show of course, it was a great experience seeing The Beatles live on stage but it got me thinking about the sound, why was it so bad for such an important artiste? I wondered what could be done about it. Maybe at fourteen I should have been thinking about other things but little did I know that a few years later I would be back in that same venue running a monstrous 10,000 watt sound system that was so loud you wouldn't even hear the girl next to you screaming.

My first personal experience of pop mania apart from The Beatles concert came when The Small Faces were asked to open the record shop next door to our TV shop where I worked. The owner of the TV shop took over the old shoe shop next door when the owner retired and converted it into a record shop. I'd been out repairing TVs and returned to the shop after my day's jobs to find dozens of young girls outside the record shop. I parked the van outside the TV shop as I usually did, my mistake. The girls thought The Small Faces were in the back of the van. I got out only to be mobbed by dozens of screaming girls. It was a frightening experience and I made a quick dash for the TV shop and just made it to safety inside. Still convinced the group were inside the van they started to bang on the side and rock the van from side to side. They didn't have to wait long though as the group showed up ten minutes later in a limousine and signed autographs before cutting the ribbon to the record shop entrance.

One of the people I worked with in the TV repair shop was Jim. He was about 25 and drove a Mini Cooper. He introduced me to blues music and lent me some of his single 45s. The first were by Howlin' Wolf, Muddy Waters, John Lee Hooker, Memphis Slim, Bo Diddley and Leadbelly. It really changed my musical interest. At about the same time he told me of a club he went to every Monday night, called The Blue Opera Club based at the legendary Cooks Ferry Inn in Edmonton, North London. That year my world changed.

I'd go down there on a Monday night and see all the upcoming blues and R&B bands. John Mayall's Bluesbreakers were regulars there which included Eric Clapton on guitar and later Peter Green and Mick Taylor. Also The Graham Bond Organisation, they had Jack Bruce and Ginger Baker in the band who later formed Cream, there was also Zoot Money, The Who, The Animals, Soft Machine, Alexis Korner, Spencer Davis, The Byrds (which featured Kim Gardner of Ashton, Gardner and Dyke and Ronnie Wood who later went on to play with The Faces and The Rolling Stones). Other regulars were The Artwoods, Peter Green's Fleetwood Mac, The Cream, Them with the young Van Morrison, Geno Washington and The Ram Jam Band; the lead guitarist in The Ram Jam Band Pete Gage later married Elkie Brooks and became best man at my wedding. It was a hugely popular club and always had a packed-out audience.

One of my favourite groups at the Cooks Ferry Inn was The Downliners Sect. They were a regular band at the club and always sold out. I expected them to make it big like the other bands that played there, but I was really surprised they never found commercial success as I thought they were easily as good as The Rolling Stones and Yardbirds. One especially memorable night at the Inn was when T-Bone Walker, a black American blues singer and guitarist, came over for a UK tour. On this tour he used John Mayall's Bluesbreakers as his backing band. As T-Bone was introducing the band one by one, he came to the guitarist and said, "The best backing guitarist I've ever worked with, Mr Eric Clapton." Eric was of course well known at the Cooks Ferry Inn as he'd been there many times with John Mayall and built up a strong fan base. Within a few months Eric came back with his own band, billed on the poster as Eric Clapton, Jack Bruce, Ginger Baker and in small print underneath, The Cream. The place was packed out and heaving and the entrance fee was only 4 shillings (20 pence in today's money). Jack Bruce and Ginger Baker were also well known as they had been there with The Graham Bond Organisation.

After Eric left John Mayall's Bluesbreakers he was replaced with Peter Green, another popular guitarist that again came back a few months later with his own band Peter Green's Fleetwood Mac. Peter Green was replaced in the Bluesbreakers by Mick Taylor who then left to join The Rolling Stones. When The Animals played there, as part of their contract the stage had to be enlarged to their minimum size and height, which was good for us because the stage was quite small, so it increased the height and we all got a better view of the bands. The Cooks Ferry Inn was a great place and hosted the best of the new bands that were up and coming, many of course went on to international superstardom; it was a great era, a part of my life I will never forget.

There were a number of good clubs in London at that time; you could go out every night for a month and not visit the same place twice. Obviously some were better than others and there were some I wouldn't go to more than once. I would have recommended The Crawdaddy Club in Richmond where I saw The Yardbirds when they took over the residency from The Rolling Stones, and a club called Klooks Kleek at The Railway Inn in Hampstead. It was upstairs above the pub and regularly featured great bands including Georgie Fame and the Blueflames, Zoot Money's Big Roll Band with Andy Summers on guitar who later formed The Police, The Graham Bond Organisation, The Nice featuring Keith Emerson who later went on to form ELP, The Family which had Roger Chapman on vocals who later had a successful solo career and Ric Grech on bass. Ric left to join Blind Faith with Eric Clapton. The club also happened to be next door to Decca Record's recording studio and a lot of live albums were recorded there. You'd often see hundreds of wires coming out of one window by the side of the stage and going through another open window into the building next door. It seemed the best way to wire the band up to the recording studio next door and it worked.

Another band who appeared regularly in the London clubs was The Steam Packet which included singers Rod Stewart, Long John Baldry and Julie Driscoll backed by Brian Auger's Trinity, a raw R&B band. They were managed by Giorgio Gomelsky, who also managed The Rolling Stones and The Yardbirds.

Eel Pie Island was an old jazz club in the 1950s that moved with the times and went over to blues and R&B in the 60s. Situated on an island in the middle of the River Thames, the only way to get to it was over a footbridge. Later when

I was called to work there I had to unload the van on the riverbank and carry or push the equipment over the bridge. I knew one roadie who tried to drive his van over the footbridge only to be shouted at by the club owner just in time before he demolished the footbridge. In later years it became a rock music venue.

I was on a bus home after a night out with my girlfriend when my friend from work jumped on the bus with some of his friends. He was going down to the Club Noreik in Tottenham High Street to an all-nighter to see The Rolling Stones and said, "Why don't you come along?" so I did. The place was heaving, the Stones played a great show that night. It was the first time I'd seen them and my first time in that club. It was so crowded there were people hanging off the balcony, climbing up the walls, perching anywhere to get a better view; the numbers must have been way over the fire limit. The venue was an old converted cinema and had a lot of famous artistes on there over the years like Howlin' Wolf, The Who and others.

Just down the road in Tottenham was The Royal, an old ballroom with a polished wooden dancefloor that had a dance band on every Saturday night; this was before discos and we had to listen to a dance band that played the latest pop songs. The dress code was smart and it was a good place to dance and meet girls. During the interval we would be entertained by what they called 'A Beat Group'. Some nights I would go down to the Tottenham Royal to see an interval group called The Dave Clark Five. They were a local band from Tottenham and they were great. Unfortunately they were too popular for their own good and when they had hits with 'Glad All Over' and 'Bits and Pieces' the audience got so big you could hardly get in the place. The crowd would be stomping their feet in time to the music and the sprung wooden dance floor couldn't take it with the whole building shaking. Despite a request from management to stop stomping, the crowds stomped even more and eventually the DC5 were banned from performing there.

Another London venue that was popular was Middle Earth, a club at 43 King Street, Covent Garden, in a basement below the vegetable market; the music went on all night until dawn. It was started in 1967 and featured some great bands of the time, Pink Floyd, Soft Machine, Graham Bond amongst others; Jeff Dexter was the DJ down there. Coming out in the morning you'd see all the foreign trucks unloading their vegetables into the market. I guess we looked a weird lot at that early hour, but they did have some cafeterias around the market that did a great English breakfast.

The basement in the Covent Garden club was getting too small for the large crowds that attended and because the popularity of the bands were demanding higher fees the basement just wasn't big enough anymore. The Middle Earth club moved to The Roundhouse in Chalk Farm, which was much bigger and I saw some amazing bands there. The building was a converted train shunting shed and used to house a revolving rail track, hence why the building was round and why they called it The Roundhouse. The shows would start at 10pm and go on all night. The Doors, Jefferson Airplane, Pink Floyd, Captain Beefheart, Jeff Beck, Crazy World of Arthur Brown, T-Rex, these were just some of the artistes who I saw perform there and a band called Tomorrow with Steve Howe who later went on to play guitar with Yes and Keith West who had a hit with 'Excerpt from A Teenage Opera.' The club unfortunately folded in 1967, a victim of its own success.

Youth culture and music would never be the same again. I was there watching it happen and realising that the old order was being swept away and was being replaced with a new culture alien to our parents.

Whilst I was attending Southgate Technical College doing my City and Guilds Electronics course I found my interests in music and electronics were beginning to merge. I started to read books on acoustics, microphones and loudspeakers, standing waves, resonant frequencies and the design of reflex speaker cabinets. These were the days that moulded my interest in music, sound and electronics and set me on the road to life in the music business.

Then one day at work someone brought a guitar amplifier into the shop to be repaired and from that day on my fate was sealed.

4

GETTING STARTED

When a Marshall Guitar amplifier was brought into the shop to be repaired I booked it in and said, "Come back in two days and it will be ready." When the owner came back we got chatting and I asked him if he was in a band. He said he was and that he had a gig on Saturday. He also told me they needed someone to drive the van to gigs as none of the band could drive. His dad had been driving them but he didn't want to do it anymore. He asked if I might do it and I asked what it involved. "Just drive us and our equipment to the gig and help with the gear and we'll split the money five ways," he also added, "You get to meet lots of girls." So I said OK, I'll do it. I suspect he had an ulterior motive in asking me, in that he knew I could repair guitar amplifiers and I might just repair them for free.

They were called Y Division and didn't have much gear, just a couple of Marshall amplifiers and a Premier drum kit that sounded really nice. They had some good gear which was unusual for a band just starting out. They also had their own Ford Thames 15cwt van which was quite impressive. They also had a pair of speakers called a PA (Public Address) system. The van felt really unstable with all the gear in the back, remember these guys were just 16 and 17 like me, didn't have much money as they were just starting out with their band and out for a bit of fun. I'd drive them to their rehearsal room in the basement of a church hall in Tottenham just down the road from the Tottenham Royal where I used to see The Dave Clark Five. There they'd practise doing some hits of the day, mostly R&B stuff from The Yardbirds, Stones, Troggs as well as some soul classics from Otis Redding and Wilson Picket.

After a while I became their unofficial manager and started phoning promoters to arrange gigs for them. One regular venue they had been playing at was a pub called the King's Oak at High Beech, which had a small stage and a dance floor. It held around 200 people so it would look empty until you had a reasonable amount of people in. The drummer Rick had made his own light show. What he'd done was to wire 240 volts mains power across the two hi-hat cymbals so whenever he hit the foot pedal and the two cymbals closed the lights would flash on and off, very basic and extremely dangerous. I told him "That is really dangerous," he said, "It's OK unless you touch the cymbals." Great I thought, so I won't be touching the cymbals, but it was 1965 and no one really cared then. Health and Safety didn't exist and you just made it up as you went along.

We would tour the local pubs in and around London. We were doing quite well in terms of bookings and then we found ourselves at a ballroom in Southend, which had a proper theatre stage with curtains and lights and fly bars and all the gear. Wow, I thought, I'll have some fun here, the band set up and did a couple of songs before the audience came in, not exactly a soundcheck, just an equipment check and a quick rehearsal. We only had one microphone and that was for the vocalist and we used the public address system in the hall. People didn't put microphones on the band's equipment in those days, if the instruments weren't loud enough they just turned the amplifiers up, that's how it was.

The audience came in and I closed the curtains so the people wouldn't see the band's equipment on stage, just like the big shows I'd seen at the London Palladium on TV where the curtains opened to the band playing. That looked really cool, I thought, I'll try that. The band were in the dressing room and as they got ready to come on stage, I flicked a few switches on the lighting board to create a light show. These lights look impressive, I thought. I'll switch on a few more. Then the band came on stage, the DJ announced the band and I opened the curtains. All was going well, it was a decent size audience and the crowd seem to be enjoying the music and dancing.

After about four songs I could smell something burning, I couldn't see anything so I wandered around the back of the set to see what it could be, maybe one of the guitar amps was overheating. Then I saw smoke coming from behind one of the curtains on the side of the stage. When I'd opened the curtains, they had bunched up directly in front of a stage light. In a panic I looked for a fire extinguisher and I found one in the corner. I tried to aim the foam at the curtain but couldn't see where the flames were. By this time the band were looking over to the side to see what the smell was. I decided the only thing to do was to close the burning curtains to get them off of the lamp, so I pulled on the ropes to close the curtains. When fully closed I discovered a huge round hole in the middle of one curtain which was on fire. I grabbed the extinguisher again and aimed it at the fire, unfortunately (for the audience that is) the foam from the extinguisher went straight through the hole in the curtain and sprayed all over the audience. I eventually put the fire out but the band had stopped playing by then and had made a quick exit off stage. The band came back on but needless to say we didn't get paid that night and were banned from ever returning, (I can't imagine why).

As I wasn't really their official manager, only performing the role of manager, I didn't get anything out of it apart from the experience and the fun of working with a pop group and the little money we received was split between the five of us which was no more than beer money really.

During this period I was approached by a professional manager and promoter called Steve who was looking for a backing band for a singer called Sandy that he was managing. It turned out the singer was his girlfriend and she needed a band to back her on stage, but to start with he didn't tell me she was his girlfriend. I arranged a two way audition, both to see if the band liked her and if she liked the band. After a while they agreed to join forces and work together. Steve promised us a lot of work and the chance to make a record with her. I wasn't so sure but it was worth a try. Sandy wasn't a bad singer and Steve did have contacts in the music business which I didn't have and I could exploit that for my own advantage. He did actually get some work for the band and he even organised a show at Acton Town Hall with Procol Harum topping the bill with us supporting them.

Not many bands had their own sound system in those days and the PA (Public Address) systems in the halls were very basic and you just had to use what was available. Just like you see in those 1950s American movies, a microphone for the singer and everything else was amplified by their own stage amplifiers, that's the way it was done in those days.

My first portable 5 channel microphone sound mixer.

That was the peak of the band's career, shortly after that Sandy left to pursue a solo career and the band broke up. I didn't see any of the band again until I met two of them down the pub a few years later after I returned from my first American tour. Matt said to me over a pint, in a sarcastic voice, "Are you still driving bands around in your spare time then?" I said "No, I'm doing it full time and I've just come back from an American tour." He looked at me like he didn't have a clue what I was talking about or else he just didn't believe what I'd said.

As well as driving the band around I started building my own PA system as I could see the need for a better vocal sound out front. Down the road was a second-hand electrical store which sold ex-government and ex-military equipment, like ammunition boxes, power supplies, two-way radios, test meters, etc. I'd go down there and rummage through the electrical stuff in case I found anything interesting. I found a huge pile of industrial audio amplifiers designed for factory Tannoy announcements, they looked in quite good condition so I bought the lot. They didn't have any input or output sockets or volume controls but that was no problem. I drilled a few holes in the front panel, put in two jack sockets, wired in a volume control and a tone control. I invited a guitarist friend of mine to try it out at their rehearsal and he said it sounded great, the sound was bright, clean and above all, very loud. He was amazed by the tone control which far exceeded the controls on his Vox amplifier giving his guitar much greater range, he liked it so much he bought it off me. I thought, I'm on to a good thing here, so I advertised these amplifiers in the Melody Maker magazine and the Exchange and Mart. I sold quite a few over the next few weeks, they didn't look as flash as a Vox or Marshall Guitar amplifier but the sound was something else. It was a pity that was all they had in the shop as I could have sold many more.

At the same time the electrical store were selling off some old Tannoy 12" speakers in a 14" box. This time I bought eight, the idea was to bolt four of them together into a column. They weren't the greatest of speakers but they did do the job and I used them at some of the gigs. We didn't have proper sound mixers in those days. The only way to mix microphones together was a small box made by Shure with five input jacks, each with its own rotary volume control and a master volume. That's what we had to work with in 1966. The only proper sound mixers were in recording studios or radio stations and were the size of a small car, not the kind of thing you would take on the road.

Shortly after Y Division split up whilst I was attending Southgate Technical College I was introduced to a someone called Paul Dobson by one of my college friends. He had a Transit van and did furniture removals and moved band equipment around. On one occasion he needed somebody to drive a pop group and their equipment to Wales in his van. He offered me some easy money so I agreed to do it for him as he was busy that day. It just involved dropping them and their equipment at a remote farm near Haverford West in the middle of nowhere and returning home, easy money I thought. It turned out the band was Black Sabbath and it was in their very early days before they were famous. I didn't know who they were and didn't realise then what a huge band they would become and that some 20 years later I would be on tour with them around Europe.

The van driving job on that day got me thinking that I could do that myself if I had my own van. So after some consideration I sold my car and bought a Transit van, placed an advert in the Melody Maker music magazine classified ads section, 'Van and Driver.' I soon started getting requests from bands in the London area to move their equipment from one place to another, usually from their house to the gig they were doing that night, then back to their house. The phone didn't stop ringing and I was getting quite a lot of work. Eventually I was working so much that I was earning more money working part-time in the evenings than I was at my full-time job during the day, so when I finished my college course in electronics I took the decision to hand in my notice and go for it full-time.

In the early days the music business was being run more like a cottage industry, people were just making it up as they went along. If something wasn't working the way we wanted it to, we'd make do and change things. The music business was being run by old men in suits smoking cigars that were a leftover from the old theatre and variety shows of the West End, they didn't have a clue about Rock'n'Roll, many thought it was a passing fad. Today the music business is run like a big corporate organisation, a slick money-making machine, never mind the music, just grab the cash. I could see how it was evolving and I saw it coming and knew when it was time for me to get out before I stopped enjoying it, although that wouldn't happen yet for another twenty-five years.

So now I was working full-time as a van driver with my own van setting up the band's equipment. Then one day someone called me a roadie, I said "What's a roadie?"

5

TURNING PROFESSIONAL

On 16th February 1969, I met Ian Knight, the road manager for progressive rock band Soft Machine, he was also lighting designer for the UFO and Middle Earth clubs and later became stage designer for Led Zeppelin, Wings and Genesis. Ian asked me to take Soft Machine's equipment to Ronnie Scott's legendary club in Wardour Street, they had just returned from an American tour supporting Jimi Hendrix. I knew of Soft Machine as I had been a big fan of theirs watching them at the Cooks Ferry Inn that I mentioned previously. When I got there I was expected to set the gear up as well, oh well, the amplifiers were no problem, just plug in the amps and connect the speakers, which was easy. But when it came to the drum kit I'd never done that before and had no idea where to start. I knew roughly what a drum kit should look like, I'd been watching bands and drummers set their own kits up, so I just put it together the way I thought it should go. I wasn't far out, the drummer Robert Wyatt arrived and made a few minor adjustments and we were away, after that I took their equipment to a cinema converted into a music venue in Ladbroke Grove called The Electric Cinema.

Following that gig I took Soft Machine to the Middle Earth club in Covent Garden, where I had spent many nights in the audience as a spectator. I did a few more shows with them around the London area over the next few months, but not enough to make it regular work. I never understood why Soft Machine never found commercial success, they'd started off in a similar style to Pink

Floyd but when they returned to England from the Jimi Hendrix tour they went into a more jazz-fusion rock direction, although more rock than jazz the albums didn't sell as well, but they always went down well at live shows.

I was disappointed when Soft Machine didn't play more gigs as I was having a good time with them and getting on well with them and their manager Ian Knight. In 1971 Ian helped to transform the Finsbury Park Astoria into the Rainbow Theatre, a 3,000-seat venue with an impressive proscenium arch, modifying the stage and installing a permanent sound system. I didn't see him again as he moved to Los Angeles and worked for Showco, a sound and lighting rental company.

As I was working freelance I couldn't rely on just one band as there was no guarantee how much work they would get, or want me to do so I was doing a lot of work around the clubs with other bands like Aardvark. They were one of the first Prog-Rock bands around, they sounded like they were heavily influenced by Pink Floyd with some heavy Deep Purple and King Crimson keyboards with a bit of blues thrown in, not too dissimilar to Soft Machine. Before I started working with Aardvark, Paul Kossoff and Simon Kirke played in the band but left to form the band Free. The band then became Stan Aldous on bass, Frank Clark on drums, and Steve Milliner on keyboards, previously with Black Cat Bones, and Dave Skillin on vocals. Their material was highly keyboard oriented, with that fuzzed-up Hammond organ which was popular at the time and more or less replaced the lead guitar.

It's a pity the band weren't recognised a bit earlier in their career as all the members went on to bigger and better things. It was Dave Skillen that first called me and booked me to do some gigs with them, I got on well with Dave, I leant him my Revox reel-to-reel tape recorder to record some demo tracks at their rehearsal studio.

During 1969 I also worked with a band called The Gods, a typical 60s pop/rock band doing the pubs and clubs; although they never made it big they did have a residency at the Marquee Club in London, which gave them some exposure and it was great fun to be working in the legendary Marquee Club.

Eventually the musicians went on to do bigger things in other bands. I got on really well with them especially guitarist Joe Konas, he left the group, moved to Canada and started a group there. One of Joe's favourite stories was telling me that Mick Taylor used to play in the band, Mick left The Gods to join John Mayall's Bluesbreakers then left John Mayall to join The Rolling Stones. Also in the band were Ken Hensley on organ, Lee Kerslake on drums and Paul Newton on bass who all went on to form the rock band Uriah Heep.

Photo: © Mike Ellen
Soft Machine at the Roundhouse, Chalk Farm

A bit earlier in The Gods' history Greg Lake (from Emerson Lake and Palmer and King Crimson) was in the band. John Glascock joined the band on bass then went on to play with Chicken Shack and Jethro Tull, Lee Kerslake later played drums with Whitesnake and Black Sabbath. It's a shame for me their talents weren't discovered earlier whilst I was still with them.

Since I took that van to Wales with Black Sabbath, Paul Dobson and I had become good friends, I helped him out a few times doing similar jobs with London bands in my own van and then returned the favour by passing work on to him when I was double-booked.

Paul Dobson introduced me to Phil Cuffley who was also doing the van hire business, he had a Commer van, bigger than a Transit but more like a local delivery van and was a beaten-up old thing, but was earning a good living with it, I became friends with Phil as well and sometimes we would pass on work to each other if we were double-booked with gigs. The arrangement worked quite well between the three of us. There weren't many of us doing that kind of work in those days.

I had been having some problems at home with my father, he was from a different generation who had fought in the First World War as a rear gunner and aircraft engineer and we weren't getting on too well. He wanted me to leave home, we argued a lot and he didn't like me having long hair and didn't understand why I had given up what he called a 'proper job' to drive a van around the country. He didn't really understand what I was doing. After one particular argument he threw a punch at me, unfortunately his punch only resulted in him bouncing off my arm and he fell to the floor. I felt terrible as my reaction was only self-defensive. I said to my mother, "It's probably better if I move out, if only for Dad's health, it's not doing him any good me being here." Paul Dobson offered me a room in his house so I stayed there with Paul and his wife for a few weeks while things settled down at home.

When The Zombies split up, keyboard player Rod Argent formed his own band called Argent, Paul Dobson was working with Argent at the time and had set up a company called RSD, (Rotary Speaker Developments). Paul had designed and built a speaker cabinet in an attempt to rival the 'Leslie' speaker cabinet used with Hammond organs. The Leslie speaker commonly used with the Hammond B-3 organ creates a Doppler effect by using an electric motor to rotate a baffle around a bass speaker with two horns on top also revolving around, making it appear like the sound is spinning around in a circle and the listener hearing a fluctuating frequency which is called the Doppler effect.

The Doppler effect is what you might also hear when standing by a railway track listening to an oncoming train. The train is making the same sound as it travels down the track but as it passes you, the tone changes from an increasing sound to a receding sound. The effect on the ear as the train passes sounds different even though the sound coming off the train itself doesn't change. The frequency is higher as the train travels towards you and changes to a lower frequency as it travels away from you. That is what is called the Doppler effect.

The Hammond organ had a two speed switch to control the speed of the revolving speakers. The Leslie cabinet was hugely popular with keyboard players from early soul and Motown artistes through to heavy rock bands. Paul had developed a similar version with more powerful speakers and a bigger motor, the result was far from what he expected and turned out a disaster. When it was being demonstrated at an Argent rehearsal, instead of the speaker baffles spinning around, the cabinet started to spin on its wheels, trouble is it span across the stage like an out-of-control washing machine and ploughed straight into a row of guitars neatly arranged on their stands. Needless to say the RSD version didn't go into production. But that was Paul for you. Later on Paul changed the name of RSD to Recording Studio Design which manufactured amplifiers and sound mixers which did have more success. I kept in touch with Paul from time to time and unexpectedly bumped into him in a hotel lift in Copenhagen some years later. We were both on different European tours and that kind of thing used to happen quite a lot with people you knew, you'd never know who you'd meet up with on tour somewhere in the world.

I had a call from a member of Junior's Eyes, a London band I had heard of doing the clubs and colleges, they booked me for a gig at Club 51 in Great Portland Street. It was a famous club in London that featured many great artistes over the years. By coincidence I had an EP (Extended Play 45 rpm record) by The Downliners Sect recorded live at Club 51, one of my favourites. I did a few gigs with Junior's Eyes around London and a few outside in the South East region but had to give them up as I was getting more work with other bands and they didn't have a lot of work. I heard sometime later they became David Bowie's backing group. It's always a gamble who you choose to work with and sometimes you get it wrong, but you're not to know the future or how well a band will do, you instinctively go with whoever is offering you the most work at the time. Over the next few months I did gigs with numerous bands around England.

Andromeda were a kind of psychedelic rock group with John Du Cann on guitar and vocals, he left shortly after I worked with them to join Atomic Rooster. One of the shows I did was at the Lyceum ballroom in London but I didn't think they were that good.

The Yarra Yarra Jazz Band came over from Australia for a few shows and hired me to take them on a gig to Tarporley near Chester. We hadn't been on the M1 more than 20 minutes when I heard a voice from the back: "Are there any pubs on this road mate?" I replied, "Sorry mate this is a motorway, there aren't any pubs until we get off in a few hours' time." A collective sigh came from the back of the van and I could hear mutterings and mumblings of discontent. I stopped at the Blue Boar service area at Watford Gap for some petrol and a coffee break only to discover that all but one of the band had scarpered out the back gate of the service area into a pub. I could see this was going to be a troubling journey.

About an hour or so later they returned to the van the worse for drink and we continued our journey. The show went as well as could be expected, I helped them load their instruments and patiently waited for them to get into the van, unfortunately in true Australian fashion all they wanted to do was keep drinking. I was waiting to go and I thought it was a bit selfish when I had an extremely long drive back to London, this was before any M6 motorway had been built so it was all A roads until the M1 motorway. Needless to say as soon as we headed off they all fell asleep in the back, just as well I thought.

Smile were a blues-rock band. It included Tim Staffell as singer and bassist, drummer Roger Taylor, and guitarist Brian May. I only did a few gigs around London with them including The Speakeasy in April and The Whiskey a Go Go in May. A year later Tim left and was replaced by somebody called Freddie Mercury. Roger and Brian changed the band's name to Queen. I wonder whatever happened to them.

In May 1969, word started to filter through the grapevine about a crash on the M1 motorway involving Fairport Convention. I knew their roadie Harvey from doing previous gigs in London. You often get to meet other bands and their roadies at gigs and I feared the worst as the story going around was their van was totally trashed as it turned over. Another roadie I knew went past the scene near Scratchwood Services just after the incident as he was driving home from a gig in Sheffield. The drummer Martin Lamble died in the crash along with Richard Thompson's girlfriend, the rest of the band suffered serious injuries. In those days we just didn't stay in hotels, we drove to the gig and then drove back to London again afterwards. We might do a series of one-off gigs linked together but not tours as we know them today. That crash sent a shock wave through the music business especially us roadies who drove up and down the motorway every week going to and from gigs. I know what it's like. I've fallen asleep at the wheel myself and you do all you can to stay awake. I know some guys started popping pills and taking 'uppers' to keep themselves awake but I steered clear of them just relying on strong coffee. Later that month a benefit concert featuring Soft Machine, The Family, The Pretty Things and DJ John Peel was held for the families of those killed.

A few days later I was asked to drive a band called Jefferson up to Leeds to do a TV show. Bad luck accrued during the trip, the van I had was rapidly knocking up the miles and broke down on the M1 just a few miles short of Leeds. After waiting for the breakdown truck to arrive it seemed likely that they would be late for the show so they used the roadside telephone to arrange for a taxi to come and collect the group and take them to the studio. I waited with the van and thankfully the breakdown truck came. It got me going again and I made it to the studio just in time for them to use their own equipment instead of the loan equipment the TV studio had organised. All's well in the end but it could have been a disaster for the band.

I did a one-off gig with Black Cat Bones in London, a blues band best known for having had Paul Kossoff and Simon Kirke in its line-up, both of whom later joined Free. Kirke also became a founding member of Bad Company.

There were a number of other bands I worked with during 1968 and 1969: Herbie Goins and the Nigh-Timers, an American rhythm & blues band, they gained a reputation as one of the hottest R&B bands in the UK and sometimes featured Alexis Korner and John McLaughlin who I would later get to know very well.

I also worked with Frank Ricotti, an English jazz vibraphonist and percussionist, who later worked with Pet Shop Boys, Leo Sayer and Rick Wakeman.

Also Freedom's Children, a South African acid prog rock band that sounded a bit like Pink Floyd, featuring Trevor Rabin who later played guitar with prog rock band Yes; I did a few gigs with them including the Fishmonger's Arms in Wood Green, just down the road from my parents' house where I used to go to watch the latest bands, they did a brilliant show that night.

Also, Sugar, which featured guitarist Laurie Wisefield who later joined Wishbone Ash and bassist Cliff Williams who later joined AC/DC. Cliff only turned up to their audition because of his friend James Litherland, guitarist with Colosseum, all names that would be a part of my story later on.

Other bands like Welcome, Bottle, Wild Mouth and I haven't forgotten The House of Lords from Scotland, who still owe me £50. In June I was called up by their management company to take them to Kiel in Germany to some really dodgy night club. It reminded me of the Star Club in Hamburg where The Beatles had a residency. I was promised payment on arrival, but they had problems getting the money out of the club's promoter and after hanging around for a day I left there with a promise that I'd get my money once they returned to England. I should have known I'd get stuffed and that the band would get stuffed as well, they didn't get paid by the promoter and I didn't get paid by them. They did get their accommodation and food supplied and I insisted on my petrol money before I left so at least I got back without losing too much. I won't get fooled again.

I found that the London club scene was very incestuous with a lot of musicians in the early days of their youth, moving from one band to another, breaking up and forming new ones or renaming bands while they found the right combination of musicians to work with. Some as I've mentioned here went on to become big stars with other bands later in their life.

When gigging around the country it wouldn't be unusual to be stopped by the police late at night on the way home. I suppose a bunch of guys in a Transit van on a country road at 2am could look a bit suspicious. If you saw blue lights behind you, those in the back of the van would be opening windows to clear the air just in case old plod would poke his head in to check the occupants. When I told them we were a band going home after playing a gig you'd get the usual reply. "Oh yeah, what's the band called then?" When I told them the name they'd say, "Never heard of you, I pulled over The Rolling Stones last week." Sometimes they'd want to see in the back of the van to check if I was telling the truth or if we were carrying anything we shouldn't. Occasionally they'd ask for records or signed photos, then we'd be on our way. Things are a lot better now but in the 60s and 70s you couldn't always guarantee to find a petrol station open after 10pm especially on some of the remote country roads in East Anglia, where there were no petrol stations open between the North Sea and London after midnight. After a few scary journeys where I nearly ran out of petrol I always made sure I filled up on the way into a town just before arriving at the venue so I had a full tank for the return journey home.

One funny story often told in the folklore of Rock'n'Roll history is how two men dressed as vicars turned up at Marshall Equipment Hire (MEH) and hired a PA system for their church village fete, they paid a small deposit and took the system away with them. After a week when they didn't return the equipment MEH discovered there was no village fete and the two vicars weren't vicars at all. They lost the whole PA system.

6

OLYMPIC STUDIOS

In July 1969 I had a call from Tony Secunda's office asking if I could take some equipment to Olympic Studios in Barnes for a recording session. Olympic Studios was originally a theatre, it was converted into a recording studio in the 1950s and has recorded many famous albums there with The Yardbirds, Jimi Hendrix, Led Zeppelin, The Eagles, The Rolling Stones, Queen, Deep Purple and many more. Tony Secunda was manager of Birmingham based bands The Moody Blues and The Move.

This job was for a recording session with musicians Denny Laine and Trevor Burton, Denny was vocalist and guitarist with The Moody Blues and sang on the iconic hit 'Go Now', despite the fact Denny had left The Moody Blues that didn't let him out of his contract. Tony still had Denny Laine signed up as a solo artiste and wasn't going to let him go. Trevor Burton played bass with The Move and had a hit record with 'I Can Hear the Grass Grow' and 'Blackberry Way'. Like Denny, Trevor had left the group but was still signed up to Secunda as a solo artiste.

It was well known that Tony Secunda was the manager of The Moody Blues and The Move and became famous when he sent a rude postcard to Prime Minister Harold Wilson advertising The Move's latest single, it got him into trouble and the story was all over the newspapers. He was fined in court for indecency but it got the band publicity, something money can't always buy. Someone told me he was a real hard man to work for and I hadn't even met him yet, so I proceeded with caution when I first went into his office. I'd heard of Olympic Studios, it was regarded as one of the best recording studios in London on a par with the famous Abbey Road Studios where The Beatles recorded. Unlike Abbey Road, which was owned by EMI record company and considered a bit old, Olympic was privately owned and had state-of-the-art equipment and was the first studio in London to install a 16 track recorder.

I was asked to drive to a farmhouse called Woolwich Green Farm in Theale, Berkshire to collect the band and the equipment and take them to Olympic Studios, the farmhouse was owned by Chris Blackwell of Island Records who rented it out to musicians, Denny and Trevor were living there together with Traffic's drummer Jim Capaldi.

I picked up Denny and Trevor and their backline gear in my van and took them to Olympic Studios, they seemed like decent blokes and I got on with them OK, they were just ordinary blokes wanting to make some records. When we got there I was told where to set the gear up and then went into the control room, the producer was none other than Jimmy Miller, The Rolling Stones' producer. I was in total awe watching him setting up this massive mixing console, the tape operator and engineer was a young guy called Andy Johns the younger brother of Glyn Johns, a name that would later become famous for working with Led Zeppelin, The Rolling Stones, The Who, The Eagles, and others, while Andy later worked with Free, Rod Stewart and a host of others. Being a tape operator is a bit of a boring job but it is a start of a journey in the recording business, everyone has to start somewhere and making the coffee, operating the tape machine whilst learning the art of placing microphones and watching a master on the mixing desk is a good way to learn your trade. I too was watching Jimmy Miller, the recording sessions would go on for hours, all night sometimes, but I would watch and learn to see what he did and the result that he achieved, sliding his fingers over the faders and adjusting EQ knobs. Of course mixing in a recording studio is totally different to mixing a live show but there are similar techniques that can be used in both areas. I spent the next few days running the two of them back and forth from the farm to the studios. The band called themselves Balls and when the recording session ended I thought that was it, but I was to work with them a few more times later.

A couple of days after I finished with the Balls recording session I received a phone call from John Hawken to do a gig with a band called Keith Relf's

Renaissance. I couldn't believe it, Keith Relf was my hero as the lead singer of The Yardbirds. I thought that all the hard graft of working in little pubs and clubs with small bands was paying off, I was starting to work with some well-known artistes at last. The other members of Renaissance were Jim McCarty, ex-Yardbirds drummer, Louis Cennamo, ex-bass player with The Herd, Jane Relf, Keith's sister and John Hawken, ex-Nashville Teens piano player.

The gig was in Hereford at a county fair showground, John travelled with me in the van with the equipment, when we arrived with the gear we were met by Keith Relf who looked at me in a strange way like he had known me for years, it was a strange feeling but I felt I was going on a journey with this band. Two days later I was lugging their gear upstairs into Klooks Kleek in Hampstead, a place I had been to hundreds of times before as a member of the audience.

To my surprise I was booked again for two more days (and nights) with Denny Laine and Trevor Burton at Olympic Studios, so much work was coming in I didn't know where to look or who to give priority to. It's easy to make the wrong decision and go with the wrong artiste, so far the work didn't clash, but I was sure that it was only a matter of time before two jobs clashed and I would have to make a choice.

Over the next few weeks I did a lot of gigs with Renaissance, including the famous Marquee Club in London's Wardour Street, Mothers in Birmingham and The Speakeasy in Margaret Street. The Speakeasy was an upmarket club in London that was open all night where all the rich and famous superstars used to hang out, musicians, actors and celebrities. The Speakeasy also used to attract some stunning looking ladies in the audience and a lot of groupies, no doubt looking to bag themselves a famous actor or musician, every time I was in there you'd see quite a few famous people. It wouldn't be unusual to see Paul McCartney at one table with friends and some members of The Rolling Stones at another table with The Who's drummer Keith Moon, all mixing with other famous musicians, actors and celebrities.

In October 1969 Renaissance did a show at the Lyceum Ballroom in London, supporting Peter Green's Fleetwood Mac; when I walked into the hall via the backstage door I couldn't believe my eyes, I saw the largest PA (Public Address) sound system I'd ever seen, it was literally a mountain of WEM speaker cabinets going up as high as you could see. On the side of the stage was their soundman and he had not one but two WEM audiomaster mixers linked together giving him ten channels to work with, you might laugh at that these days but ten channels was a lot in 1969.

The sound that night for Fleetwood Mac was exceptionally good, the best live sound I'd ever heard, it was a crystal clear sound the likes I had never heard before, the sound that night became my benchmark as to what all bands should sound like live.

Not only was I impressed, but Renaissance were impressed as well and Keith Relf said to me during Fleetwood Mac's set, "We have to get one of those WEM PAs." I told him that would be great and a good investment for the band. I decided that the next opportunity I had I would go down to talk to Charlie Watkins, the founder of Watkins Electric Music to discuss buying a WEM (pronounced Wem) PA system off him for Renaissance.

For a time during the late 60s and early 70s it would be unusual to see a live show by a major act that didn't use a WEM PA system. Charlie was the originator of the modern British PA system and all the big bands used them. Charlie started WEM in the 1950s making guitars and guitar amplifiers and was an innovator whose ideas were picked up by others like Vox and Marshall. He also invented the WEM copicat, an echo unit first used by Johnny Kid & the Pirates on 'Shakin all Over' and later used by thousands of guitarists over the years. He built the WEM Audiomaster sound mixer, the first portable mixer with foldback control and the only alternative to the boring old Shure microphone mixers used in theatres. He also built the first 100 watt amplifier that was linkable, so that ten linked together would produce 1,000 watts of power, unheard of before the 1960s. The WEM column speakers which contained four 12-inch speakers were used by all the big bands, The Who, Pink Floyd, Fleetwood Mac, Cream and countless others. The first Isle of Wight Festival with Bob Dylan and next year with Jimi Hendrix used a WEM PA system as did the Reading Jazz & Blues Festival; The Rolling Stones free concert in Hyde Park used a 1,500 watt WEM.

Charlie Watkins and I worked out a budget and the size that we considered big enough for the venues we were playing in, of course I would have liked a bigger system but there were financial restrictions on what I could spend. So while I waited for the PA to be delivered I carried on doing a lot of gigs with Renaissance, around four to six a week with the old PA system.

Between those gigs I still found time to slot in a few odd jobs that kept coming my way. King Crimson were rehearsing in Fulham for their upcoming American tour and needed some equipment delivering, so after

I dropped off the equipment I hung round for a while and listened to their rehearsal. What a band, I was really impressed with their stage sound and that huge distorted fuzzed-up organ that made them famous and was copied by many others.

I also slotted in a gig with a band called KA that had Andi Banks on bass and Robin LeMesurier on guitar. They were a group of lads from London, although I didn't do many gigs with them I ended up becoming good friends with them and stayed in contact with them for many years. Andi Banks, the bass player, called me to do a gig at Roehampton College in London and when I later needed someone to help me on the road setting up the sound equipment I called on Andi and asked if he wanted to help, he agreed to come on the road with me. We spent many years on the road together doing gigs with several different bands which are mentioned later in this book. I will always remember we had some great times together. I stayed in touch with Andi for a long time and he even came to my 60th birthday party.

Meanwhile Renaissance's WEM PA was delivered and we spent the next few weeks doing more gigs around England including the Marquee again. To be at the Marquee when the club was so packed with an enthusiastic audience was a great experience, the place where so many great bands had once played, from The Rolling Stones to Pink Floyd, The Who and countless others. We also played at the Friars club in Aylesbury, Klooks Kleek in Hampstead, the Roundhouse in Dagenham, and the Boathouse in Nottingham, a club that I would go into years later with Def Leppard.

The new WEM PA system consisted of four bass cabinets which had two 15-inch speakers in each, eight high-frequency cabinets which had four 12-inch speakers and two cabinets for on-stage monitors. I had a WEM five-channel mixer which had a separate foldback control to send a signal to the monitors, (don't laugh now, this was high-tech for 1969), to have a separate monitor send on your mixer was a luxury even though we had to use the same EQ (tone control) as the front PA.

Previously bands who wanted to hear more of the sound would just turn one of the main PA speaker's inward towards the stage. The other thing to remember was that bands didn't mic up everything in those days, microphones were just meant for the vocalist to sing into, it wasn't until later that we started to put mics on drums and in front of guitar amps, so in that respect you didn't need big mixing desks.

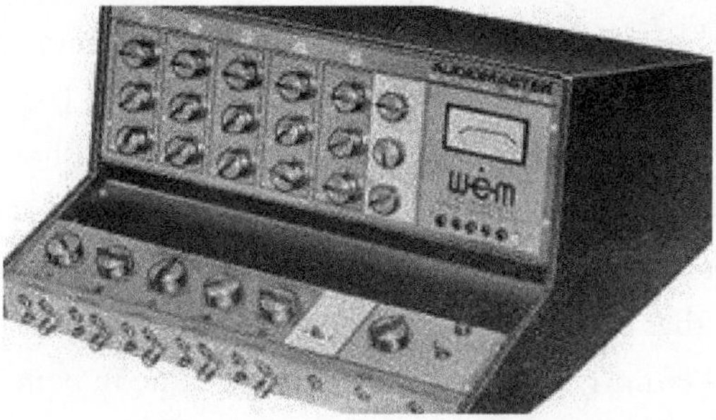

WEM 5 into 2 Audiomaster mixer

WEM 15" Bass cabinet

WEM 4 x 12" Speakers.

Renaissance's music was considered at the time as "very original" a phrase often used, this time they were different. Classically trained John and Louis and ex-Yardbirds Keith and Jim blended with the female voice of Jane. Jane told me she only joined the band for a joke to start with. The whole show was linked with pre-recorded electronic sounds, that's where I came in, it was difficult finding enough channels to plug everything up including the tape machine so I built a switching box that switched between tape machine and microphones as and when I needed them. My electronics experience came in handy.

Meanwhile I was back at Olympic Studios again, this time with Renaissance to record their first album, the producer was Paul Samwell-Smith (ex-Yardbirds bass player). I had to lug all the equipment up the stairs and into studio 2, set it up and was just getting comfortable in the control room when the engineer Andy Johns walked in and checked out the tape recorder, only to discover that the studio was set up for 8-track recording instead of the new 16-track recorder which had just been installed, one of the first studios in London to have a 16 track recorder. Andy went into a fit and said, "I can't work with that," stormed out and went home, the band were not happy they had to cancel the recording session and they also went home. That left me on my own to pack all the gear up, lug it downstairs and load it back into the van, all in a day's work, never mind I was getting paid by the day so wasn't going to complain.

A few days later we went back into the studio and started recording the album which this time had been set up for 16-track, the album was released later in 1969.

In November 1969 we were booked to do a show at the Greyhound in Croydon supporting Atomic Rooster, who consisted of Vincent Crane on keyboards and Carl Palmer on drums who had recently left The Crazy World of Arthur Brown band and who would later form ELP (Emerson, Lake and Palmer). They were joined by Nick Graham on bass and vocals, although they were not a popular or brilliant band they did later have a hit record in 1971 with 'Tomorrow Night'.

The venue at the Greyhound is upstairs in a pub, it was a good-sized room with an old-fashioned ballroom dance floor, but it was up two flights of stairs and I had a lot of gear including the WEM PA system. I unloaded the van and left the gear on the dance floor in front of the stage while Atomic Rooster were going through their sound check. When they'd finished their sound check I went up on stage to set up my equipment but was shocked to be told by their crew that, "We're not moving any of our gear." I said, "But there's only two feet left at the front." Their unhelpful crew had a really bad attitude and wouldn't move a thing, not even the guitar pedals. It was totally impossible to get anything in two feet of stage especially a drum kit and piano. I phoned the manager and told him what was going on then waited for the band to arrive, they had no luck in changing the situation either so I ended up taking all the gear back down the stairs again and had the night off.

It was always a custom that the headlining band would clear some room at the front of the stage so the opening act could put their equipment on, it didn't require a total stage set-up or strip down, it only required a few guitar pedals to be moved and the guitar amps to be slid back a foot or two. But Rooster's crew were a bunch of jobsworths and just couldn't be bothered to move anything, not only was it unhelpful it was just plain lazy on their part. I took note of that incident and marked their cards just in case I came across them again in the future.

John Hawken (Renaissance and ex-Nashville Teens piano player) asked me if I would do the sound for a 50s revival concert at the London Palladium with Gene Vincent headlining with the original Nashville Teens on the bill supporting who came out of retirement just for the show.

I went down there and did the sound on what was a really weird old-fashioned sound mixer, obviously set up for theatre shows not Rock'n'Roll concerts, but we did ok and the show went well. Emperor Rosko was the MC for the evening and as to be expected from Rosko he played the part by coming on stage all dressed up in a 1950s leather motorcycle suit with a huge quiffed wig and winklepicker shoes. Sadly Gene Vincent passed away in 1971 at the age of 36 of a ruptured stomach ulcer, so it was a real pleasure and a privilege to have worked with this great Rock'n'Roll master.

In December Renaissance had five nights in a club in Lausanne in Switzerland which involved an overnight drive through the Swiss mountains, a beautiful sight with lots of small villages all lit up with real Christmas trees and Christmas lights along the narrow streets, a bit scary as well coming down those mountain roads in the snow and ice at night. When we arrived in Lausanne the club was already open so I unloaded the equipment onto the stage ready for the five-night residency.

This is where I came across my first ATA Carnet (ATA meaning *Admission Temporaire* or Temporary Admission). The ATA Carnet is a temporary admission document which acts as a kind of passport for commercial freight, goods or equipment normally used at trade fairs, shows, exhibitions, sports events including music shows and concerts. ATA Carnets are now regularly used for everything from F1 racing cars to exhibitions and rock concerts so that goods can cross borders without paying import tax.

The purpose of a Carnet is to allow travel through various countries so that Customs officials can satisfy themselves that all the equipment that you bring into the country is the same that you take out and not sold, for example if a guitar is sold then duty has to be paid on it since it then becomes an imported item.

Using a Carnet eliminates the use for a customs declaration at the borders of foreign countries. So long as the goods are re-exported, no duties or taxes are paid. Failure to re-export the goods listed on the Carnet or failure to get the Carnet stamped on exit results in the payment of duties and taxes.

That was the idea but it has always had its problems especially when you turn up at a border post at midnight and the border guard has never seen an ATA document before and hasn't a clue what to do with it. Many times I've had to tell them where on the document to sign it and put their rubber stamp just so we can get out of there and go. Unfortunately there is always a jobsworth who dislikes anyone English and will keep you there for hours in a deliberately uncooperative way just because he can. He then wants a bribe or some free gifts just for doing his job, once he realises you're carrying band equipment he starts asking for records, T-shirts or photographs of the artiste.

Sometimes the jobsworth says he has to wait for his boss to arrive and that won't be until 8am, by which time the road is clogged up with a tailback of trucks and the customs hall is full of European long distance lorry drivers wanting their papers signed, so guess who gets left until last.

A few times the truck has been unloaded just so the border guard can check something he randomly picks off the list. The list must contain everything you're carrying right down to every plug and cable, every guitar and every light bulb, if you can't produce it off the list you could be in trouble. Similarly the customs man may point to something in the truck and ask you to identify it from the list, if it's not on the list you could also be in trouble. Once or twice I've had to blag my way out of trouble by claiming something on the truck is different to the list because someone in the office didn't list everything properly. Joining the EU had made things a lot easier to travel across EU borders but that only applied to EU countries.

It was always a struggle to find somewhere to put the sound mixer at a gig, traditionally up to the 1960s the sound mixer would be on the side of the stage, I guess that goes back to the old days of theatre when everything was on stage, it was always difficult trying to mix sound from the side of stage as you didn't really know what it sounded like in the audience. I would routinely walk out into the audience wherever possible to have a listen and then go back and make a minor adjustment to the sound. I was already thinking of using a long multicore cable and putting the mixer in the audience, but the technology hadn't arrived yet, so meanwhile I would put the mixer behind the PA stack and hide behind there trying not to be seen on stage too much.

Our residency of five nights at the night club in Lausanne ended on December 23rd and I headed back to England for Christmas and a well-earned rest and prepared myself for my first tour with an American band.

7

THE FIRST TOUR STATESIDE

The 1970 New Year started off as 1969 ended, Renaissance had plenty of gigs booked and I wasn't taking any work from any other bands. I wanted to stay with Renaissance and was thinking that as Keith Relf and Jim McCarty were ex-Yardbirds and that three other major guitarists, Eric Clapton, Jeff Beck and Jimmy Page all played in The Yardbirds and went on to become international superstars I would do well to stick with Renaissance. Keith had moved from lead vocals in The Yardbirds to guitar and vocals in Renaissance. Although Keith was no Eric, Jeff or Jimmy, he played well and was a competent guitarist. I enjoyed the music and working with these guys, I was hoping they would go on to bigger things.

The first gig of the year was back at Mothers in Birmingham and then straight over to Paris for two nights at the Olympia, a 2,000-seat theatre that looked quite impressive from the front stalls but the backstage area left a lot to be desired, old and dirty and in need of a facelift. I was constantly being reminded by the French stage crew that The Beatles once played there in 1964, possibly, but I don't think it had ever been cleaned since then. Then it was back to the Country Club in London, which was always a favourite venue of mine.

Next up was something that was a cultural shock and changed my whole view of the way sound was delivered to the audience. Renaissance got themselves on a UK tour and opened the show for American blues-rock band Canned Heat, starting off at Newcastle City Hall, a venue that would become a very fond and memorable place. Canned Heat had just had a hit record 'Going up the Country'.

By this time I had got rid of my old Ford Transit van as it was becoming uneconomical to run and unreliable so I told the band's management that I would rent a hire truck. For this tour I rented a 7.5 ton truck with a tail lift, the tail lift made my job of transporting the gear around a lot easier.

Canned Heat had bought their own sound system over from the States, Jack their roadie told me they heard that English venues didn't have very good sound systems installed and there weren't any sound rental companies in the UK at that time, that may have been true.

This was an eye opener for me, the first time I had direct contact with an American band and their equipment, everything they had was bigger and heavier than the English equipment, for a start all their equipment was packed in 'flight cases' as they called them, we in England never 'flew' anything around so we didn't need flight cases. I guess this was due to the fact that in America they have to travel vast distances between shows and flying is the only practical way to do that, flying in America is just like getting on a bus in England as I was to find out later.

Even though I was happy with my WEM PA, I was surprisingly impressed with their PA system which consisted of a single bass reflex cabinet. I had seen bass reflex cabinets before but only behind cinema screens and they were 6 feet high, 3 feet wide and 3 feet deep. Canned Heat's bass bin was a lot smaller, and on top of the bass bin was a single radial horn. To be honest the Canned Heat system was only one small box either side of the stage but it blew my WEM system away, the bass coming out from that one cabinet was twice as loud as the WEM system and the horn threw the high frequencies all the way to the back of the hall.

In those days bands didn't share PA systems, each band carried their own just like a guitarist would carry his own guitar amplifier, a vocalist would carry his own PA, it seems crazy now but that's just the way it was done then.

After Renaissance opened the show for the first half I would pull the WEM PA down along with the other backline equipment and store it backstage while Canned Heat's road crew got the stage ready for the headliners. I'd then start packing the equipment away and if possible load it into the truck then watch the show from the side of the stage. The next morning we headed off to Liverpool Philharmonic Theatre, and then on to Brighton, Croydon and Birmingham, we actually had hotels on this tour, luxury.

Over the next two weeks we did nine shows around England including a dash over to Bremen to do a German TV show, *Beat Club*. This was a German version of *Top of the Pops* in its format but more like an *Old Grey Whistle Test* with the type of bands that performed, showcasing the best English and American acts in rock that were around at the time rather than top ten chart groups, unfortunately it was only broadcast in Germany.

The last show of the Canned Heat tour ended up with our manager having a punch-up with one of the Deep Purple crew. The Royal Albert Hall in London is a magnificent building with a huge amount of history, but unfortunately not designed for electric rock music. The acoustics are all wrong. Go to see a full acoustic orchestra and the sound is phenomenal, but rock music just bounces off all the walls. Aware of the problem, the Albert Hall installed some upside down mushrooms in the roof of the building which has helped the reflections a bit but not by nearly enough. Anyway, top of the bill was Canned Heat supported by Deep Purple and lastly Renaissance who opened the show. As I said, in those days each band would have their own PA system and again each would dismantle their equipment after their set, the PA as well as the backline equipment, that meant at the Albert Hall three PA systems all stacked up on stage, one in front of the other.

In reverse order Canned Heat used their American bin and horn system positioned where they wanted it. The biggest PA for some reason belonged to Deep Purple who were using a Hi-Watt system supplied by Hi-Watt themselves, a British sound company who until now just made guitar amps and thought they would now move into the PA market. Finally came my WEM system which had to fit somewhere in front where I could find space, totally insufficient for a room like the Albert Hall but that was still bigger than the PA The Beatles had used when I saw them at the Hammersmith Odeon in 1965.

During the sound checks or in Deep Purple's case a long rehearsal, I got talking to my old friend Phil from Hi-Watt, I knew him from being the salesman for Hi-Watt guitar amps and we always got on well, as Hi-Watt guitar amps were used by many of the bands I had worked for. He was showing me his new combined six-channel sound mixer and amplifier, he was proudly showing off a new control knob on the mixer he called a 'Presence' control, I'd never heard of that before and asked him what it was and how it worked. Basically it was a mid-range frequency boost in all but name, most mixers including my WEM only had two tone controls, a bass and a treble just like you would have on your home hi-fi system, this Hi-Watt mixer had three tone controls, bass, treble and presence (or middle), he showed me what a vocal mic sounded like with the presence turned off and then turned it on. I had to admit the clarity and volume from the mic was double what it was, I was impressed.

The time came for Renaissance to go on stage, we were first on, it was a packed house and the atmosphere in the hall was electric, the band could rock hard with the best of them and I had no hesitation they would go down well as they had been doing over the last few months. Halfway through the first song my WEM system cut out and stopped working, as I jumped up to find what the fault was, a microphone and stand suddenly appeared in front of Keith and it was live, of course he started singing into it as that was the only mic working. Phil came over and said, "You might as well turn your system off now you're not using it." I never did find the fault. After our show when Deep Purple were setting up their gear our manager John Michelle tore into Phil and accused him of sabotaging our PA system, the argument got out of hand and a scuffle broke out between John and Phil. I managed to pull them apart and I refused to suspect Phil of doing that deliberately. But John was convinced it was sabotage, the next time I used the WEM PA everything worked OK, so we will never know the truth.

GOING STATESIDE

After the Canned Heat tour finished and the cultural shock of touring with an American band, Renaissance headed off on an American tour which exposed me to an even bigger cultural shock. Going to America took me by surprise as it was the first time a band had actually asked me to go on tour with them as their soundman. The band wanted me along but their manager John Michelle seemed a bit reluctant to let me go with them and tried to make out he was doing me a favour by paying me a salary. I was learning what tricks managers try on and I wasn't standing for that. I knew the band wanted me to go with them. One of the deciding factors for me going was Keith Relf told me one evening that because he had done eight American tours with The Yardbirds he was determined we take our own PA system with us. I thought that a bit weird and asked him, "Do we really need to take a PA, don't they have PA systems in the States?" Keith said the American systems installed in the clubs and theatres were nowhere near as good as the WEM system we had and the venues we were playing would not have the kind of sound quality he wanted. I was still surprised after hearing Canned Heat's sound system but that was because the band had their own PA and did not have to rely on house-installed PA systems. The first thing I did was to go out and buy a trunk to carry all the cables and accessories, not exactly a flight case but it did OK as a road case.

The day came and I was given the address of the air freight company at Heathrow to take the equipment, they kept me hanging around at the hanger for most of the day waiting for temporary export paperwork, documentation and the ATA Carnet but I got it all in the end, the next time I would see the equipment would be at Philadelphia airport a week later.

We arrived on 6th February 1970, in Philadelphia, the first time I had experienced jetlag, and it was weird that my body was telling me it was 10pm yet it was only 5pm local time. I was only 21 and it wasn't something I had experienced before, one of the first people I met outside the airport asked me if I knew the way to a location I had never heard of, I had to tell him, "Sorry mate, no good asking me I've only been in the country for an hour." America was a culture shock, I had of course seen numerous Hollywood movies and watched American TV shows and I knew roughly what to expect but actually being here was a different experience.

The manager John Michelle gave me a wad of American cash and sent me off to pick up a rental truck so I could collect the equipment from the freight terminal. I went to the airport U-Haul truck rental company to rent a truck for the equipment, but no one bothered to tell me that in America they require a credit or charge card, I told them I don't have one of those I'm paying cash in advance. They said "No, No, we need a credit or charge card," I said, "I'm paying cash in advance." I couldn't understand why they wouldn't accept cash and they couldn't understand why I didn't have any cards. In the end I had to leave a hefty cash deposit. This was 1970 and I never even thought of using cards, of course today it's normal to use cards. John Michelle though should have known better.

I picked up the equipment from the airport fright terminal and drove it to the venue called The Electric Factory in Philadelphia for two nights, it was a huge converted warehouse, not exactly designed for acoustics but it had a big stage.

When we arrived, America was still recovering from the 'British Invasion' of the 1960s with the legacy of The Beatles, Rolling Stones etc. America in 1970 was probably not the best place to be for a 21-year-old English boy brought up in a strict Methodist family, confronted by pretty girls wanting to chat you up just because you spoke with an English accent and worked with an English rock band. But I got through it in one piece.

After Philadelphia we flew down to New Orleans to perform at another venue called The Warehouse for three nights. I was met at the airport by two of the stage crew from The Warehouse who helped me load my equipment onto this huge ten-wheeled truck. With the equipment loaded and the back doors closed I proceeded to walk towards the passenger door when one of them threw me the keys and said, "This is your gear, you're driving." I was a bit taken aback because I had never driven anything this big and to be honest I didn't even know if I had a licence to drive something this size, it was enormous, just like one of those huge monster trucks you see in the movies, but I didn't mind having a go.

As I got into the driver's seat I realised that although I had driven in Europe on the right-hand side I'd never driven a left-hand drive vehicle before. As I put it into gear and started to pull away I was told this monster had eighteen gears, a six-way gearbox with three gear sticks, I was told to ignore the first six gears as those were for going up the side of a mountain. I was a bit nervous at first but soon got used to the size and the height. It was a bit over the top for the small amount of gear I had in the back but they were probably used to American acts with their huge boxes and flight cases.

When we got to the venue it really was just a warehouse, it seems that was what Americans used for music venues. The band headlining on the first night was Sly & The Family Stone, the second night the headliner was Jack Bruce with his friends Larry Coryell, Mike Mandel and Mitch Mitchell on drums from the Jimi Hendrix band, also on the bill was American rock band Pacific Gas & Electric. We were third on the bill each night and first on, the show went OK and after I cleared the stage of our equipment I went backstage. I was waiting in the backstage lounge area where the bar was when a girl came up and started talking to me, she was very friendly, so much so I thought that she might be chatting me up, but when the next band came off stage she introduced me to her husband, the guitarist with Pacific Gas & Electric. He was a nice guy and I was surprised how friendly everyone was, the guitarist even gave me one of his albums, I didn't expect to meet people so friendly. On the third night we were second on the bill supporting The Rascals originally called The Young Rascals who had hits with 'Good Lovin' and 'Groovin'.

This was Mardi Gras day in New Orleans and during the afternoon I went down town to see the Mardi Gras festival, very impressive, never seen anything like it before. My visit was cut short though when a mini riot broke out. Two police motorcyclists decided to ride down a pedestrian street almost knocking a man down, the man shouted some insults at them for nearly hitting him and they quickly stopped, came back and started to beat the hell out of this poor guy. I'd seen it in the movies but I'd never seen police brutality like this ever before. I was quite shocked.

From there we flew to a night club in Boston and performed at The Tea Party, then on to Bridgeport University, that was weird as it was just like an English university where you performed in the canteen hall after dinner. Next down to Washington DC and a show at The Emergency Club, the smallest venue we had played so far in America, it was just a small nightclub.

On to Columbia University in New York and then two nights at Bill Graham's famous Fillmore East. We were on the bill with The Kinks, one of my favourite bands from the 60s, but I was very disappointed with their performance, they sounded road tired and just went through the motion of going through their set of songs. Headlining the show on the first night was Savoy Brown, an English blues-rock band who were bigger in America than in England and selling more records in America than The Kinks so were top of the bill, one of the few bands from the 1960s who are still touring to this date.

The Fillmore East was a great venue, a 1920s movie theatre converted for live shows in 1968, its art deco interior was something to admire. The Joshua Light Show who put a psychedelic lighting backdrop onto the stage was an integral part of all the performances although it looked a bit dated by then. This was before bands carried their own light shows around. In the foyer there was a poster advertising forthcoming events for the next few days and weeks. There would be Ten Years After, Neil Young and Crazy Horse, Steve Miller Band, Miles Davies. John Mayall, BB King, Taj Mahal, Moody Blues, Argent, Joe Cocker and The Grease Band, Brian Auger Trinity, Stone the Crows, and that was just in the next few weeks, it must have been a great time to live in New York.

From here I picked up a U-Haul rental truck and was given an assistant roadie to travel with me, the band thought I would need someone to help me because we had a lot of overnight drives to do in the next few days. A guy called Max, he helped me with moving the gear and the driving, a good bloke and very helpful, we had a good time. We went on to Stony Brook State University on Long Island, The Music Hall in Cincinnati, East Town Theatre in Detroit, here we had armed police for security on the backstage door and in the hall, reminded me of the movie *Blues Brothers* where they lined the front of the stage to stop people enjoying themselves. I was chatting to one of the cops telling him that English police don't carry guns, he replied, "Well, you're more civilised over there." That may have been true but he probably wouldn't say that now.

Backstage the band wanted tea in the dressing rooms so a runner was sent out to buy a kettle, he came back and was really excited saying, "Look guys I've got an English teapot" I said, "That's not a teapot it's a kettle," he then corrected himself saying, "Look guys I've got an English tea kettle." I said, "It's not a tea kettle, it's just a kettle for boiling water," he looked unsure and confused, I said, "Don't you guys have kettles in America?" It was actually an English Swan kettle with an automatic switch-off that were popular in the 1960s and 70s, but they had never seen one before, that surprised me. After Detroit we drove to the Auditorium Theatre in Chicago. After the Chicago show I said goodbye to Max at the airport as I made the long flight to San Francisco, the band wouldn't pay for his air fare so for the next two weeks I managed on my own which was OK as it only involved two venues.

California seemed like a dream to me and most English guys of my age, with what we saw on television and in the Hollywood movies. I had visions of The Beach Boys, The Byrds, Crosby, Stills & Nash, surfing, beach parties, glamorous girls, big cars and sunshine, which it was of course but for most American musicians and would-be actors heading to Hollywood it would be a broken dream, many of them ending up working in a car wash.

We did four nights at Bill Graham's other famous venue the Fillmore West in San Francisco and five nights at the Whiskey a Go Go in Los Angeles. At the Fillmore West in San Francisco we were on the bill with The Butterfield Band and Savoy Brown again and stayed at a hotel across the Golden Gate Bridge in Sausalito. The Fillmore was originally a ballroom and they did have their own sound system which wasn't too bad. I met some interesting people who introduced me to some green tobacco, he said it wasn't marijuana and it was legal, I tried some and wish I hadn't, it turned out to be horse tranquilliser. I found out the only reason it was legal was because it hasn't yet been made illegal, it got me high as a kite, and I never took it again. We had a few days off here and I did a lot of sightseeing, doing the tourist bit and hanging out at the local nightclubs even though it was only March, it was lovely weather, really warm and sunny.

Considering the venue's world-famous reputation I was disappointed with the two Fillmores, the light shows were good but a bit dated, old-fashioned now for this new decade and the venues that once had impressive architecture were now looking tired, old and dirty as some old venues get when they've been through a lot, but the experience was good and I was glad to have been able to work in them. Whilst I was in the USA I took the opportunity to check out their sound systems and sound mixers. I was surprised how old-fashioned and basic they were, mostly Shure equipment, old theatre sound mixers with rotary volume controls instead of faders, basic tone controls and no outboard effects.

In Los Angeles we stayed at the Tropicana Hotel located on Santa Monica Boulevard, one of the more notorious hangouts I was told. 'The Trop' as it was called seem to cater to the cheaper end of the rock band hotel market. On arrival reception staff would say that so-and-so stayed here last week and so-and-so was booked in next week, names that went over my head at the time.

We had some days off before the next show so some of us went down to The Troubadour club for a night out, one of L.A.'s first nightspots, originally opened as a jazz club in the 1950s, changed to a folk club in the 60s and it didn't even permit amplifiers on stage until 1967 when Buffalo Springfield was the first 'electric' band allowed to play there.

It looked like the hangout for all of L.A.'s rock stars and those 'wannabe' rock stars along with their hangers-on and some very glamourous ladies or should I say groupies.

We performed for five nights at the famous Whiskey a Go Go club on Sunset Boulevard, famous because a whole list of big name acts have performed there over the years including Led Zeppelin, Jimi Hendrix, The Doors and too many others to mention. It's only a small venue, about 250 capacity, a typical night club with a stage at one end, the audience were mostly day trippers who went there because it was the groovy place to be and be seen at, more interested in being seen there than who was on stage that night.

I spent most of the time during the five days at the Whiskey while the band rehearsed some new songs. Kathy, one of the waitresses, invited me to stay at her apartment for the week down on Venice Beach. I stayed there for a few days and after the tour finished Kathy asked me to stay on for a few extra days. She showed me around California in her beaten-up old VW Beetle, we would drive up and down Sunset Boulevard and we took a trip to Hollywood's Disneyland. America really is a giant playground for adults, as nice as it is to visit, I wouldn't want to live there.

Back stage at the Fillmore West, San Francisco.
From left: Me, Jim Mc Carthy, John Hawken, Louis Cinamo.

John Hawken (piano player) stayed on in L.A. as well after the tour and I flew back to England with John and got ready for the next batch of UK gigs.

Keith was very particular about the band's sound balance and seemed happy with what I was doing, I asked him if he regretted taking our sound equipment from England for the tour, he said it was worth it. He kept telling me he had toured America eight times with The Yardbirds and the sound systems that were supplied were awful, which is why he insisted on taking our own WEM PA.

The first show back in England was at the BBC theatre in London for a live radio recording to be broadcast later in the week; there was this weird little fat piano player who opened the show and did a 30-minute set to warm up the audience, turns out it was someone called Elton John, I wonder what ever happened to him?

On 28th March we drove over to Europe for three open-air festivals: the Easter Pop Festival in Le Mans, France; the next day Le Bourget Pop Festival in Paris and then The Evolution 70 Festival in Hamburg Germany. Five more dates followed in Germany in Lubeck, Hamburg, Kiel, Salzgitter and Bremerhaven, then back to Mothers in Birmingham. I was getting quite used to playing Mothers, a club that was formerly a ballroom upstairs above a shop; some famous people have performed there including Deep Purple, Led Zeppelin, Fleetwood Mac, Black Sabbath, and The Who. Pink Floyd recorded their live album 'Ummagumma' there.

A week later we were back over to Europe performing at The Casino Pop Festival in Montreux in Switzerland, this time I was 'instructed' by the manager John Michelle to leave the sound to the locals as it was being recorded for Swiss television and they did not want anybody mixing sound in camera shot on the side of the stage. That's when I decided I needed to get out into the audience with the mixer, for this I needed a multicore cable with multiple pairs of screened wires, I decided to investigate this when I got home. There were six more shows in May including Bath University and London's Roundhouse where I remember seeing many good bands in the early 1960s.

Since coming back from America I could sense some tension within the band, things hadn't been right, nothing was said, at least not in front of me but I could sense an atmosphere and could tell things were not right and there were signs that this might not last much longer.

After one of the outdoor festivals at Breda in Holland, I started to dismantle the mics and backline after the show and saw what I thought was a stagehand take a guitar amplifier off the stage and run with it down the ramp. I suddenly realised that the guy wasn't actually a stagehand and was trying to steal it. Without thinking of the consequences I took a running leap and dived head first off the stage and landed on top of the thief, I grabbed the amplifier and the thief ran off. The festival was on Liberation Day and was supposed to be a celebration of the Allied forces liberating Holland from the Nazis, we were a British band whose Army helped liberate their country and someone tries to steal off us, there's gratitude for you.

I suspected the band were having problems with their manager John Michelle and he had his own problems with the band but he was on my back all the time for no reason. I could do without that. I suppose it came to a head one day when I went to his office to hand in some receipts and collect my back pay when he started on me again. I said, "You know what, I don't need this hassle from you." I threw the truck keys onto his desk, walked out and got the bus home. I felt a huge relief with what I'd done, I didn't have any problems with the band, I loved them all to bits and we all got on well. But that manager was out of order, it was not the first time, but it certainly was the last time. I knew it was time for me to jump ship before the ship sank.

I'd only been home a few minutes when the phone rang and it was John Hawken, he'd phoned to see what had happened. I said I was sorry I didn't speak to the band first but I hadn't gone to the office intending to quit. I said, "I can't work with him anymore, it's either him or me and I don't expect you to sack your manager for me so I walked away before I ended up punching the guy." John was sympathetic and disappointed I had left and he wished me well. The end of an era and the start of another, but not the last time I would work with John.

Sometime later I heard my old group Renaissance were on tour in France and had cancelled their show because the venue was too small, the stage too small and there was not enough AC power to supply the stage equipment. So not all promoters get away with ignoring the 'rider' (see below). Unfortunately when the audience heard the show had been cancelled, they found the band and crew at the local hotel and caused a riot setting the hotel on fire; everyone managed to get out OK.

RIDERS

A rider is a document attached to a contract which sets out certain requests that an artiste requires to perform their show. This will include a 'Technical

Rider' stipulating minimum stage size, sound, lighting and other equipment. A 'Hospitality Rider' will include requirements for the dressing room including food, drink and anything else the artiste requests. A 'Venue Rider' will request the number of stage crew, security, venue staff, guest tickets, and a variety of other items. Most rider requirements have been listed to avoid problems that have arisen from previous shows.

Riders can be a waste of time on small tours unless you're dealing with a well-established and reputable promoter. There are some good promoters but many will ignore the rider with the expectation that you will do the show anyway, no matter what you asked for. Some promoters cut corners to save money, leaving the crew with no food or drink. One such promoter on a tour I did with Def Leppard decided that we didn't need 6 stagehands to unload the 20 tons of equipment in the back of our 40-foot trailer, on this occasion we did the show but only after we did the unloading and loading ourselves. But the band only got half the equipment and the audience only got half the show.

Some riders have become famous for the wrong reasons, Van Halen asked for a bowl of M&Ms with all the brown ones removed. At first people thought that the band were egocentric rock stars being awkward, but in fact it was done deliberately to catch out promoters who didn't read their riders properly on the assumption that if they ignored that item, what else had they ignore? Of course there are always divas who ask for ridiculous things just because they can.

8

RADIO GERONIMO & THIRD WORLD WAR

Walking out on Renaissance was an end of an era for me and I started to wonder what I would do next; during the rest of May I didn't do anything.

One gig that I had done the previous year had changed my life, a gig at the 100 Club in London's Oxford Street, the headliners on that night were The Deviants. In the crowd I saw two stunningly beautiful girls walk across the dancefloor and sit down at a table, they looked about 18 or19 and didn't seem to be with anyone. I figured they must have been models, they stood out from the crowd and were easily the best looking pair in the room. After a while I just had to make contact and walked over, sat down and started talking to them. Becky was tall, slim and blonde, Estelle was tall, slim and brunette with a fuzzed up Afro hairstyle and both were very beautiful. Although I was talking to both of them I was especially attracted to Estelle but Becky was doing all the talking. I wondered whether I was directing my attention to the wrong person as Estelle was so quiet and shy.

After a while I said I was working for the band here tonight and had to go to work. I asked Estelle if she wanted to meet up again another time and to my surprise she said yes, we dated each other on a regular basis for the next few months, by this time though I'd discovered she wasn't 18 at all but just 16. Being away from home so much working on the road was difficult to keep a relationship going and somehow over time I lost contact with her until a few months later when she made contact with me with some surprising news. She told me she was pregnant and I was about to be a dad. That was a huge shock to me and I spoke to her on the phone a few times over the next few weeks and when our daughter Tamzin was born I went to visit them both and we struck up the relationship again, eventually getting married two years later.

SKY

In July 1970 I got a call from the office of Denny Laine and Trevor Burton's manager Tony Secunda; the last time I had worked with Denny and Trevor was in July 1969, a whole year ago. Those in Secunda's office were totally unaware that I had been busy with Renaissance for the past 12 months, but suddenly Tony needed someone to work with an American act he was managing, they were coming over to record an album at Olympic Studios with The Rolling Stones' producer Jimmy Miller. Oh, Olympic Studios again. "I know that place" I said to Sam who ran Tony's office. I asked what was involved and was told I had to pick them up at Heathrow, take them to their hotel and basically ferry them and their equipment to and from the studio as and when they were booked to record. I said I would do that and we agreed a price. It was basically a babysitting job. I was over the moon with that, I had no idea who this band were, they were called Sky, a three piece band from Detroit sounding not too unlike The Police who came along some years later.

The band comprised Doug Fieger on bass and vocals who later went on form a band called The Knack best known for their hit single 'My Sharona'; John Coury on guitar, keyboards and vocals who I later bumped into when he was playing guitar in the support band touring with Van Halen in 1978, he also worked as a guitarist on albums by Don Henley and Randy Meisner from The Eagles; Rob Stawinski on drums and vocals who later worked with Badfinger, and toured with The Who, Bob Seger, Traffic and Joe Cocker. But for now they were a new band recording their first album. I was unsure at first why they'd come to London to record their album until I was told that Rolling Stones producer Jimmy Miller wanted to produce the album at Olympic. Once again I would be sitting in with the maestro Jimmy Miller, what an honour.

The day came to pick them up at Heathrow; I went there and was looking out for three guys walking through arrivals with guitars, so I was surprised to see another six hangers-on who'd come along for the ride. I told the extra six they had to take a taxi as I was only taking the band, they were not part of the deal.

The hotel address I had been given was a private hotel in Earl's Court; when I rang the doorbell, a little old lady answered the door and asked who we were. When I explained we were the American guests come to book in she took one look at us, then took one look at the entourage who had just arrived by taxi and said, "Oh no, I was told to expect three American businessmen, I'm not letting you in." I can't say I blame her, the band looked OK and quite decent enough but the rest of the rabble looked like a bunch of hippies from San Francisco. I telephoned Secunda's office and Sam told me to go to the Ambassador Hotel in Notting Hill, she would tell them to expect us, but only the three musicians; I told the others to get lost. After that I didn't see the others again, I guess they went off on a sightseeing holiday, I'm relieved to say.

The recording was going really well and I was impressed with the quality of the songwriting and the performance of these guys, they were truly professional musicians in the way they worked and the way they acted. I thought these guys was going somewhere, if not now then later. I was right but not with this band, even though they only recorded two albums they all went on to perform with other artistes. When I heard The Knack some years later on the radio singing 'My Sharona' I thought, *I know that voice.* I found out it was Doug Fieger and his new band.

By now the band had suggested I stay at the hotel with them, which seemed like a good idea since I was spending so much time with them anyway, both working and socially and it saved me time commuting.

After one of the recording sessions at Olympic we were invited back to Jimmy Miller's house for some food and drink. Jimmy put on a reel-to-reel tape straight from the studio with some brand new Rolling Stones tracks that he had just recorded for their new album. I thought this sounded great, this was a studio tape played through a studio quality hi-fi and I was listening to the Stones new album before it had even been finished. After consuming some food and drink sitting around chatting he changed the tape, at first I thought it was another Stones track as it sounded just like them. Doug asked who the band was, Jimmy said it was a track by a band called Balls. John turned to me and said, "Hey, that's the band you'll be working with after us." So that's what they sounded like, it sounded just like a Stones track and in fact I thought it was the Stones. The single 'Fight for My Country' released on Wizard records was not a commercial success, partly I believe because of the name of the band and the fact the BBC wouldn't play it. I did say to them later that the name Balls was not really a radio-friendly kind of name to pick, but they didn't listen.

Sky sightseeing outside Abbey Road Studios:
From left, John Coury, Doug Fieger, Rob Stawinski

Sky finished their album and it was released on RCA records, not a commercial success but it did have some good tracks on it.

RADIO GERONIMO

As well as a management company Tony Secunda was also running a radio station Radio Geronimo from the top floor of his Harley Street offices. I would go up there sometimes and listen to some of the tracks being recorded for the next show although it was not a live transmission. If I was in the office at the right time (or in my case the wrong time) Tony Secunda would get me to collect the master tape from upstairs and take it over to Heathrow Airport where it would go on the next flight to Monte Carlo for transmission. It was then transmitted over the airwaves of Radio Monte Carlo on 205m medium wave which rented out airtime at the weekend during the night. Hugh and Terry were the DJs and it was a mix of 70s rock, blues, folk and oddball stuff they would find. Tony was financing it along with Jimmy Miller (although I don't know why Jimmy got involved). Tony wanted a more commercial sound to attract more listeners but there weren't that many listeners and the radio station didn't seem to be making any money. They tried to sell records, T-shirts and even roll-your-own cigarette papers but they didn't sell much merchandise.

Geronimo wasn't a pirate station, nor was it broadcasting from a ship in the North Sea and it wasn't illegal, it was broadcasting from a legitimate radio station in Monte Carlo, but the BBC didn't like it and tried to jam it with another transmitter (typical of the BBC who don't like competition). After a few months Geronimo closed down through lack of money.

BALLS

When Sky flew back to Detroit I started working with Denny Laine and Trevor Burton again, it was good to see them after a year, they were a good couple of blokes to work with and very sociable as well, treated me like one of the team.

One of the first jobs I had down at the farmhouse in Theale was to make sure the barn was weatherproof and watertight for the band to use as a rehearsal room and recording studio. Tony Secunda had sent down ten large rolls of thick plastic sheeting, a staple gun and some gaffer tape. Single-handed I had to climb a ladder and cover the inside roof with plastic sheets and fix them in place to keep the weather out.

I set up the guitar and bass amps, a drum kit and a small PA system. We were joined by guitarist Steve Gibbons from The Steve Gibbons Band and drummer Mike Kellie from Spooky Tooth. A mobile recording studio came a few times to the farm to record or we drove to Olympic Studios. At Olympic two girl singers came in a few times who had been recording next door in studio 1 with the Stones to record the backing vocals, names that I knew but I'd never seen before, P.P. Arnold and Doris Troy, no messing there, they were legends and great singers.

Twelve tracks were recorded on the Balls album, but it was never released. One of Denny Laine's songs 'Say You Don't Mind' was a hit when it was recorded a year later by ex-Zombie, Colin Blunstone.

After spending most of July, August and September in the barn at Theale or at Olympic Studios we set out on the road doing a few small clubs around England, nothing special. I don't even think the audiences knew who the musicians were that were performing for them, it was only supposed to be a low-profile warm-up for bigger things. In October we went over to Frankfurt and did four nights at The Zoom club, a seedy nightclub on the first floor where American military police would come in each night looking for off-duty squaddies on a night out who had been told that The Zoom was off limits, you could always tell a GI by his haircut. One night two GIs got dragged out by a couple of real hard-looking MPs, hate to think what happened to them.

During one of my visits to the farm Trevor Burton had just brought home a preview of the new album by George Harrison, 'All Things Must Pass'. We sat around and listened to the whole album totally amazed at what this guy had just recorded, as soon as it was released at Christmas I bought it and played it non-stop.

Over the next few months up to January 1971 we did a few more club gigs and universities and the Royal York Hotel on the Isle of Wight. One day I was asked to take the band's backline to a new rehearsal room in London, there was a different drum kit already set up when I arrived, I thought it looked a bit flash, but who did it belong to? I found out when Alan White walked in; until recently he had been working with John Lennon's Plastic Ono Band and later went on to join the prog-rock band Yes. As they rehearsed with this new drummer nothing was said but to me it looked like an audition.

The next week we were flying to Nice in southern France for a TV special. We met at Heathrow airport and got as far as Paris for a connecting flight, but as we were waiting to check in Tony heard a Tannoy announcement to call his office. The message was that the TV show had been cancelled and we should come home, but Tony decided to take the band anyway and told me that I wouldn't be needed. He asked me to change the tickets so I queued up at the ticket desk waiting to be served, about ten minutes later he came over and asked why I still hadn't changed the tickets, I told him there was a queue. He gave me such a filthy look and looked at me so viciously as if to say I should have gone to the front of the queue, which was the first time I saw him as he really was in a new light. He may have intimidated some people but he didn't intimidate me and I was all ready to tell Tony that if anyone tried to push in front of me they wouldn't get away with it. He just turned away and went off in a huff. I guess he wasn't very impressed with me for not forcing myself to the front, but I did get the tickets changed without getting into a fight.

This reminds me of an incident sometime later when I was flying out of Stansted Airport on my way to a festival in Germany, I was on my own, there were about 20-30 people in the queue and I was about eight from the front. I saw this young German man in his twenties about six feet tall slowly shuffle into the queue and push in front of an elderly lady two places from the front, I waited for a few moments to see if anybody was going to say or do anything but nobody did. I left my bag in line and walked up to the elderly lady and said to her, "Has this man pushed in front of you?" She said, "Yes he did," so I said to him in a loud voice so everyone else could hear, "Oi, you, there's a queue, get to the back, if you want to be at the front you'll have to get out of bed earlier." He looked at me in shock and shuffled himself to the back of the queue, then to my surprise there was a spontaneous round of applause from the rest of the queue for what I did.

The band split up shortly afterwards, Denny Laine joined Paul McCartney's Wings and Trevor Burton formed his own Trevor Burton Band.

KA to REIGN

I received an unexpected call from my friend Andi Banks who had been helping me on the road with Renaissance and was playing bass guitar in the band KA; for some reason they had just changed their name to Reign and I was booked to do a few gigs with them, including a gig upstairs at the legendary Ronnie Scott's Club in Frith Street, Soho, which I really enjoyed. Coincidently they had just recorded their first single written by Keith Relf and Jim McCarty from The Yardbirds and Renaissance.

Along with Andi Banks on bass, there were Tim Renton on guitar, Andy Renton on drums and Robin LeMesurier on guitar, Robin was the son of actor John LeMesurier from 'Dad's Army' fame and actress Hattie Jacques who appeared in many 'Carry On' films.

Andi, Robin and I used to hang out together, sometimes I would visit Andi at his place and Robin at his house and they would sometimes come round to my house. One night at my house Robin told me he got kicked out of The Wombles for being caught with some marijuana. I guess it wasn't considered a good message to send to children if one of The Wombles was caught smoking dope. I'd often call round to Robin's house at Eardley Crescent in Earl's Court for a social visit. His mother Hattie Jacques was one of the friendliest, most generous and lovely people I've ever met, she even invited my wife Estelle and me to a Christmas meal on Boxing Day and again the following two years. After a great meal with Hattie and her guests we would go downstairs to Robin's apartment in the basement and listen to some music.

Mike Batt the songwriter for The Wombles asked the guys in Reign if they would dress up in Womble outfits and do some Womble gigs including *Top of the Pops*, of course no one knew who was inside the costumes but it was a good gig for them. After The Wombles, Robin joined The Rod Stewart Group as a guitar technician, changing strings and tuning guitars for the band; unbeknown to him a film crew was recording him playing guitar under the impression he was actually in the band rather than just one of the road crew.

Another night at my house when Robin and Andi Banks called round for a social visit, Robin would tell us about his time on tour with Rod, but you can't always believe what you read in the press. When I asked him what happened on that flight to Australia when the band got arrested for having a food fight on the plane, he said, "There was no food fight and we weren't arrested."

Andi Banks later worked with me on the road in several bands and Robin went off to live in Los Angeles and got a gig playing guitar with Air Supply, Strider and eventually playing guitar in The Rod Stewart Band. Tim and Andy Renton went to form a band 3AM.

GRAHAM BOND

The next day I was asked to do four shows with another great blues man, Graham Bond, who I used to see perform at the Cooks Ferry Inn back in my younger days. He is best known for fronting the band in which Jack Bruce and Ginger Baker played before they joined Eric Clapton in Cream.

THIRD WORLD WAR

It was almost a year ago to the day that I did my last gig with Renaissance. I received a phone call from John Hawken the piano player to ask if I was working with anyone. I said, "I've been working with various people, Sky, Balls, Reign and Graham Bond." John told me he had joined a band called Third World War and they needed someone to mix their front-of-house sound. I asked the usual questions: are they any good? What do they sound like? How much work do they have? etc. I thought they had to be fairly good otherwise John wouldn't be with them.

He suggested I come down to their next rehearsal to meet the band and listen to what they were doing. I was in for a shock; what I was listening to was England's first ever punk band, this was 1971, long before the word 'punk' had even been invented. They were rude, crude and raw and sounded like it, but I also heard something different to the normal rock bands of the past and despite their appearance they were really nice guys.

They had a raw urban sound, more than any other band of its day, what made them different was their aggressive anti-popstar, anti-establishment working class attitude and revolutionary left-wing working class lyrics, typically what future punk bands would adopt.

What did impress me though was the fact that they had a WEM PA and not one WEM sound mixer but two, this was great, I actually had ten channels to work with, that sounds ridiculous these days but believe me it wasn't in 1971. The only time I'd seem two WEM mixers linked together was when Fleetwood Mac used their WEM PA at the Lyceum Ballroom in 1969. They also had what I wanted, a multicore cable to connect the microphones to the mixer, I had actually got the mixer 'out front' in the audience and to the back of the hall at last.

The band had two other roadies, a guy called H who drove the band around and Roger Manifold, also known as Roger the Hat. Roger came across very possessive at first, saying things like, "I'll let you mix my band if you're any good." Sorry Roger that's the band's decision, not yours, but despite that initial first meeting, we became good friends and worked well together. I think Roger just wanted to lay down some ground rules by making clear it was 'his' band, he was here first and he was the main man. OK, Roger.

I listened to the album they had just finished recording and they had tracks like 'Ascension Day', 'Working Class Man', 'Shepherd's Bush Cowboy', 'Teddy Teeth Goes Sailing' (after PM Ted Heath), it reminded me of The Who's first album. The main men were Terry Stamp, an ex-truck driver and he looked like one as well, who played what he called a 'Chopper' guitar, and ex-Thunderclap Newman bass player Mick Avery. Also Paul Olson on drums, John Knightsbridge on guitar, and of course John Hawken on piano. John was a piano player, not a keyboard player, and there were no electronic keyboards in 1970 that sounded like a piano so John insisted he would only play a real piano.

During John's time with Renaissance the promoter had to provide a tuned upright piano at each venue, but this was becoming impractical and unreliable so John bought himself a Lindner upright piano. He stripped it down to its bare metal frame to save weight and fitted three pickups specially built for the piano. I think they were just modified guitar pickups. I fixed them on with drawing pins at each gig. The best thing about it was that it had a folding keyboard that supposedly made it a bit easier to move, ha-ha. It was as heavy as hell but I managed to get the thing in and out of the truck with Roger's help by putting it on a trolley board.

The first venue was the famous Marquee Cub in Wardour Street, a venue I knew well and had been to many times. Terry Stamp (lead vocalist) with his Chopper guitar strutted around the stage. John played his stripped-down piano which made it look real mean, the first time I'd taken a real acoustic piano on the road, and Paul hammered away at his massive double drum kit with two kick drums and what looked like a hundred cymbals, which took up a lot of stage space.

The Marquee Club was a good gig and they went down well. The next show was in France at The Piblokto Club in Dourges, it was a typical French nightclub, dark, dirty, dingy, smelt of stale beer and French cigarettes. The show went OK but I'm not sure the French knew what to make of the band, they weren't exactly Johnny Halliday, and I don't think they had seen or heard anything like that before. I do remember the unisex toilet in the building which didn't have any doors on it, to my surprise nobody seemed to mind.

Straight back to England into the Lyceum Ballroom in London supporting the mighty American rock band Mountain, it was a good gig but we didn't get much help from the Mountain crew and my PA system wasn't set up where I wanted it. The music magazine journalists were all down there, *Melody Maker* did a hatchet job on the band. Roy Hollingworth of the *Melody Maker* was in the crowd and declared it was the worst band he ever heard, to which the manager Paul Fenton's reaction was to blow up the MM review into a poster and fly plaster it all over London on billboard sites just to show that the band didn't care and to make a point; it was like saying bad was good, and there's no such thing as bad publicity, the publicity was a brilliant masterstroke and created a lot of interest.

After six months of doing gigs around the UK the manager was experiencing financial problems in that he couldn't pay the band or the crew. A decision was made that Roger had to go to cut costs. I felt guilty as I was the new guy on the crew. Soon after he left I heard he got himself a job with Pink Floyd and had a talking part on one of the tracks on the *Dark Side of the Moon* album.

Third World War was without doubt the first punk band in England, although there has been some dispute over the claim; the phrase 'punk' hadn't been invented then but Clash guitarist Joe Strummer acknowledged some years later that TWW were out there doing punk long before anyone else was.

During May, June and July we did a lot of gigs around England and a tour of Finland was scheduled for July and August. The day after a gig at the Rugby Club in Skewan, Wales, I drove the band's truck from Wales overnight to catch the ferry from Harwich to Hamburg and then drove across Germany, Denmark and Sweden and then caught another ferry across to Finland.

The Finnish promoter put us up in a 4-star hotel the first night and bought us all a nice meal in the restaurant, I thought this was going to be a good tour, but alas he was setting us up into a false sense of security: that was the last we saw of civilisation and the only decent hotel we saw all trip. The very next day we set off across Finland to an open-air festival just outside Turku, the weather was glorious and I hadn't expected Finland to be so hot or so picturesque. Over the next three weeks we worked back-to-back which involved 28 shows in 23 days travelling from festival to festival and a few halls which were built at the end of long dirt tracks in the middle of nowhere. As they were so remote I didn't think anyone would turn up, but they did by the thousands and the gigs were packed out, on one occasion doing four shows in a day. We also did a live Finnish TV show in Helsinki.

When we got to Lapland in Northern Finland the sun didn't set all night. In Lapland, the sun stays above the horizon 24 hours a day for two months of the year. We experienced the 'Land of the Midnight Sun' and it was literally sunshine all night; driving back to our hotel at 1.00am after the night's shows the sun was shining in a clear blue sky. Temperatures reached 30 degrees Celsius some days, something I never expected in Finland.

The gigs were weird; sometimes we used our WEM PA and sometimes I would use the festival PA system, which was usually a hotchpotch of different speaker cabinets; one stage was floating on rafts on a lake which bobbed up and down causing a wave every time Terry jumped up and down. Most of the time the local audience were out of their heads on the local moonshine, similar to vodka, a brew they distilled in the forests of Finland, made out of pine trees, a lethal alcoholic drink as strong as jet fuel. I never touched it, not after I saw what it did to the locals. Although alcohol was legal in Finland it was only available from Government shops.

Finland like Sweden at that time was full of American Vietnam army deserters. They made their way from Vietnam to live in Sweden because it was neutral; some got bored in Sweden and moved across the Gulf of Bothnia to Finland, which was less densely populated, and some of them formed American rock bands.

One American GI we met had a cabin in the woods next to a lake, he invited us all down to his cabin on one of the few days we had off. We had a great time, and we all took advantage of the facilities he had there, a sauna we would sit in for ten minutes then run and jump off the jetty he had jutting out into the lake, a barbeque where he cooked reindeer steaks; reindeer is common in Scandinavia and a popular dish, similar to the way we eat cow or sheep. There was no electricity so he didn't have a fridge but he did have a cool box full of beer which he kept cool in the lake. He also had a canoe and a speedboat, which came with waterskis. Of course I had to try this, never having waterskied before, I failed miserably, although I put that down to the fact that the speedboat driver insisted on pulling away at full speed which left me flying through the air like a rocket and once I hit the water I was being dragged along underwater like a torpedo until I eventually managed to let go; it was fun though.

Whilst the band took the ferry from Helsinki to Copenhagen, my return trip with the truck was on a drive-on drive-off freight ferry across the Baltic Sea. I had to share a cabin with a Finnish truck driver; he was quite insistent that I shared a bottle of Finnish vodka with him, despite trying to decline the offer. I got the impression that my refusal was being seen as an insult, he couldn't speak English and I couldn't speak Finnish so I reluctantly had a few vodkas with him then I slept the rest of the journey, but not before witnessing a brilliant sunset across the horizon on a sea that was so still it was like a mirror, the only ripple on the surface was the wake created by the ship. I'd never seen a sea so still and tranquil.

Back in England after the Finnish tour we did a couple of dozen gigs around the UK, and then we were called into a meeting with their manager Paul Fenton at his flat in Brompton Road, Knightsbridge for a band meeting to discuss the future. Halfway through the meeting Joe Cocker walked in from a tour he had just finished; Paul was also manager for Joe Cocker as well as for us. Paul said, "Don't mind Joe he's just staying here for a few days." It turns out the band were experiencing further financial difficulties and there wasn't enough money to pay the band or me; although the band were prepared to work for nothing, I had to tell Paul and the band that although I wanted to stay I couldn't work for nothing, I would be looking for something else. I continued to do gigs with the band whilst looking for another band to work with, but typically when you want one you can't find one. When you're not looking for work the offers come from all angles and you don't know which to take. So I continued to work with TWW until the day came when I received an unexpected phone call from an old friend and the last show I did with the band was at the Marquee on 20th September 1971.

9

SOUL, ROCK AND VINEGAR JOE

In October I received a phone call from a friend of mine, Norman Dugdale, who had been doing some van driving jobs with various bands at the same time I was, and I used to pass some of my jobs on to Norman when I was overbooked. He had got himself a job as road manager with a band called Vinegar Joe who had just re-formed from the remnants of the band Dada. He asked me to come and work with him with the new band. The band changed musicians a few times over the years but the line-up I first met was: Robert Palmer and Elkie Brooks on joint lead vocals, Pete Gage on guitar, Tim Hinkley on keyboards, Steve York on bass, Rob Tait on drums.

I was asked to go down to Olympic Studios (that place again), a place I knew well by now to meet the band, they were busy finishing off their debut album called 'Vinegar Joe' although it wasn't released until 1972.

As I walked into the control room Elkie was hammering out a vocal track. I hadn't heard Elkie sing before except at The Beatles concert some years ago and I couldn't remember what she had sung then, but my first impression was she sounded like a cross between Janis Joplin and Maggie Bell. I was introduced to the band with: "This is Wilf our new soundman." I hadn't been called a soundman before and didn't expect to be given that title but I thought it sounded good.

Norman was their road manager and although they'd done a few warm-up gigs, Norman didn't want to mix their sound and lug their gear around, so he asked me if I wanted the gig and brought me in to take care of their stage equipment, do the sound and drive the truck while he drove the band.

The first gig we did was at the Black Swan in Sheffield; luckily for me it had really good acoustics so for a first show the sound in there was really tight and punchy. The band were really pleased with what I did; I thought the band played well, which helped me. The system wasn't anything special, just four full-range HiWatt cabinets each side and a HiWatt mixer, which put me back on the side of the stage again, just like the system used by Deep Purple at the Royal Albert Hall. I really missed having Third World War's multicore cable.

It wasn't long before Elkie had her picture splashed right across the front page of the *Melody Maker* magazine; Robert Palmer was a bit miffed that his picture wasn't on the front page as well, as they were both lead singers in the band. For the next eight months I worked for this band full-time, not taking any work from any other bands, that suited me fine at the time as there was plenty of work and I enjoyed the routine of working with just one band. We did practically every town in England, every pub, club, ballroom, university and college, the band really worked hard, we did a BBC radio show at the Maida Vale Studios, an *Old Grey Whistle Test* TV show, a few shows at the Marquee Club including one supporting Wishbone Ash, one of my all-time favourite bands.

I got on well with the band and enjoyed doing the shows with them; Pete Gauge the guitarist was telling me he once played guitar for Geno Washington & the Ram Jam Band, the same band I used to see down at the Cooks Ferry Inn years before. Pete told me that one night backstage Geno said to the band, "From now on everybody in the band is going to wear black on stage," so the next gig everyone got changed into black shirts and black trousers to go on stage, then Geno, to everyone's surprise (or not), suddenly appears wearing a bright white suit. No surprise there then, a 6 foot black man in a white suit with a white band wearing black, who's going to stand out on stage more? Rod Tate the drummer was a nice guy and he once played for Pete Brown's Battered Ornaments and The Crazy World of Arthur Brown. Which reminds me, my friend Mick was the roadie for Pete Brown, in those days the band used an ex-army ambulance as their equipment truck and he told me that one night on the M1 on the way to a gig he was late, so decided to put the blue light on. It didn't take long for a police car they passed to realise this was no army ambulance, with a long-haired hippy at the wheel and driving on civilian registration plates, he was pulled over and given a ticket.

One particular night that I won't forget at the Marquee Club, Elkie was belting out her usual stuff, stomping her foot and banging the mic stand down on the stage as she always did, when suddenly she stopped singing and all went quiet. I looked up to see Elkie had disappeared from the stage, she had smashed a hole in the stage with the mic stand and disappeared into the hole, luckily she wasn't hurt and the show continued. We all had a good laugh about it and it was the topic of many conversations for weeks to come. That would have made a good Spinal Tap sketch. I must have done a dozen or so shows at the Marquee with Vinegar Joe. Elkie would get through a bottle of brandy each night before she went on stage, I dread to think how much she drank after the shows.

Robert Palmer was the other lead vocalist, he had just left a band called The Alan Bown Set. Robert and Elkie would do alternate songs and each go on backing vocals when they weren't doing lead vocal, they sounded good together with their blend of harmonies. I tried to keep the vocals 'out front' as much as possible, to keep the harmonies clear, clean and distinct, as close to the record as possible.

Another memorable night was in February at the Top Rank Suite in Sunderland when we did a show supporting Free with Paul Rodgers on vocals. It was a packed out ballroom, no seats, standing room only with security barriers across the front of the stage. I had my sound mixer in the security area in front of the stage. After our set I cleared the stage of our backline gear and went back down into the security area to watch over my mixer and watch the rest of the show. Before the first song from Free was over, the crowd were pushing so hard against the barrier it started to bend; the security men decided to evacuate as it was too dangerous to stay there and advised me to get out. I unplugged the mixer and handed it up onto the stage, quickly scrambling up onto the stage myself as the only safe way out; as soon as I had got to safety the crash barrier collapsed and the crowd were pressed right up against the stage. Lucky escape.

Another supporting role for us was at the Top Rank Suite in Cardiff supporting Argent and Caravan, two great bands. At Leeds Polytechnic we had a support band called America. I was very impressed with them and they eventually became international stars.

My wedding in 1972 with guests Elkie Brookes, guitarist Pete Gage, Road Manager Norman Dugdale and members of the extended family.

In 1972 I married my girlfriend Estelle. I invited the band to the wedding and I asked Pete Gage to be my best man and Tim Hinckley to play the church organ. When the day came, Pete and Elkie arranged to pick up Tim first and then collect me on the way to the church, which was about an hour's drive away in Shenfield, Essex.

I waited anxiously for them to pick me up and after an hour I was getting worried. I telephoned Pete but got no reply; eventually Pete and Elkie turned up but without Tim. Pete said he went to pick up Tim but he was nowhere to be found, so we headed off to Shenfield without an organist. With the congregation sitting in the church waiting without any music playing, the bride's car had to do two laps of the village until I arrived with Pete and Elkie. It was very embarrassing for me arriving late. Thinking about it, it was a bad idea asking Tim in the first place, something I will not forget. (Thanks Tim).

After the wedding I overheard Pete saying to Norman Dugdale, "Now he's married I'll give it six months before he quits the music business." He didn't know I'd heard him and it turned out he was wildly wrong on his prediction by about twenty years.

When Tim Hinkley left the band I wasn't disappointed, not after what he did on my wedding day, I didn't even get an apology. The band were talking and thinking about a suitable replacement, I suggested to Pete that he might consider John Hawken who I'd worked with in Renaissance and Third World War; I told them his experience with The Nashville Teens would go a long way in this band. I called John and asked him if he was interested as I knew TWW had eventually split up after completing a few contractual obligations. He said he was interested and I put him in touch with Pete Gage. Soon afterwards he joined the band and away we went again. This was now the fourth band with whom I had worked with John on piano; I later learnt that Elkie Brooks had supported The Nashville Teens on a few shows when Don Arden had managed both the Teens and Elkie years earlier; luckily for Elkie, she didn't sign a contract with Don so she was able to walk away when a better offer came along.

One of the weirdest experiences of working with Vinegar Joe was doing the May Ball at Cambridge University each year, the end of term bash that goes on all night and features a variety of bands and assorted amusements including a string quartet, a trad jazz band and a headlining rock or pop band. The corridors are decorated out and transformed into tunnels of different themed styles. The lavish black tie ball is the biggest event of the student calendar and marks the end of their exams. Students have a lavish five-course meal followed by music and dancing. An ox roast was laid on but to my horror the animal was delivered alive and slaughtered in the grounds where it was to be cooked, I was told it's easier to walk it in rather than carry it in.

These students are supposedly the country's future leaders, the country's next generation of politicians and leaders of business, but for one night a year there is champagne flowing, dancing in the street and punting down the River Cam, many making a right fool of themselves. After the show the celebrations continued well into the morning with girls in full ballgowns and guys in their tuxedos right Hooray Henrys and Henriettas all getting drunk, and as the sun came up students walked around barefoot, ties askew and ball dresses crumpled, with many dancing in the street swigging from bottles of champagne.

Previous acts who have performed at the May Balls around Cambridge have included The Who, The Moody Blues, Pink Floyd, Soft Machine, Fleetwood Mac, Deep Purple, David Bowie and Genesis before they all became mega-famous. It was an interesting gig to do, I did three in all.

During one of the band's gigs at Bumpers Club in London I happened to see a sound mixer being used by one of the other bands on the bill similar in design to a studio model, but much smaller and more compact. Remember we all used our own PAs in those days. I spoke to the soundman operating it and he told me it came from a British manufacture called Midas; it was a 16-channel mixer with sliding faders instead of the old-fashioned round knobs. I decided to investigate further with a view to buying one myself.

WEM had dominated the PA market until now and every big band was using WEM, but others were emerging in the wake of WEM's success; unfortunately WEM didn't bring out their 9-channel audiomaster until 1975, by that time it was too late, they had lost the market to Midas, Studiomaster and Kelsey-Morris. Crown were building more powerful amplifiers and Dave Martin was developing the bin and horn speaker system similar to the one used by Canned Heat. But more on that later.

After a few months with the heavy workload getting busier, Pete suggested I get someone to help me out with the driving and heavy lifting, it was getting to be a two-man job, so this guy Dave came in and he helped me out setting up the equipment and driving the band's truck.

In April 1972 as a result of a few speeding fines I accumulated twelve points on my driving licence and was banned for six months; that was devastating for me but I guess I deserved it after getting caught three times in three years. Considering the mileage I did up and down the country I had been lucky to get away with it for so long. As a result of this, Dave, my side kick took over driving the truck, which worked out fine for a while because I would get a train into London to meet him on the way to the gig, he would drop me off home afterwards, but this was getting too much for Dave and he was getting resentful of having to drop me off at home in the early hours of the morning when there was no public transport. I don't blame him for that.

It came to a head one day when Dave told Pete Gage he didn't want to be doing all the driving on his own. I spoke to Pete about the situation and Pete asked if I would 'stand down' until I got my licence back, in other words I was being sacked, it hit me quite hard although I was expecting this might happen for some time since I'd lost my licence.

The last show I did was on 27th April at the Marquee, so I took some time off while I decided what to do. I could wait out the remaining time of the six-month ban or I could do something else. I had a wife, a baby and a mortgage, so I couldn't just sit and wait to get my licence back and even then I still didn't know if I had a job to go back to. Vinegar Joe brought in someone else to do their sound and I wasn't even guaranteed I'd get my old job back.

Leaving Vinegar Joe was the end of another era and again I wondered what I would do next but I didn't have long to wait.

Photo: briancooke.com
Vinegar Joe at a BBC Studio.
Front Row from left, Pete Gage, Elkie Brookes, Robert Palmer.

10

THE MIDAS TOUCH

After losing my licence I considered what to do next. I thought about going back to my old trade in electronics, but there were not many jobs being advertised. Then I decided to pay a visit to Midas Amplification where I had previously been looking at buying a mixer I'd seen at Bumpers Club.

I spoke to Jeff Byers, the owner and brains behind Midas. I told him what had happened and we talked about whether there was something I could do at Midas with both my experience in electronics and having mixed sound for a few bands. He was interested in my background and asked me if I wanted a job on production helping to build the mixers. For me this was a perfect combination, it gave me unprecedented access to the workings of a modern sound mixer combined with the understanding of how they worked, and it kept me in the music business.

So in June 1972 I started working at Midas Amplification, travelling across London by train to a small workshop at 87 North Grove near Seven Sisters tube station. The building had previously been a corner shop and had all the windows blacked out so there was no indication from the outside what went on inside. Inside was a single room downstairs with workbenches around the outside of the room, a storage rack of parts down one side, in the corner was a staircase which went upstairs into what was Jeff's office and where he also lived in a single bedroom. Jeff's business was his whole life and he spent 24 hours a day working at it, that devotion and dedication to his business was to prove highly profitable for him in the future.

Also working at Midas was Chas Brook whom I had previously met when he was working as a roadie for a group called Egypt; they didn't do much apart from a few college dates around London. Chas was an experienced electronics engineer with a university degree and helped Jeff design some of the electronics for the mixers they built. Chas would be better known later for forming the company 'Brooke Siren Systems' (BSS) which developed DI (Direct Injection) boxes, compressors, noise gates and other assorted audio processors for the professional audio market.

There was also Nigel, a good guy who was busy wiring up mainframes and printed circuit boards. I was put to work with Nigel assembling the printed circuit boards, wiring up the mixer mainframe and doing the internal wiring. Each channel was hand-wired including the printed circuit boards (PCBs), which we hand-populated with all the components. This suited me fine as I was familiar with this type of work; the next best thing to mixing live sound was building the actual mixers, which gave me a great insight into what made them work, how they are made and how to repair them when they went wrong, something that other live sound engineers didn't get the opportunity to experience.

Midas was very much a cottage industry at that time, PA technology didn't really exist before 1969 in the UK and most bands used Selmer or Vox speaker cabinets which were derived from guitar speaker cabinets. Charlie Watkins of WEM came up with the 4 x 12" speaker column; it was revolutionary then and everyone from Pink Floyd down bought them with the WEM 100-watt amplifier until Midas and Martin came along.

We were building Midas sound mixers for a variety of bands including Mud, Supertramp and others, including one for HMS Ark Royal for their ballroom, (no, I didn't know they had a ballroom either), and for a few sound equipment rental companies, which was a new and fast growing industry at the time. Companies like Entec, Britannia Row, Colosseum Acoustics, Concert Sound, ML and others had started up in business supplying sound systems to bands on tour; quite often these started out as a PA system owned by a band and then expanded into renting their equipment out for others to use. This was a new concept.

One of the first generation 12-channel Midas mixers I built.

Until then, bands had owned their own PA systems but as the equipment was steadily getting bigger and more sophisticated so did the expense, and it was increasingly out of reach of most bands except for the biggest and most successful. Along with the sound mixers, Midas also produced a powerful amplifier block consisting of 4 channels of 500 watts to drive the speakers. This amplifier 'block' as it was called delivered a powerful 2,000 watts, making it a big beast. Even though it looked big and ugly I still rate this as the best amplifier ever manufactured for delivering bass due to its huge power transformer.

Midas was considered at the top end of the mixer market at this time mainly I think because they used lots of input and output transformers, real line output stages and quality integrated circuits rather than cheap transistors like some other mixer manufacturers at the time.

Other new manufacturers on the market pushing WEM aside were Soundcraft, which made a small and compact mixer, but not modular like Midas, and Kelsey-Morris, a good desk that worked well but was cheaply made. One early feature of Midas consoles was a built-in two-way electronic crossover, an unusual feature in a mixer at the time but very useful as active crossovers were becoming more popular in sound systems.

Whilst I was at Midas, Jeff collaborated with Dave Martin, who founded Martin Audio, who I got to know really well over the years. After many years of WEM having dominated the PA systems for the live music industry, PA systems were about to go modular with a revolutionary bin and horn system pioneered by the likes of Dave Martin and Bill Kelsey (of Kelsey-Morris).

Dave Martin in particular had taken a basic American bass bin design and modified it to include a flare on the front of the speaker cabinet. Dave told me he had seen the RCA W cabinets being used at an Iron Butterfly concert, just like the ones I had also seen around the back of cinema screens. Iron Butterfly had brought some W cabinets over from America for their UK tour but didn't want to pay the air freight back to the states, being seven feet high and weighing 500lbs I can understand why, so they were sold off to prog-rock band Yes.

They were called 'W' cabinets because the sound from the two 15-inch speakers would travel in a W direction (back-forward-back-forward) inside the cabinet; this produced a much bigger, deeper and louder bass response than just a forward-facing loudspeaker like WEM.

Dave Martin took the RCA W cabinet and cut it in half, reduced the length of the horn and fitted just one 15-inch speaker. Dave also invented the mid-range Philishave speaker, so-called because it looked like a Philips electric shaver which had two 12-inch speakers inside.

On top of the bass and mid-range cabinets were the high range horn cabinets which housed a Vitavox horn with a JBL driver on the back, creating a powerful high-frequency sound. I'd often go down to Dave's workshop in Covent Garden to discuss over a cup of tea the different stacking variations. He had his recommendations and I had my own ideas which I put to him.

Pink Floyd who had used WEM speaker cabinets for the last few years now used Martin, so did Supertramp, King Crimson, ELP and many others, and it wasn't long before PA rental companies such as Concert Sound, Colosseum Acoustics and Entec bought Martin speakers; they were so successful that bands were ditching their WEM speaker cabinets like yesterday's technology.

There is more to speaker cabinet design than just bolting a loudspeaker into a wooden box. It all goes back to physics and basic speaker design that I learnt at college. A horn-loaded device can transfer sound energy much more efficiently than just a forward-facing speaker. Just think about when you shout at someone, placing your hands around your mouth like a trumpet increases the range, volume and direction of that sound; so with a speaker cabinet as well.

With the early PA systems the high-frequency horns were just placed on top of the bass bins because it was somewhere convenient to put them, but with systems getting bigger I started to stack the bins in vertical columns and the horns in vertical lines, this threw the sound to the back of the hall much better.

After four years in Covent Garden, Dave Martin moved to Stanhope Street, right next door to Midas Audio who had also moved there, even though these were two totally separate businesses. The 'Martin-Midas' combination became the standard PA package for professional sound rental companies and for rock and pop groups, so being placed side by side in Stanhope Street was very convenient for everyone.

A few years later in response to a call for a one-box system that could fly as well as stack on stage, Martin developed the F2 system with easy-to-fly rigging hardware, a forerunner of line array systems long before others ever thought of it.

Dave was a wacky character and a bit of an eccentric but behind all that he came up with some amazing engineering ideas; although a brilliant designer he was not a businessman so he brought in an MD to run the business side of things while he concentrated on design. Today, Martin Audio is not only known for its touring PA systems, but it also has a huge presence in the fixed installation and contractor markets across the world, in particular in pubs, clubs and cinemas.

SPIRIT

After about 2 years at Midas I received a phone call from one of the sound companies who had bought a Midas mixer asking me if I could go on tour and do the sound for an American band called Spirit, a Californian underground rock band touring the UK. I'd got my driving licence back by then and was thinking of going back on the road anyway so this offer was very tempting. I did ask Jeff Byers if he would let me go on 'unpaid leave' for a month and he agreed he would let me go for this tour, but he looked a bit worried in case I didn't come back. I said I would come back.

I turned up at Waltham Forest Technical College in Walthamstow to meet the band and check the sound equipment being supplied. I knew to expect a Midas mixer and a Martin speaker system. I had no rehearsal time and only a 20-minute soundcheck; it went pretty well for a first show and I continued with the tour. It was great to be actually using a Martin-Midas system, the mixer was one I had actually built.

Spirit evolved from a Los Angeles band The Red Roosters, which included Randy California on guitars & vocals, Mark Andes on bass and Jay Ferguson on vocals & percussion. I did 20 shows with them around the UK in four weeks including an *Old Grey Whistle Test* TV show at the BBC. The venues were mostly colleges, universities, clubs and small theatres, the usual kind of UK tour venues, ending up at London's Rainbow Theatre, which I remember as being the old Finsbury Park Astoria before it was converted from a cinema into a live rock venue. It was one of the first venues converted by my old mate Ian Knight, who had managed Soft Machine a few years ago, a nice venue and one of the first to have a Martin-Midas PA system permanently installed. Not so good was the sound mixing position, which was hung in a cradle underneath the balcony, not the best place to be but it didn't take up any seats in the venue, which is probably what the promoter was thinking.

The band's most successful single was 'I Got a Line on You'. The guitarist Randy California was a weird guy but quite friendly and quite harmless despite being stoned out of his head most of the time; he would sit and chat to us quite a bit. His favourite conversation was about when Led Zeppelin had supported Spirit on his last American tour before they became famous. Randy claimed that Led Zeppelin had 'stolen' his song 'Whole Lotta Love'. I hadn't heard Spirit's version but I do remember hearing a song called 'You Need Love' written by Willie Dixon and recorded by Muddy Waters in the 1960s which is probably where Zeppelin (and Spirit) had both stolen the song in the first place.

Randy had also played guitar in the band Jimmy James and the Blue Flames, which was actually Jimi Hendrix before he changed his name.

The Spirit tour ended in March and I returned to Midas. I carried on there until June when Vinegar Joe suddenly called me out of the blue and wanted me to fly to Lisbon in Portugal and mix their sound for a gig in the massive 50,000-seater football stadium supporting Blood Sweat and Tears. This was a two-day event and both shows were sold out. It was a complete surprise to hear from them again and they didn't explain why they wanted me to do those two shows instead of whoever was doing their sound after I'd left, but it was a pleasure to see them all again and I was pleased they hadn't forgotten me.

Vinegar Joe recorded and released another album 'Rock'n'Roll Gypsies' later in 1972 and their last album 'Six Star General' in 1973, but although the band were hugely successful doing live shows and always got packed out audiences, the popularity was not reflected in record sales. Their record company Island Records were not bothering to promote the albums properly, a familiar story which has affected many artistes. Island Records didn't really care that they played to thousands of kids every week and went down a storm. The band eventually broke up, John Hawken went on to play keyboards with The Strawbs until 1975, Robert Palmer decided to pursue a solo career, he went on to have top ten hits with 'Addicted to Love' and 'I'll Be Your Baby Tonight'. Elkie also decided to go solo having chart hits with 'Pearl's a Singer' 'Lilac Wine' and 'Fool If You Think It's Over'. Surprisingly in 1997 Elkie was listed in The Guinness Book of Records as the most charted female album seller in the last 25 years.

I hadn't worked with Soft Machine for a while but I heard the drummer Robert Wyatt broke his spine whilst leaving a party through a window, climbing down a drainpipe and falling three storey. It left him paralysed and permanently confined to a wheelchair. Pink Floyd and Soft Machine did a benefit concert for him at the Rainbow Theatre in 1973.

Again I returned to Midas wondering if I might stay here permanently or go back on the road. I didn't have to wait long for my decision.

11

THE SOUND MIXER

Some of the things said to me at the sound mixer by the audience:

Are you the DJ?
Do you do the lights?
Do you know what all those knobs are for?
What would happen if I pressed that button?
Do you ever get to meet the band?
Can I leave my handbag under your desk?
I suppose you're off to the party now?

In the 60s and early 70s, before digital sound enhancement and other tricks were used to recreate live music in front of an arena audience, it was at best a bit 'hit and miss'. More than one group has failed trying to compete on tour with their own recorded sound. Some artistes use their sound and lights to add to the overall show; that may look good and some may say it's to make up for what they lack musically, but I'd never suggest such a thing.

Before 1969 there wasn't much in the way of purpose-designed PA systems, PAs were for vocalists to sing into, not for a full band to be miked up. The only choices you had were Vox or Selmer speaker cabinets originally designed for guitars. So when Charlie Watts invented the WEM column it took off like a house on fire especially with bands like The Who and Pink

Floyd who took their sound seriously, although the mixers were still very primitive.

Once monitor speakers started to appear on stage, we sound engineers started having a problem trying to mix a sound for the audience and to give the band something they could hear on stage. Early mixers only had a volume feed from the front of house audience mix so the band had the same mix as the audience.

Realising now that bands wanted more from their monitors, separate EQ (equalisation or tone controls) were inserted into the mix and sent to the stage. I came up with the idea of splitting the vocal mics into two channels. I'd use one channel for the audience mix and another channel for the stage mix so that I could give each channel separate EQ, this worked well. Eventually special monitor mixers were used on stage and operated by a separate monitor engineer, although initially these were just modified front of house mixers until dedicated monitor mixers were produced.

Use of outboard equipment for live concerts was beginning to grow. Front of house racks now included graphic equalisers, electronic crossovers, echo, reverb and harmonisers. Later on we used noise gates and compressors, it now looked like a mobile recording studio on the road. Effects have now gone into a totally different universe with digital technology.

The one thing that baffles most people when they first see a full-sized sound mixer at the back of the hall or in the middle of an arena are the hundreds of buttons, switches and knobs with lots of flashing lights, and the most common question asked was, "How do you know what all those knobs do?" It's not as complicated as it looks although it could look a bit bewildering when first viewed from a distance.

Let's take a look at what's on a sound mixer in simple language. A mixer is split into two halves, the inputs and the outputs. The inputs are the microphones, instruments and effects. The outputs are where you send the sound mix to, whether it's to the main PA, a monitor speaker, or a recording device.

All you need to know is what each vertical line does (see picture below). A vertical line is known as a channel and corresponds to one microphone or instrument, each of the other vertical lines or channels does exactly the same thing for a different microphone or instrument.

One of Concert Sounds Yamaha 40-channel mixers

A channel is divided up into four basic sections. Starting at the top working down, the first part is the input section where you adjust the level of the signal coming into the channel.

The next section is the EQ (equalisation or tone controls). On your home hi-fi you might have two tone controls, bass and treble, on a mixer you could have four controls, bass, low mid-range, high mid-range and high (or treble). As well as being able to turn the four tone controls up or down, you can also select where you want to fix the frequencies that you control. This is known as parametric equalisation.

The third section on the channel is the AUX or auxiliary routing, where you send the signal. The AUX mixes would typically be used to send a signal to a reverb-echo-delay, effects unit or to a monitor mix.

The fourth and last section is the main control area where the fader is and the routing for the sub-groups; this section also has the PFL (pre-fade listen) switch so you can listen to the channel on your headphones and it also has the channel mute switch which will turn the channel on or off. The sliding fader sets the volume for that channel in the main mix.

So now you know what one channel does, all the other channels are exactly the same only they apply to a different microphone or instrument. That's the input section.

The output section is where you have your main master left and right stereo faders and eight sub-group faders. A sub-group is used to group different channels together. For example you could put all your drums on one sub-group and therefore you can bring the whole drum kit up and down on one fader instead of trying to use ten fingers to do all ten channels together. You can also set the send and return volume levels for your effects, and routing for external recording devices.

The first thing to do when you jump onto a mixer for the first time is to zero all the pots (potentiometer knobs), that means turning all the level controls down to zero on the dial just like the volume control on your radio. Once you have set each channel to the required input level and adjusted any EQ settings you want, set the channel faders to the required level; there is no right or wrong way to do this, it's like baking a cake. You could give ten chefs the same recipe and end up with ten different looking cakes. You could have ten sound engineers and end up with ten different sounding mixes, each with their own preferences.

There is no right or wrong way to mix sound, the sound balance is in the ear of the listener and what might sound right for one person may not be right for another. In an audience of 10,000 you won't please everybody. The main thing to consider is that you are trying to replicate how the musicians want their sound reproduced and that may not always be what you think may be right. Most of the time the musicians will allow you to do what you think is right, or they simply don't know what they want, so it's up to you to interpret how you think it should sound; often you can suggest effects to improve the sound that they wouldn't even have thought of.

Microphone positioning and channel EQ can all affect the individual instrument sounds. The band has to trust the soundman to do what he feels sounds right. On some occasions when working with a young band who hasn't had much experience of performing live, I have actually told the band what I am going to do and why, in those circumstances they rely heavily on your experience and knowledge. With an experienced band who have made records you might need to replicate as closely as possible the sound on the studio recording. Having said that there have been many soundmen who have failed miserably in attempting to replicate the studio sound, mainly because the recording studio has perfect acoustics and the tracks have had multiple layers of processing over several days. Live sound has to be captured instantly as it happens there and then, there's no second chance.

There are no rules to mixing except rules are meant to be broken or at least bent. I always remember the story of Keith Richards when recording the Stones' first album, confronted with elderly studio engineers wearing white coats who insisted that the VU meters should *never* go into the red because it would cause a distorted sound, Keith replied, "But I *want* a distorted sound." That was a totally alien concept to engineers brought up recording classical musicians where everything is clean and within the parameters they were taught.

If you start with a good instrument sound, you don't (or shouldn't) have to change anything on the EQ. Changing EQ on a channel is only to correct an error that shouldn't be there in the first place. If an instrument or voice isn't sounding like it should do, start with correcting the source of the problem first and only then adjust the channel EQ. Sometimes EQ is used to compensate for something bad, but that's just covering up a mess rather than fixing a problem.

Musicians can be temperamental beasts and this means that if the sound isn't right for them then the show will suffer and could cause friction between musicians and sound engineers.

THE MONITOR MIXER

Once upon a time bands didn't have monitors nor ever thought of asking for them. Then as volumes started to rise on stage, so the need to hear themselves became a problem. There was never a battle between the stage volume and PA volume, bands were able to hear themselves clearly by keeping the stage level down and could hear themselves from the backline and what they could hear coming back from the front PA. The solution to start with was to turn one of the front PA speakers inwards so the band could hear more of the sound from the PA system.

When wedge-shaped monitor speakers started to appear on stage I would send a separate mix from the FOH mixer; I soon realised I had a struggle to separate the audience sound from the stage sound. Higher monitor levels on stage now required a separate on-stage mixer to do a separate monitor mix, the trouble is no one had invented a proper monitor mixing desk at that time, so a FOH desk was used. For Thin Lizzy's 'Live and Dangerous' album I used a Soundcraft 16 into 4 FOH mixer for the monitors. The main left and right master mix became the left and right side fill cabinets, the four auxiliary mixes went to the three front-of-stage wedges and a drum mix at the back. I used the headphone jack socket to listen to the mixes with my own wedge.

Eventually Midas and others came up with a real monitor mixer, but instead of having faders on each channel we had eight rotary knobs, each going to eight different mixes. Inserting a 27 or 31 band graphic equaliser into each mix created a huge leap forward in sound quality and volume.

DIGITAL MIXER OR ANALOGUE MIXER?

It's horses for courses, depending what you're going to use it for. The main difference between digital and analogue is digital mixers are more compact than the old analogue mixers.

Analogue mixers are also cheaper and easier to use but don't have built-in effects so you need to plug analogue effects in. The effects built in to digital mixers are just a software copy of the analogue hardware version, which can sound very clinical, so if you don't like what's being offered, you end up plugging in analogue effects units the old-fashioned way, which defeats the object. As we know, computer software can go wrong, become corrupted or freeze.

Effects are now built into digital mixers, but that means going through a list of parameters on a menu and you make the adjustments on a touch screen. The old outboard effects racks may look big and ugly but I can lean over and make an adjustment instantly on a control that's already active and guess what, I can make a change to another input channel with my other hand at the same time.

Digital mixers don't need heavy effects racks alongside you when you're mixing, but I actually prefer to have an effects racks alongside me. Digital mixers also have the facility to be controlled by a tablet or smartphone so you can walk around the venue and tweak the system in each corner of the hall from your phone. Finally once you've set the mixer to how you like it you can download the settings to a memory stick and take it with you. Another advantage of digital is that they can run off a Cat 5 computer cable instead of a two-inch-thick multicore cable which is a pain to run out to the mixer every day. Not forgetting that promoters will like the fact you're not taking up ten seats with a 48-channel analogue mixer.

Although digital mixers are constantly improving, I don't feel they have that natural sound, just like those who prefer vinyl to CDs or those who prefer Betamax to VHS, guitarists prefer valve amps to transistor amps, it's what you prefer and it's what you instinctively feel is superior. Different engineers will have different preferences but I prefer the warm, natural sound of analogue, some might prefer the clinical and sterile electronic sound of digital, it's up to you.

The choice is yours. Whatever your preference, whether you like it or not, the future is going to be digital.

12

THE RISE OF SOUND RENTAL COMPANIES

COLOSSEUM ACOUSTICS

In February 1974 whilst working at Midas I received another unexpected phone call, this time from one of Midas's customers, Colosseum Acoustics. This was basically a sound company set up by the roadies of Jazz-Rock band Colosseum founded by drummer John Hiseman, sax player Dick Hextall-Smith and bass player Tony Reeves, who had all previously worked together in John Mayall's Bluesbreakers. When the band were not working, the road crew hired out the band's PA and lights, which was now becoming a common practice. Pink Floyd set up Britannia Row, The Who set up ML Executives, The Man band set up Concert Sound and Colosseum set up Colosseum Acoustics.

There became an increasing number of sound rental companies to supply the ever increasing demand for high powered sound and lights which were too expensive for the average band to buy outright, so hiring a system for a short tour made financial sense. Other rental companies were Asktam, Entec, Wigwam, Tubosound and TFA.

In America it was becoming big business as the venues there were larger than the average European venue, companies like Showco, Tasco and Clair Brothers dominated the market. In America the idea started with the Woodstock Festival, which required a monster PA for a huge audience, the like of which had never been built before; it was there that the idea of a PA rental company was born.

Colosseum Acoustics (abbreviated to Col-Ac and then rebranded as 'Colac') already had a 32-channel Midas mixer and a Martin speaker system for use with their band Colosseum and were expanding into a sound rental company. They had also purchased a new 24-channel Midas mixer for a European tour with American band Dr Hook and the Medicine Show. The owner of Colac, Scott Thompson, asked if I wanted to join the company and start off with a Dr Hook tour across Europe with a full Martin-Midas PA system. Of course I agreed to it and within a couple of weeks I was down in New Ash Green, Kent, checking out the PA system that I was to take with me, along with the new truck they had just bought. I was given an assistant in the form of Marc. He was a young lad of about 20 who hadn't been on the road before and hadn't had any experience with sound equipment, but had been instructed by Colac on how to wire it up.

The trouble with working for just one band is that your ambitions are limited, you're relying on their success for your success, if they fail you're out of a job. Working for a sound rental company gives you more experience and a wider range of musical exposure, you don't have to listen to the same songs year in year out, every tour is different and every artiste is different. When one tour ends you hook up with another artiste doing their own tour.

Just a quick note on lighting rental companies. Their emergence came shortly after the sound rental companies, mainly using old theatre type equipment not really meant for Rock'n'Roll touring and some even used film lighting equipment as it was more durable on the road. Rank was a well-known brand for lighting dimmers but were not very reliable when transported around every day. In 1974, lighting company Keylites changed its name to Showlites; they came up with a new zip-up lighting truss with Socapex connectors which meant the lighting trusses went up really quickly compared to the old lamps which had to be plugged up individually by hand. Unfortunately (for sound crews) it didn't mean that lights went up any quicker it just meant that more lights were used and bigger rigs could be designed for the same amount of rigging time.

The music business is not just about bands and solo artistes, it is a multi-billion pound industry which supports a vast fringe industry. Apart from the obvious record labels, recording studios and concert venues, it includes truck hire, air freight, equipment manufacturers and hire companies, record, CD and tape distributors, insurance companies, rehearsal studios, T-shirt printers, travel agents, case makers, musical instrument manufacturers, suppliers of spare parts like guitar strings and drumsticks, security, journalists, ticket agents, caterers, chauffeurs, body guards, hotels, even bar staff and cleaners. Not to mention sound, lighting, backline and stage crews. It employs a huge number of people.

DR HOOK & THE MEDICINE SHOW

In March I headed off to Germany for my first gig with Dr Hook & The Medicine Show in the Zoom Club in Frankfurt, it was a two night residency. I had been there before with Balls a few months before so I knew what to expect. It was a small room upstairs above a restaurant that looked like it was run by Korean gangsters. Dr Hook had their own sound engineer, John Draper, whom I got to know very well over the next 10 years, the first thing he asked me when looking at the mixer was, "What does the Presence control do?" I had to explain that it was a mid-range tone control as not many people had seen one on a sound mixer before. I asked Jeff Byers at Midas why he didn't just call it a mid-frequency control, which later on he did, and now all mixers are marked up as Bass, Mid and Treble.

The second night ended badly: while I was packing up the equipment, a lone robber came into the club with a handgun and attempted to rob the box office of its night's takings, the staff were having none of it and attacked the gunman with kung-fu, battering him half to death. The gunman tried to defend himself with anything available including my cable drum, which was solid steel and ended up with a big dent in it; the gunman eventually managed to flee the scene leaving a trail of blood behind him. Ten minutes later he came back with a knife demanding his gun back, silly man. The two Korean staff members delivered the same treatment as before with even more deadly force. The band members and I kept well out of the way. Again the gunman left covered in blood leaving both his gun and his knife behind. I doubt whether he returned a third time.

From there we went to Amsterdam and did a show at The Royal Concertgebouw where the band was keen to go off sightseeing and in particular to the legal pot-smoking cafés in town. In the cafés you were presented with a sweet shop-style counter and a selection of different brands of hash and marijuana sold by the gram. Looking around were seated a mixture of business professionals, tradesmen, students, housewives and your average citizen on a day out to the shops. As it was legal in Holland it was quite a culture shock to the Americans who couldn't believe their eyes seeing people smoking a joint in public.

Dr Hook at the Musikladen TV studios in Bremen, 1974

The next day we travelled to Bremen for a television show called 'Musikladen'. This was an easy gig as I didn't need to put any PA in the studio. I helped the backline guys unload their equipment and had an easy day watching the television sound crew do a sound check and the camera crews run through their camera checks.

Three gigs in Denmark, then a ferry across to Sweden for a show in Stockholm, a drive up to Oslo in Norway and back down to Gothenburg. Another ferry back over to Copenhagen and then onto Germany where we had a problem. After the show in Aschassenburg, which was attended by about six people, I received a telephone call from Colac back in England saying that they hadn't been paid by the German promoter for the hire of the sound equipment. I was to await instructions on whether to carry on with the tour or bring the truck and its sound system back to England. I told the band's road manager Nineyear Wooldridge of my instructions and he looked really worried I would abandon them halfway through the tour without a PA. I told him that as I really liked those guys and wouldn't want to see the shows cancelled I would leave early the next morning so as to avoid the telephone call. Nineyear was so grateful, he never stopped thanking me for that for the next ten years.

We did a few more gigs around Germany, Austria and Luxemburg, which all went well except for a show at the Kongresshallen in Saabrucken where we had to scuttle the gig whilst the audience were already in the hall. It's not an easy thing to do, trying to dismantle the stage equipment with a few hundred fans wanting to know why the band were not going to play. It turned out the promoter had gone bust and done a runner with the money, the band wanted to do the show anyway because the audience had paid for their tickets and we were already set up, but the venue hadn't been paid for and with no promoter showing his face they were preventing us from using the hall. Something to do with insurance and public liability. Try explaining that to a crowd of Austrian fans who wanted their money back. We escaped out of there without any damage to body or equipment but it looked as though it could have turned nasty.

At the end of the European leg of the tour we headed back to England. We did our first show in England at Stoneground in Manchester, an old converted cinema. The first thing the American road crew wanted to try was English fish and chips, they'd never had it before and were keen to try it. After the sound check I took them all down to the local chippy and introduced them to our national delight, naturally they loved it.

As was to be expected throughout the tour the audiences thought that one of the lead singers, the guy with the eye patch Ray Sawyer was Dr Hook, in fact Dr Hook is the name of the group and not the name of one person. The name came about because in the early days when they were thinking of a band name, someone suggested Captain Hook from the Disney film but said Dr Hook by mistake and it stuck. It had nothing to do with Ray Sawyer other than the fact he wore an eye patch. Another question which constantly came up was does Ray wear the patch as a stage prop? No he actually lost his eye in a car crash when the steering wheel shattered and lodged in his eye socket. He never takes his patch off in public but I am one of the few people who have actually seen his eye and there is nothing there except a scar. Dennis Locorriere is the other joint lead singer and the voice of the band who sung all the hit singles. He took exception to Ray being seen as the face of Dr Hook. He may have been the face but he certainly was not the voice.

A near sell-out show at London's Rainbow Theatre followed by Barbarella's in Birmingham and Newcastle City Hall completed the first European tour of many with Dr Hook over the next ten years. For my first tour with Colac it went pretty well, no major problems except they weren't paid for the shows in Germany.

RICHARD AND LINDA THOMPSON

My second tour involved a folk act, Richard Thompson and his wife Linda Thompson with their band. Richard had just left folk heroes Fairport Convention. We did three shows in Scotland doing small theatres and after that nice and easy three-day mini tour, where all the band were friendly and happy, to a difficult three-day experience that was far from enjoyable.

COCKNEY REBEL

I did three days in Belgium with Cockney Rebel; the first show in Hasselt nearly ended in disaster when the house electrician wrongly wired my power cables into the wrong phase and blew up the PA system. Instead of connecting my wires up to a 220-volt supply, he wired me across 380 volts of three phase power. The idiot took out half of my amplifiers. I spent the rest of the day trying to fix some of the Midas amplifiers, luckily I had built those very same amplifiers whilst I was working at Midas so I knew how they worked and what parts to replace. I managed to use enough parts from each amplifier to get the system up and running in time for the show although it did start late. Steve Harley in front of the audience decided to blame the delay on the PA system rather than the electrician. I'd had a really bad day and that was the last straw; as he passed me in the corridor I told him what I thought of him and his comments, it wasn't necessary to involve the audience. That didn't go down too well but I didn't care by then after I'd spent all day fixing something that was not my fault, and may not have worked at all in time for the show without my intervention.

Before I'd left England I had been told to collect the cash for the PA before the show. I phoned back to Colac to tell them what the Belgium electrician had done and I was again told to collect the cash before the show or don't let them use it. After two requests for the cash and two replies that I would get it tomorrow, the last show was bound to be confrontational. After the sound check I asked for the cash and was told I'd get it later so I took the fuse out of the power supply and put it in my pocket. Ten minutes before the band were due to come on stage, their soundman said to me, "Can I have the fuse for the power supply?" I said yes it will cost you £300. He looked at me with rage and stormed off backstage; eventually he came back and handed over £300 in cash and I gave him the fuse. Needless to say I never worked with Cockney Rebel again, nor would I want to.

COLOSSEUM, TEMPEST & THE MAN BAND

After the band Colosseum broke up, Jon Hiseman formed a new band Tempest with fellow Colosseum member Mark Clarke on bass and Ollie Halsall on guitar. In May 1974 I did a show with them at the Marquee and a week later at the Nightingale in Wood Green.

The Man band were doing a show at the Rainbow Theatre and wanted to increase their PA system to something more powerful. The crew working for Man were in the process of doing what a lot of bands had started doing, including Colosseum, and that was using the band's PA to set up a sound rental company to hire out when their own band wasn't using it. Their PA eventually became one the biggest sound rental companies in Britain, Concert Sound, later merging with Clair Brothers to become Clair Global, now the biggest in the world. But for now they had a small Martin-Midas PA the same as Colosseum had, so by combining the two systems together it became a respectable-sized PA. It's easy when everybody uses the same make of equipment, it can be coupled together to make one large system. This went on quite a lot over the next few years, sound companies would rent equipment to each other, we called this 'Dry Hire', where you just hire the equipment but not the engineers, and it seemed to work well for all concerned.

STEELEYE SPAN

In 1969 a bunch of English folk rock musicians formed a band called Steeleye Span to revitalise the traditional folk music scene with a rock concert theme in an attempt to make folk more popular.

Using Morris dancers, sword dancers and a rock band sound and lighting system we went on tour, some said it couldn't be done. But with a gold album, five silver albums and two hit singles ('Gaudete' going to No 14 in the UK singles charts and 'All Around My Hat' to No 5) they proved them wrong, taking the music out of folk clubs and into theatres and concert halls making folk-rock popular.

The band were now being managed by Tony Secunda. Tony Secunda popped up again after working with him and his bands Sky and Balls, it's a small world in the music business and I wasn't expecting to run into him again. They were booked to play two sell-out nights at the Royal Albert Hall.

Steeleye Span were one of the most influential bands in English folk music at that time. It was Tony Secunda who transformed them into a folk-rock supergroup. It was a great show, I'd never seen them before and was surprised at how good they sounded, not so much a folk group as much as a rock band playing folk music, very professional and I got on really well with them all.

ROSKILDE FESTIVAL

In June I set off to Denmark for the annual Roskilde Festival just outside Copenhagen. A three-day event that went on 24 hours continuously, I did the 6pm to 6am slot and Scott did the 6am to 6pm slot, while his partner Clive Davis did the lights when it got dark. With a couple of crew members to help run the stage, it looks like I drew the short straw, but Scott and Clive ran Colac and I was just an employee and I didn't mind.

Running a festival sound system can be really boring at times, the only bright side is you occasionally get to see a really good band. For the most part the bands that turn up don't have a sound engineer so you're doing the sound for them, during a changeover you would leg it up to the stage to help put the mics in position. I would decide what mics to use and where to put them, then leg it back to the mixer halfway down the field to the control tower. The control tower is like mission control, on the first level about 5 feet above ground is the sound mixer, and above that on the next level is the lighting mixer, and on the top level are the follow spots but that's only manned during the hours of darkness.

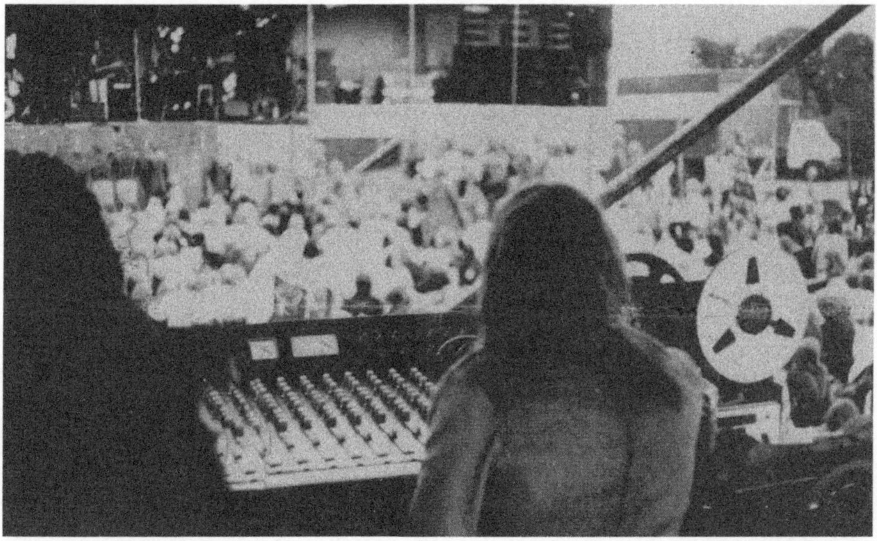

Roskilde Festival with me at the front of house mixer

The first night Status Quo were the headliners and I was operating the monitor mixer from the side of stage; their backline roadie was putting on a show all by himself and may have inspired the Spinal Tap movie. He was running around the stage like a ferret fixing the backline, untangling guitar cables and tightening up loose cymbal stands. I'm sure he left things loose on purpose just so he had an excuse to run on and fix things. Status Quo were a great band to see working, The rest of the bill were local Danish and other European bands, some rock and some folk groups, all types really, no one that I had heard of.

The second day was the same local European acts with the English rock band Camel headlining, a progressive rock band from Guildford who a year later would sell out a concert at the Royal Albert Hall, with the London Symphony Orchestra.

The third night was headlined by The Incredible String Band. After three long nights at the festival site I was ready to sleep for a week but the stage had to be stripped down and loaded into the two trucks; I was driving one and Scott the other. This was the first time Colac had put together their entire sound system on one stage and it was a great sounding system, 10,000 watts of Martin speakers blasting out across the Danish fields.

COZY POWELL

When I got back to England I was told I had a tour with Cozy Powell's new band Hammer. Cozy had been the drummer in The Jeff Beck Group and for his own band Bedlam. Cozy had three solo top-twenty hit singles: 'Dance with the Devil', an instrumental track which got to No 3; his second single 'The Man in Black' reached No 18 and his third 'Na Na Na' which got to No 10.

He put a band together to tour the UK comprising of Bernie Marsden on guitar who previously played with UFO, Clive Chaman on bass previously with the Jeff Beck group, Don Airey on keyboards who was a classical musician having spent some time on cruise ships and Frank Aiello from Bedlam on vocals. When I started working for Cozy he was promoting his new single 'Na Na Na'. We were doing respectable-sized venues and the first one was Sunderland Locarno which I had previously done with Vinegar Joe supporting Free. Cozy's style of drumming was phenomenal, when he was in top gear it was like listening to a machine gun, if you stood in front of him it was like being kicked in the chest with his double kick drums thundering away, it was so loud. I could always tell when Cozy was playing on a record, he had a unique style that sounded like no other drummer, in my option the best rock drummer there has ever been (including some well-known overrated rock drummers I won't mention).

Cozy had a huge Yamaha drum kit, double kick drums, four rack toms and two floor toms. I was using 12 mics on his kit and it sounded great. We spent quite a while sound checking and tuning his drum skins. His drumsticks were an amazing 20mm (3/4 inch) thick, I called them telegraph poles.

The highlight of the show was a ten-minute drum solo which featured the 1812 overture complete with cannons. The cannons were of course on a soundtrack played back over the PA from a cassette tape with Cozy playing along with the 1812 orchestra, he later used this in his act with Rainbow. Bernie Marsden had played in a blues band called Skinny Cat who once supported Vinegar Joe, it's a small world.

Over the next six months I did over fifty shows around the UK with Cozy mixing his FOH (Front of House) sound, mostly clubs, ballrooms, universities, theatres and seaside pavilions, they were very enjoyable times but not everything was plain sailing. We had two 3-ton trucks, I was driving the sound truck and Graham was driving the backline truck. Coming back from Liverpool on our way to the hotel, I was coming off a slip road approaching a roundabout when I heard a screech of brakes and a crash; when I looked in my side mirror I saw Graham's truck on its side. I think he may have fallen asleep whilst following me, he was alright but the truck was a write-off.

Photo care of RAK Records.
Hammer: from left,
Clive Chamen, Bernie Marsden, Cozy Powell, Frank Aiello, Don Airey

Cozy would usually turn up to the shows in one of his sports cars; as well as being a drummer he also had a career in motor racing, which took up a lot of his time, and he raced for Hitachi on the UK saloon car circuit. One particular night he turned up in a Ferrari and after the show on a freezing cold night, he started the engine up and revved the hell out of it. Without warming the engine he drove away like a bat out of hell; he drove his cars just like he played his drums.

The last shows of the year were at seaside pavilions doing eight shows in December ending at Lea's Cliff Hall in Folkestone on 21st December; from there we all went home for Christmas.

It didn't take long for the story to cross the Atlantic, whilst I was on tour with Cozy. We were talking about a fight which had broken out at a Lynyrd Skynyrd concert in the US after their sound engineer was accused of turning the sound off for the support band Blue Oyster Cult. The Cult's roadie claimed the sound was turned off during their set and the sound engineer had a fight with Skynyrd's engineer to get the sound turned back on, it got so bad police had to be called in. This story at the time didn't surprise me as a lot of these things went on in those days, I personally never gave the support band a rough deal when it came to the sound equipment. Many engineers working for the main band would place restrictions on the opening act or support band, like switching half the amplifiers off so the main act sounded louder and better. Another trick was only giving them the faders to use but none of the other controls, I know what it's like, and I've been the victim of such techniques. I was once told that I had to use the same channels as the main band, but I couldn't touch any of the settings in case it upset the main band's sound. Any good sound engineer could and should be able to reset the mixer after the support band has been using it without affecting their own sound. I suspect that they restricted the mixer's use so their band sounded better and didn't want to be blown off stage by the support band. Either that or they were insecure about their own competence of allowing their mixer to be used. Sabotage was commonplace; when I was mixing Renaissance at the Royal Albert Hall, although there was no evidence to suggest anything was done deliberately, our manager had a fight with Deep Purple's soundman accusing him of sabotaging our PA.

In the early days, bands would each have their own PA system but as the PAs were now getting larger and more expensive there was no room on stage for more than one system and support bands were now using the main act's PA which left them at the mercy of the main act's engineer.

Working for the opening act was always a bum deal if you didn't carry your own mixer; you never knew what you would be allowed to use and how helpful the main act's engineer would be towards you. It did help if you knew the crew members involved and got on well with them, but if they wanted to screw you up they could do so without doing very much, you were totally at their mercy. Opening up for Atomic Rooster at The Greyhound in Croydon was another example as I mentioned in chapter 6.

Lights were no exception either, support bands were usually told they could only have a small percentage of a lighting rig to use so the main act looked better and brighter. To some extent I can understand the lighting rule because the main act has paid for the entire rig, which is designed especially for their show.

My attitude to support bands has always been that 'today's support band is tomorrow's headliner', I never forgot that and I've worked with many support bands that eventually became bigger than the band they first supported. A few examples I can think of are AC/DC and Van Halen who both opened for Black Sabbath. In 1972 Genesis were third on the bill behind Lindisfarne and Van Morrison. Chris Rea supported Lindisfarne, Deep Purple supported Canned Heat, Elton John supported for Renaissance, The Beatles supported Helen Shapiro.

THE LOCAL STAGE CREW

Loading in and loading out is like a well-oiled machine and the stage crew are a vital part of the operation. At best the stage crew are as good as the road crew and know exactly what to do with the minimum of supervision, and they've done it before. At worst you get a bunch of students who have volunteered to do it for free, don't know how to lift a case, have a lazy attitude and are generally only there so they can get in to see the show without paying. You're lucky if they even stay around after the show to help you load out, it's better to pay them, that way they have an incentive to stick around after the show to help with the load-out.

Whereas the load-in might take four to six hours to unload and set up the stage, wire it all up and check it's all working, the load-out is a strip-down, just pack everything away in its cases and go. As a rough guide you can generally say that a 40-foot trailer will take about an hour to load depending on the stage access: if the truck can back straight onto the stage it will take you less time, if you have to carry the equipment up or down a set of stairs or have a long push along corridors then it will take longer.

When I was production manager, I had one security guard standing watching the show and dancing when he should have had his back to the stage watching the front row for anybody getting crushed. I told him twice, he was not here to watch the show, he must watch the front row. Another security job for the local crew is guarding the dressing rooms, the stage door or fire exits, which can be a boring job. This is to make sure no-one opens the doors and lets all their mates in without buying a ticket. I would rotate the crew every 30 minutes or so in each spot so at least they get to see something of the show instead of just a cold dark corridor. On large shows dedicated staff from a security firm would do this job.

In the early days promoters used anybody off the street to do these jobs. Thankfully on big productions professional 'event staff' are now employed by organised companies and have turned the whole industry into a corporate business.

13

BLOOD, SWEAT AND MUD – THE FESTIVALS

1975 carried on as 1974 ended, which was with Cozy Powell's Hammer and some TV shows including Granada's *Hard Rock* music show from the Manchester Studios. Interestingly enough we were on the show with a new band Pilot who were promoting their first single called 'January'. Although Cozy Powell was a bigger name, Pilot's single went on to sell many more records. We played the Marquee Club again to a packed-out audience and the usual universities, clubs, colleges and town halls.

At one town hall, I had to wire in the power for the sound and lights to the mains electrical supply. You can't just plug into a 13 Amp socket, the sound equipment required a 30 Amp supply and the lights required a 60 Amp supply. What I always do when the venue doesn't come up with a house electrician, is go into the main fuse box and isolate the supply. In order to do that I had to turn the main fuse box off, in doing so unbeknown to me I'd also turned off the town hall clock which was situated 40 feet above our heads. I didn't realise what I'd done until a few minutes later when the council jobsworth came in wanting to know why the clock had stopped. I pleaded ignorance and he went off saying I'll have to report it, I said OK!

At Woolwich my wife Estelle and four-year-old daughter Tamzin came along to the show. Tamzin was very excited to be at a show and see a live band for the first time, she spent most of the day running around the venue, I have to say the band were brilliant and really looked after her. By the time the band went on stage she was so worn out she'd fallen asleep in the dressing room and completely missed the concert. Oh to be young.

One amusing show we did was at an agricultural college for their end-of-term party, the car park was full of farm vehicles as young students turned up on their tractors borrowed off the farm for the drive into town. I can just imagine the last dance, "Would you like a lift home on my tractor darling?"

The last show of the tour with Cozy was on 8th February 1975 at St George's Hall in Exeter. I'd expected to be doing more shows with Cozy on his next tour as he'd said he looked forward to seeing us all again later, but later on that year Hammer broke up. Cozy went on to play in Rainbow, Whitesnake, Black Sabbath and ELP (Emerson, Lake and Powell). Bernie Marsden went on to play with Whitesnake. Initially Neil Murray who'd replaced Clive Chaman on bass and Don Airey joined the new Colosseum, ,called Colosseum II, who I later worked with doing their sound with Gary Moore on guitar. Don Airey also worked with other artistes including Black Sabbath, Rainbow, Gary Moore, Ozzy Osbourne, eventually replacing Jon Lord on keyboards in Deep Purple.

I didn't see Cozy again until a show at Hammersmith Odeon where he was playing drums with Richie Blackmore's Rainbow. I managed to get myself on the guest list that night with a backstage pass; I wasn't very impressed with the show and the sound was terrible. The Odeon has a backstage bar for guests and after the show I managed to grab Richie Blackmore as he was passing and told him politely that I wasn't very impressed with the drum sound; he looked a bit shocked but I had to tell him, not that I had an ulterior motive of course. To be honest I just couldn't hear the drums over the rest of the band. Richie was very polite and thanked me for my comments.

On 5 April 1998 I heard a BBC news report that Cozy Powell had been killed following a car crash on the M4. According to a later report, Cozy was driving his car over 100 mph near Bristol, crashed into the central reservation barriers, hit a bridge and was ejected through the windscreen and died at the scene. Cozy's blood-alcohol reading was over the legal limit, and he was not wearing a seat belt, in addition to that he was talking to his girlfriend on his mobile phone. Not a very good combination when you're driving at that speed. He really did drive his cars like he played his drums, right to the end. A very sad ending.

RALPH McTELL

Two weeks after the last Hammer gig I got a tour with folk legend Ralph McTell, quite a difference in musical tone to Cozy Powell's Hammer but nevertheless very enjoyable. Again it was a small-low-budget production tour. Ralph had always toured as a single artiste travelling with his brother and road manager Bruce in an estate car with his guitar in the back using the house PA system in each venue, not that he needed much of a PA in small folk clubs. This time it was different, he'd just had a top 10 hit with 'Streets of London' which reached No 2 in the UK charts and the album remained in the charts for twelve weeks, so he took a band on the road which included Rod Clements of Lindisfarne on bass, folk/jazz violist Mike Piggott who later played with Bert Jansch, Stefan Grossman and Pentangle, Sammy Mitchell on slide guitar who played with Rod Stewart on two of his albums, American drummer Danny Lane with Joy Askew and Sian Daniels on backing vocals, we called them the McTellettes.

The first half of the show Ralph would come on alone and do his usual acoustic set with just a guitar. His brother Bruce would stand behind me and drop a pin on the floor, if he couldn't hear it hit the floor he'd tap me on the shoulder and tell me to turn the volume down, that's how quiet it was. For the second half he would bring his electric band on stage for a more rounded performance, occasionally you'd get an old-time folkie call out, "Play on your own, Ralph," which was a bit off-putting, you can't please old folkies who are so extreme they don't like electric instruments. Just like when Bob Dylan brought over his electric band to the UK for the first time, it was so loud Pete Seeger (another old folkie) tried to cut the power line to the stage. Despite an occasional old folkie heckler he went down really well everywhere and it was a real pleasure touring with him. Ralph was a true gentleman and a nice guy to be with.

We did 32 shows during February, March and April during which time my son Alex was born. I was planning to be home on one of the scheduled days off but he arrived three days early so I didn't get to see him until he was three days old. Ralph and the band all congratulated me for a job well done, I said, "It was easy for me, my wife Estelle did all the hard work."

I had a problem with the sound in the Victoria Hall at Hanley. I was getting interference from the fire station next door when radio signals would break through onto the PA system; at first it was amusing, then it just became annoying as the show went on. There wasn't anything I could do.

Founder members of Steeleye Span Gay and Terry Woods were the opening act on that tour, a nice folk duo whose style was called Celtic-Rock, playing mandolin, dulcimer and guitar. An extra show was slotted in at the Dorking Halls with a pleasant surprise having Jo Ann Kelly as a support act that night.

ROAD CREW MAGAZINE.

In April 1975 a magazine was launched called *Road Crew*, it was an A4-sized 27-page edition with a glossy colour cover and packed full of useful information and cost 10 pence (with a suggestion you take it out of your float). It was published by Event Publications. The first edition featured a truck hire survey with a breakdown on the best ten truck hire companies in the UK; a true life experience of a tour across America by a roadie working for a band called Puzzle, (no, I haven't either); a Birmingham gig guide featuring the nine music venues around town, including important information like stage sizes, venue capacity, load-in access, sound and lighting facilities, number of dressing rooms and so on, quite a comprehensive guide and worth keeping. The largest venue in Birmingham at that time was the Odeon Theatre which doubled as a cinema and had a capacity of 2,397. I think the magazine planned to do all the towns in the UK, which sounded like a good idea.

The magazine also included a 'Roadie of the Month' feature and this month featured Jane Smailes who worked as roadie for The Mike Absalom Band (no, I haven't heard of them either). It also included a survey of twelve PA companies although disappointingly it didn't feature some of the more well-known ones, and a three-page article about ATA carnets. Plus it featured an article on the 'Frankfurt Fair 1975' which was attended by all the big music and equipment manufacturers. Finally, there were numerous adverts for sound and lighting suppliers, some music shops and equipment manufacturers. For a first edition, all in all, a very well-presented magazine with a great potential for the future.

Issue 2 contained more of the same but mysteriously failed to include a 'Roadie of the Month'. This month it featured a Bristol gig guide and more adverts as people got to hear about it. By the time we got to issue 4 there were many more adverts and an article on the 15th Reading Festival and strangely a New York gig guide on the city's top seven venues making it more of an international magazine; why they did New York before completing a UK guide I don't know. I don't know how many months the magazine lasted but I didn't see any more after that.

DR HOOK

No sooner had the Ralph McTell tour finished I was straight off again with only three days inbetween en route to Denmark to start another Dr Hook tour. By this tour Dr Hook & The Medicine Show had dropped the Medicine Show part of their name and were now just called Dr Hook. The Fyns Forum was the first venue and the Danish crowds were going mental, there was definitely a build-up of excitement in the air. Twelve different venues followed across Denmark. Two more in Sweden including a special unadvertised gig in the very small Hard Rock Café in Copenhagen which was no more than a large restaurant and apparently have had some very big named bands play there as unadvertised gigs.

This time the sound company Colac had sold the band the idea of taking a lighting rig along, two Genie towers with 16 lamps on each tower. Of course this also meant a different crew member and the company found someone called Robin Gomer. I had the pleasure of working with him for the next few years, a young lad with no experience of the road or any experience of touring with a band, it was like a holiday for him; he soon learnt that it wasn't a holiday though when I set the pace of working. On this tour load-ins were at 12 noon so we could be leaving the hotel by 7am to travel, which came as a shock to Robin. It didn't do him any harm though, he later went on to do the lights for bands like Thin Lizzy and others. For many of the shows we had to take a ferry to cross between Denmark and Sweden and 12 ferries were used on this leg of the tour alone.

On arrival we would set the sound system up first, then I would tell Robin where he could put the lighting towers. Dr Hook's backline crew travelled separately to us and arrived after lunch to set their equipment up on stage, then I would place the mics and do a line-check (line-check means checking that all the microphone lines from the stage to the mixer were working) while waiting for the band to arrive for their soundcheck.

Another change to the sound system was the addition of a monitor mixer, I say monitor mixer but actually nobody in 1975 had built monitor mixers yet.

I had been given a Soundcraft front of house mixer designed to do a stereo PA mix for the audience, not for the band. I had to adapt this to provide six mixes, the left and right stereo mix became the left and right side-fill speakers on each side of the stage, the four auxiliary mixes would feed the three wedges across the front of the stage and one mix for the drummer at the back.

I would listen to my own monitor wedge by pressing the PFL switch, (pre-fade listen). John Draper was still, for now, mixing the front of house sound for the audience so I did the on-stage monitor mix for the band. Dr Hook had two lead singers. Ray Sawyer's mic was the most difficult as he kept swinging his mic around by its cable sometimes causing it to squeal in the speakers, Dennis Locorriere who sung the lead vocals on the band's hit records didn't move so much so was easier to set. The PA was the same size as last time, just 3 Martin bass bins each side and 3 Hi-frequency horns each side, back then we were still running the sound on a two-way crossover (high frequency and low frequency).

For most of the tour we based ourselves at the Plaza Hotel in central Copenhagen and by the end of the tour we thought of this as our home as we spent so much time there, very expensive and it seems 'the' place to stay. Mostly entertainment people stayed at the Plaza; in reception is a plaque with all the names of famous people who have stayed there, singers, musicians, actors, film stars and bands have all stayed there and some really big international names. It wouldn't be unusual to see someone famous walk through reception or hang out in the luxurious bar.

We had a new guy as guitar tech, Mark from Macon, Georgia, a lovely bloke but he spoke with such a southern drawl that he sounded like he was in slow motion. Is he slow? I was told, no that's what he's always like. I really liked him and we got on well. One problem Mark seemed to be having was tuning his guitars, they just didn't sound right and he couldn't understand why. Then I noticed that he was using an American Strobe tuner to tune his guitars and he was using a transformer to convert from 220 volts to 110 volts. I asked him if he realised that American equipment worked on 60 Hertz and European equipment worked on 50 Hertz. He didn't realise this and that's why his tuner was tuning guitars to the wrong key. I suggested next time he came over I would get him a UK Strobe tuner for 220 volts 50 Hz.

The after-show parties were getting to be a bit of a habit; as we didn't have that much equipment, just a 3-ton load, we were packed up and out of there in under an hour. The promoter had arranged for the band and crew to get free access to the town's most popular nightclubs, bypassing the queues at the front door, we were treated like VIPs.

Travel around Scandinavia involves a lot of ferries. On this trip we went on the Ebeltoft to Odden once, Dragor to Linhamn twice, Nakskov to Spodsberj twice, Knudshoved to Halsskov three times, Helsingor to Helsingborg twice, Ebeltoft to Sjaellands once and finally Harwich to Esbjerg to and from England.

At the end of April we returned to the UK for seven dates starting off at Dingwalls Club in Camden Town, a small funky little club but very popular and always packed out regardless of who was playing. People went because it was a popular venue to be in, not to see the band, although there have been some really good acts performing there and some very well-known artistes despite the small size of the place. Despite its small size it was a prestigious place to perform.

The next day I had to load the equipment into the BBC for an *Old Grey Whistle Test* show presented by Bob Harris. A totally manic show that I will never forget, as well as Hook's backline I put a monitor system in and operated that. We did a soundcheck in the morning, camera check in the afternoon and the live show in the evening. The support band for the UK part of the tour was John Otway and Wild Willy Barrett from Aylesbury. They also performed on the *Old Grey Whistle Test* with us and performed their hit song 'Really Free' where Otway decided to jump onto a guitar speaker causing it to fall over resulting in Otway crashing to the floor on to his back destroying the stage set. Everyone just stood around not believing what we had just seen on live TV.

There were five more shows around the UK ending up at the Victoria Theatre in London, the biggest venue we had played in the UK so far, but it was only half full due to the fact the band were still relatively unknown in the UK at that time.

BARRY WHITE

The rest of the year was strangely different, a lot of outdoor festivals starting with a collaboration with another sound company 'Entec' who needed enough speakers to fill Aston Villa football stadium for a concert with Barry White and the Love Unlimited Orchestra. I turned up and stacked my Colac equipment next to their Entec equipment; as we were both using Martin speakers the sound systems were compatible and worked together.

Just before sound check I heard this loud bellowing bass voice coming through the side gate, it was Barry White, he sounded like an empty oil tanker. His voice was so recognisable and bellowing out with that familiar bass sound, he had such a loud voice he hardly needed a microphone. The show started with The Love Unlimited Orchestra which was not as you might expect, they were not American musicians flown over from Philadelphia famous for that 'Philadelphia Sound' but the local philharmonic orchestra conducted by an American working for Barry White. I guess when you're a classical musician reading sheet music it doesn't matter where you come from, great sound though, just like the record; the second part of the show featured Barry White performing all his hits.

ALAN PRICE

The following week I did four shows with Alan Price at Hanley, Birmingham, Bristol and London's Victoria Theatre. A strange fellow Alan Price, having once played keyboards with The Animals and had a massive hit with 'House of the Rising Sun' he now goes off into a cabaret act, not a very friendly sort of bloke and not the sort of person you could have a laugh with, in fact I'd go so far as to say he was a right miserable git.

ROSKILDE FESTIVAL II

In June I was back over in Denmark again for the second Roskilde Festival, this year the three-day event featured Procol Harum, Focus, Swinging Blue Jeans, Ravi Shankar, Loudon Wainwright III and dozens of other unknown local acts.

An unfortunate incident happened one afternoon whilst I was on stage placing mics in position for the next act. We suddenly heard this enormous explosion I looked behind me into the backstage area where the explosion had come from to see a human body being flung into the air across the backstage enclosure. There then came a huge plume of black smoke billowing out of one of the caravans that had been parked in a circle for makeshift dressing rooms. This person had decided to use one of the dressing rooms as a factory for his

Barry White stage being set up with a Colac-Entec PA.

firework display later that evening; unfortunately he made a tragic mistake and blew himself up and the caravan as well. Luckily (for him) the explosion threw him clear away and probably prevented him being killed. He was covered in black soot; as there was an ambulance on standby at the festival site he was rushed off to hospital almost immediately. Later we heard he lost four fingers but he was lucky it wasn't more serious than that.

HYDE PARK CONCERT

At the end of May we supplied the sound for a free open-air concert in Hyde Park, London with Don McLean headlining with Caravan and Joan Armatrading supporting. 85,000 people were reported to have attended. One of the biggest shows so far, although by today's standard we could have done with a bigger PA system. It was a cold windy day but Don McLean and Caravan put on a great show.

STEELEYE SPAN

In July I was asked to do a short mini tour of five shows with Steeleye Span. The first one was an open-air show at Blackpool football stadium with Roy Harper and then three more theatres; great band, very underestimated, more like a rock band than a folk group.

This seemed to be the year of European festivals along with all the mud and backstage toilets. I never really enjoyed doing festivals but it all came with the job, long hours and not much pleasure except for the occasional good band that might appear once in a while.

If you're working for a band and you're doing the European festivals it is always a bit of a challenge, whether doing the big stage at Roskilde Festival in Denmark or the smaller beer tents of Austria. It's a case of turn up and make the best of what's available. 99% of the time you don't get what you ask for. The mixing desk is smaller than the band needs, the outboard effects are primitive or not working properly, the speakers are inadequate and the microphones get plugged into the wrong channels. But as long as you go with an open mind and accept what you have to work with, you can have a good time. I am pleased to say that I know I can always get the best sound out of a sound system that it is capable of producing.

With festivals, you might be using a strange system you've never seen before and you don't get a soundcheck, you just plug in and go, no second take, it's live and it's now. I'm pleased to say at Colac when we supplied sound to a festival we always had good equipment.

There's usually a strange smell of marijuana at festivals as it wafts across the audience with huge funnels of smoke coming from various parts of the crowd. There's always the ever present 'idiot dancer' waving his arms around wildly pretending to look cool, scantily clad young girls dancing, even when everyone else is sitting down there will always be a few girls standing up dancing topless without anyone taking the slightest bit of notice. You often see groups of people staking their claim to their patch of territory by placing a blanket or sheet down on the ground and staying there all day for fear of losing their space. I would stand on stage and look out over the audience or watch from the backstage area and wonder what makes people sit in front of a stage all day listening to second-rate bands just to get a good spot for when the main acts come on later in the day.

Another open-air festival I did was part of the European 'Startruckin 75' European Tour, which was a touring festival just like a circus with its own stage, truckloads of equipment and many bands. For some reason we had to supply the sound system on just one show as their trucks couldn't cross the continent in time, so the sound trucks leap-frogged us and went straight onto the next show while we filled in. Acts featured over the three-day event were Ike and Tina Turner, Wishbone Ash, Mahavishnu Orchestra (who I would later tour with in the USA), Soft Machine (who I previously worked with in the UK), Caravan, Climax Blues Band, Cockney Rebel (who I stayed away from), John Cale, Sailor and Fairport Convention.

BILLY CONNELLY

From August until the end of October 1975 I was on tour with Billy Connelly. I'd never heard of him before, he had a big tour though, longer than some big name rock bands. The tour consisted of five nights at the Music Hall in Aberdeen, twelve nights at the Apollo in Glasgow, six nights at the Usher Hall in Edinburgh, two nights at the Caird Hall in Dundee, six one-nighters across England plus six nights at the Victoria Theatre in London.

Who, I thought, could sell out that sort of tour? I noticed that most of the venues were in Scotland, there's a clue there. I soon found out who he was, I was warned he was a Scottish country/folk singer, that's all I needed, two months with a country singer, not that I'm against country music, some are good, but I was sure he was no Johnny Cash or Glen Campbell.

I only had a small PA and Robin came along with two lighting towers, all packed into my 3-ton truck. To make it even more boring he played solo with just a guitar and a banjo, so there was no backline to set up as he didn't have a band. The first three weeks I couldn't understand a word he was talking about because of his strong Scottish accent; the following three weeks I got used to his accent and began to understand him and even laughed at some of his jokes. The remainder of the tour I was so sick of the same old jokes each night I was getting bored and wanting it all to end. We did have a support act, New Celeste, to add a bit of music to the evening and relieve some of the boredom. Having said that he was a great guy and quite enjoyable to be with, if he stayed at the same hotel as us he would buy us drinks and have a good laugh with us in the bar, quite hyperactive and wouldn't sit still for long.

Having just two channels of microphones to work with wasn't a very stimulating or challenging kind of tour and there was nothing very exciting about the tour. During the twelve long days at Glasgow, we would spend most of the time hanging around Glasgow town centre or playing the latest video game, Space Invaders, situated in the theatre's foyer. There were a mind-boggling twelve shows at the Glasgow Apollo with just one day off in the middle because the venue had been previously booked by another artiste, so rather than break down the sound and lights and have to load them back in again the following day, I came to an agreement with the promoter that I would do the sound for Hank Locklin, an American honky-tonk country star for a reduced fee to save us the hassle and I was already in Glasgow so it's not like I could go home for the day. It turned out quite an enjoyable show and nice to listen to something different. After five venues in Scotland, a surprise visit to Corby in Northamptonshire which was the only venue apart from London outside of Scotland. This also happens to be the largest population of Scots outside of Scotland in the UK. Most of the audience were as to be expected Scottish workers employed by the British Steel works set up in Corby.

DR HOOK.

A welcome relief came in November with the return of Dr Hook and their third UK / European tour. I was getting to know them quite well by now and because

I was arranging the sound, lights and backline for the tour I was given the job title of Production Manager. This time their manager and record producer Ron Haffkine came along for the ride, and I mean a ride. If you thought Tony Secunda and Don Arden were unpopular you hadn't met Ron Haffkine yet. The band hated him, even though he discovered them and put them where they are today, he did his job well but at a heavy price to the band. Mr 50% they called him because he would slice 50% off the top of everything they earned, this was before expenses so by the time they paid for their production costs, travel and hotels and living expenses there wasn't a lot left. So it was no wonder that their 1975 album release was called 'Bankrupt' because the band really had actually gone bankrupt.

Ron Haffkine hadn't realised how big Dr Hook were in Europe until he saw the size of the crowds. I think he was just coming along for a holiday (at the band's expense) to do his manager bit. When he saw the crowds in packed out halls, 2,000-3,000 capacity venues, he was blown away, you could see the dollar signs spinning around in his eyes like a fruit machine.

Throughout Europe we would normally pick up a local support act to do the first half of the show. When they had finished and we were setting the stage for Hook to come on, Ron Haffkine liked to strut around the stage like a prat doing his peacock impression, much to the annoyance of the road crew who were trying to work and to the amusement of the crowd who probably wondered what the side show was. Why he had to be on stage was a mystery as he didn't actually do anything except get in the way.

Whether the crowd thought the same as the crew I don't know. I was still checking the vocal mics while Haffkine was on stage when I heard a thump and a twang. I looked around to see a six-inch hunting knife embedded in the stage just where Haffkine was standing. Gary yelled over to me, "Get off the stage," I did so very quickly.

This part of the tour consisted of twelve shows across Denmark, Norway and Sweden. For some reason Dr Hook became very popular in these Scandinavian countries where they were selling huge numbers of records long before their popularity in the UK. I persuaded Colac to give me a bigger PA system this time as we were doing bigger venues. I was doing the monitor mix from the side of the stage, using a 16-channel Soundcraft mixer along with six 27-band graphic equalisers.

Whilst taking the ferry across from Dragor to Malmo in Sweden the band's bus got pulled over and searched by Swedish customs; unfortunately the border guards found some marijuana on the bus and that led to the whole band being strip-searched. This could have blown all the shows in Sweden, so a few diplomatic phone calls from the Swedish promoter were made to some of his friends in Government and the band were allowed in to perform due to the amount of money that would have had to be refunded if the shows were cancelled. The band got away with it this time but the news spread and they were given extra scrutiny at every border from then on. Fortunately for me I was driving the equipment truck with the sound and lights ahead of the band bus so it didn't affect me or my lighting man.

The next leg was back to the UK for nine shows including another *Old Grey Whistle Test*, I was getting to know Bob Harris by now, he was a friendly bloke who would generally take an interest in the band and wander around the studio whilst we were setting up the backline and monitors. The BBC didn't have monitor speakers in those days and BBC sound crews weren't very good at doing a live sound anyway so I always took Hook's monitor system in with their own backline equipment.

The last chore of the tour was the dreaded sales conference for the EMI record company staff, a bonus I suppose for all the hard work the record company people had done in helping the band and themselves sell records. It was held at Heathrow Hotel next to the airport in their Wessex Ballroom. Dr Hook was supposed to be a surprise show after the banquet for EMI staff. That meant we had to hide all evidence of the band including covering up flight cases with their name on and disguising the stage set so it wasn't recognisable as Dr Hook's. It worked and the staff were totally in shock when the band came out and did a very 'up close and personal 'show. I put a small PA system in to cover the room which was only 72' x 72' and luckily, with a ceiling clearance of just 11', no lights were needed. The next day the band flew back to the States and I went home for Christmas.

14

THE BOYS ARE BACK IN TOWN

BLACK SABBATH

January 1976 started off with rehearsals for a Black Sabbath tour, with two days in Studio C at Shepperton Studios where we did a full production rehearsal. This was more for the benefit of the production crew than it was for the band and we set up the entire production on the studio floor, sound, lights, stage risers and backline gear. This was to promote the 'Sabotage' album which had just been released, it was the first time I had been on tour with an articulated truck and 40-foot trailer with the crew travelling in a 15-seater mini bus.

I was asked by the sound company Colac to work as system tech and monitor engineer. The two owners of Colac, Scott who was looking after FOH sound and Clive who was looking after lights, went along on tour as well. We loaded up the truck with a monster PA which this time included six monster Vitavox 'W' cabinets and headed off to Studio C at Shepperton Studios. Studio C is called a sound stage but in fact is just a huge warehouse totally soundproofed with flying facilities for overhead props and more importantly for us, lighting rigs, so this was a full technical rehearsal with all the equipment we would use for a full show. Although it was supposed to be a 'stage', in reality there was no stage, the room was completely empty, we just used the entire ground floor as a stage and marked out on the ground where the edges would be, that saved us having to go up and down to get on and off the 'stage'. We spent the next two days at Shepperton; first the lighting rig went in, and once that was flown up out of the way above our heads the sound equipment went in and then the stage set and backline gear.

The second day we played around with the gear, fine-tuning the sound and the lighting guys spent their time changing lamps and setting the colours they wanted, setting up the lighting board with pre-set cues for special effects and mood depending on the songs. The backline guys changed guitar strings and polished the drum kit, we then waited for the band to arrive. Eventually they turned up one by one, first was Tony Iommi (guitarist) who came and looked around, plugged in his guitar and checked his amplifiers, then Geezer Butler (bassist) turned up and rolled a joint, Bill Ward (drummer) came in and started adjusting his drums, tuning the skins and generally hammering the hell out of them, his kit was loud as you would expect from one of the loudest bands in the world. It was painful to stand in front of it. Ozzy Osbourne (vocalist) eventually arrived looking like death and tried out his mic. They didn't say a lot to each other but spent the time just jamming and going through some tracks off the album.

My job on this tour was to mix the on-stage monitors, I knew I had my work cut out after seeing the size of the backline. A wall of bass guitar cabinets on one side of the drum riser and a wall of Laney guitar cabinets the other side. Bill was perched high up on a six-foot drum riser way above everybody's heads. Ozzy although being the band's vocalist was positioned stage left bang in front of Tony's guitar stacks. I thought that was strange. I'd never seen that before, normally the vocalist goes centre stage, not in this band. It was clear right from the start who the band leader was, not Ozzy but Tony. Tony took centre stage position and he wanted two monitor speakers in the centre so he could hear his guitar. When I jokingly asked why he didn't stand in front of his stack so he could hear his guitar louder, I realised I had said the wrong thing and I got a look that should have killed me dead, I considered myself lucky to have survived the rehearsal let alone the tour. Tony didn't want to stand in front of his stack as it was too loud for him (that's his own fault), but then standing in the centre he couldn't hear his guitar because he was directly in front of Bill's drums, so Tony wanted two stage monitors at the front to drown out Bill.

Ozzy couldn't hear his vocal monitors because he was directly in front of Tony's guitar cabinets, which caused me a problem, so I gave him a double side-fill stack in his left ear and three floor monitors in a semicircle on the floor in front of him. By the time I had EQ'd (equalised) his mic I couldn't stand in front of it, it was so loud, it actually hurt my ears. It was a case of everybody trying to outdo everybody else on volume, except the louder it got the worse the problem became; it was a vicious circle.

We hit the road the next day starting at the Portsmouth Guildhall. The stage there was a lot smaller than the Shepperton sound studio and of course the acoustics were a lot different.

The show was a belter. Ozzy kept looking over to me at the side of the stage where I had the monitor mixer asking me to turn the volume up, so I did, trouble is he kept asking for more and more volume because Tony's guitar was so loud, so each time he asked I gave him more volume. Only doing what I was asked. Ozzy came off stage clutching his ear and giving me a thumbs up, but the next day at the Ipswich Gaumont I was told by his road manager that Ozzy had to go to hospital with a perforated eardrum. I said to his road manager, "Don't look at me, I only gave him what he asked for." Ozzy was OK about it.

There were three more dates on this mini tour, The Kurzal at Southend, Birmingham Odeon and finally Hammersmith Odeon. It was obvious that the band weren't getting on, Don Arden who I knew of from previous bands had just taken over management of Black Sabbath after they realised their old manager had been ripping them off for years. They had just come back from the States after recording their latest album *Sabotage*, this was a warm-up tour to promote that album. All the old favorites were on the set list including 'Paranoid' that reached No 4 in the UK singles charts, 'War Pigs', 'Iron Man' and others. Tony didn't seem to like Bill, he got on OK with Geezer as he co-wrote some of the songs and was the main lyricist. I got the impression Tony didn't like Ozzy either but saw him as a necessary evil in that he could work the crowd. Whatever you think of his vocal talents he was a brilliant showman and had the audience in his hands, he only had to raise his arms and the crowd would follow him. What amazed me most was the age of the audience, although there were older fans from the early days of Sabbath, the kids in the front rows were mainly 15-to-17-year-old boys, many were probably too young to remember when 'Paranoid' was first in the charts six years previously. We also got these weird satanists turning up all dressed in black like something out of an occult movie, weird lot hanging around the backstage door trying to find a way in like a bunch of half-dead zombies, I didn't like the look of them much, they were spooky. Black Sabbath were never into the occult despite the band's name and even though they played it up in the press they privately hated the satanic thing, which distracted from the music. The name of the band actually came from a Boris Karloff low budget horror movie.

Birmingham was a homecoming for the band and the home crowds certainly let them know it, during the last song of the encore the power went off plunging the stage into silence, the crowd whistled and booed as if the band had stopped playing. I rushed down to the main power board under the stage to discover a blown fuse. I didn't have a replacement so I wedged a screwdriver across the contacts and held it there for the duration of the last song. Looking back it was a dangerous thing to do but you do some crazy things in the name of Rock'n'Roll. The last show at Hammersmith was also a brilliant show but I have to admit, being on stage left near Tony Iommi's guitar stacks did some damage to my ears.

SYDNEY DEVINE

From one extreme to another, February saw me back in Scotland for a seventeen-day tour with another Scottish country singer, Sydney Devine, Scotland's very own rhinestone cowboy, complete with cowboy hat, boots and tasselled shirts. The highlight of the tour though was working with a very nice female singer Kimberly Clarke, who opened the show for Sydney.

THIN LIZZY

From the end of February until April 1976 I was told I would be doing a tour with a band called Thin Lizzy. I'd heard the name but I didn't know who they were or what they sounded like except for a single 'Whiskey in the Jar' I'd heard in 1972. I knew the song 'Whiskey' was an old Irish folk song so I assumed they were another Irish folk group, I was thinking I didn't want to be doing folk and country, my passion was rock with big productions. So I was surprised to hear that we had four days of technical rehearsals at Shepperton Sound Studios using a cut-down Sabbath PA. When I saw the backline equipment being unloaded into the studio I realised this was no folk group. Another 40-foot trailer was used so I was thinking this looks like being the norm with the crew travelling in a 15-seater mini bus again.

I was doing on-stage monitors again with the same set-up, stereo side fills and three floor monitors across the front of the stage and a drum fill at the back. For the monitor mixer I was using the standard front of house Soundcraft mixer, very basic by today's standard but that was high-tech in 1976. I did have the luxury of some 27-band graphic equalisers, which helped me tune the sound for maximum volume. The guys were immediately very friendly and happy to see us and couldn't wait to get started. The band spent the first half an hour just jamming and trying out their equipment and I spent some time with their front of house engineer Pete Eustace. They had just recorded their new album 'Jailbreak' and this was the promotional tour for the album; when I heard it for the first time I realised this band was going to be big, really big. The support band for the tour was Graham Parker and the Rumour who were a good bunch of guys and put on a good show, they were no trouble at all and a pleasure to work with.

When the tour started 'The Boys Are Back in Town' was released as the first single from the album and as the tour went on it slowly went up to No 8 in the UK charts, audiences were getting bigger and noisier and it wasn't long into the tour that shows were selling out. We were doing the usual second-division venues, town halls, colleges and universities, 28 shows in 35 days ending the tour at the Victoria Theatre in London. The band were great and we always had a few drinks at the hotel after the show; it was a low-key tour as they hadn't yet made it to superstardom and the guys were just happy to be where they were.

Bass player Phil Lynott's favourite story was when guitarist Eric Bell left the band some time earlier and then Gary Moore joined and left the band (twice). Phil then decided to audition for two lead guitarists to join the band. Phil said, "It's just in case one of them left," which everyone found amusing as guitarists seem to be leaving on a regular basis. It was a formula that worked, which gave them that unmistakably famous twin guitar Thin Lizzy sound.

A week after the Lizzy tour ended I was driving home after a night out when I heard on the late-night BBC news that Keith Relf, singer of the Yardbirds and Renaissance, had died of an electric shock at his home. I later heard that he was electrocuted when he plugged in his electric guitar, which had an electrical fault on it. I was really upset to hear about Keith, I will always remember the good times I spent with Renaissance, he was a really nice guy and being a vegetarian he used to mock us meat-eaters for damaging our health, but he was a heavy smoker and Keith only had one lung. So I would jokingly mock him back and say. "So is it alright to smoke cigarettes for your health then?" I remember one warm sunny evening at the Cooks

Ferry Inn in Edmonton after the sound check, we were sitting outside having a beer. Keith went into depth about when Eric Clapton was in the Yardbirds. The conversation inevitably went on to what it was like having Jeff Beck and Jimmy Page in the band and he thought that what the Yardbirds were doing then was the forerunner of what Jimmy Page later did in Led Zeppelin.

15

LIVE AND DANGEROUS

In April I managed to squeeze some dates in with Andy Fairweather Low, the vocalist and guitarist with Amen Corner who had a hit with 'Bend Me Shape Me', and a No 1 hit 'If Paradise Is Half as Nice'. It was just small clubs but included Dingwalls in London and Newcastle Mayfair. Andy later went on to play in various bands with Eric Clapton, Bill Wyman and Roger Waters as well as pursuing his own band, a nice guy and easy to work with.

DR HOOK

In May I started another Dr Hook tour, the fourth tour so far. The band were doing well in the charts with a hit single and the album 'A Little Bit More' which reached No 5 in the UK charts, No 1 in Denmark and No 18 in the US country charts. As production manager I tried to persuade the band to put the drums on a drum riser. Gary Doon was against the idea as he thought it would look too much like a rock band. I suggested using an 18-inch riser, not a 6ft riser, so the drummer's head would be the same height as the rest of the band when they were standing. They were persuaded with that argument and I got my way. Another suggestion I made was when we were asked by a theatre tech what colour drapes we wanted to hang at the back of the stage, I could see Gary was thinking about it, so I jumped in and said, "Black." I always used black as a backdrop, mainly because the band stands out more and the lights look more impressive.

With 'A Little Bit More' at No 1 in Denmark and with their previous single 'Bankrupt' reaching No 2 in Denmark they were a huge band in Scandinavia. The first show of the tour was at the Tivoli Theatre, a nice venue situated inside a theme park in the middle of Copenhagen, very handy for the hotel as it was just across the road from The Plaza Hotel. There aren't many big towns in Denmark but we packed out another six venues mostly large sports halls and arenas.

The after-show parties were getting to be a bit of a habit again, we didn't have that much equipment so we were packed up and out of there in less than an hour. The promoter had arranged for the band and crew to get free access to the town's most popular nightclubs again, we just walked straight in bypassing the queues. After Denmark there were ten shows in the UK including Hammersmith Odeon and then one show each in Holland, Belgium and Germany, for some reason Paris and Frankfurt were cancelled.

After the show in Germany at the Gurzenech in Cologne, I had a 900-mile overnight drive to Oslo, Norway with Robin Gomer the lighting man, to do a show at the Isle of Calves Festival. Scott and Clive from Colac were already in Oslo but they only had half the PA, I had the other half and Dr Hook were headlining the festival so it made sense to combine the two PA systems together to make one big PA.

I left Cologne at midnight and we got to Hamburg at about 8am, it's not that far except the truck I was driving was limited to 55mph. I had driven all night so Robin took over the wheel to give me a break. At about 9am coming off an Autobahn exit to go on to another Autobahn, Robin slowed down to take the all-too-familiar 360-degree exit slip road, he had trouble changing down the gears and ended up coasting around the bend in neutral far too fast. I called out to get it back into gear but the truck continued to gain speed as he wrestled with the gear stick and I could feel the truck starting to tip. Like a slow motion movie it went up on two wheels and started to tip further. Next I heard the wing mirror crack and smash into the ground with an almighty bang, then the side passenger door was on the ground, the side window smashed in and I could see grass sliding along the ground at 50mph. Before we knew it the truck was on its roof and we were still sliding along the ground upside down and I was wondering when it would ever stop. Eventually it did stop and I heard this enormous creaking and cracking and bits of metalwork blowing out, a really frightening experience. For a short moment it went deadly silent, then I heard diesel gushing out of the upturned diesel tank, I really thought we were going to die there. I was lying on my back and the windscreen was lying right across my chest, there was no way I could get out. I called across to Robin, "Are you alright?" fearing he may have been seriously injured more than I was, but he said he was OK. Relieved that we were both alive, I started to think what we should do.

I don't know how long we lay there, it only seemed like a minute or two when a German ambulance crew were talking to us through the small hole in the crushed door, one got a hold of my arm and pushed a syringe into my hand between my knuckles giving me a shot of something, I don't know what. Next on the scene were the police asking if we were OK, I said, "No, we are trapped and can't move." Next on the scene with typical German efficiency were the Customs Officers, someone must have alerted them to the fact it was a British registered vehicle and wanted to know if we had our paperwork, that was the last thing on my mind. As we waited for what seemed like hours but was probably just minutes a large crane was pulling alongside and I could hear them connecting a winch on to the back axle, which was the highest point on the vehicle. They raised the truck up into the air just enough for the ambulance crew to drag us out feet first. We were put straight into an ambulance and driven off to the local hospital.

Colac's truck after the crash with my equipment lying on the grass.

We had a medical check-up and after lying on a hospital bed for quite a while I decided we couldn't stay around here all day, we had a gig to do in Oslo tomorrow morning and Scott was waiting for the rest of the PA. I discharged myself and told Robin we were going, the nurse said we should stay longer but agreed to let us go as there were no serious injuries. I contacted the police and they were really great, they arranged for a rental truck to be delivered to the crash site and they gave us a lift back there in their police car. Everyone was really good to us and with perfect German efficiency.

When we arrived at the crash scene I couldn't believe what I saw, our truck was suspended hanging in the air by this crane with all the equipment spewed out onto the grass embankment in a big pile of flight cases and speaker cabinets. I couldn't believe we'd survived in what remained of the crushed cab. When the replacement truck arrived I signed all the paperwork and we started to load the gear as best we could into the new truck, to my surprise there didn't seem to be any damage to the equipment except for a few scuffs and scratches.

With the gear reloaded we set off for Oslo, no longer feeling tired: after that wake-up shock I was buzzing. Robin wasn't feeling so good though, still in a state of shock, feeling totally afraid of what Scott and Clive would say and disheartened that he had wrecked the company truck, he was quiet for the rest of the trip.

In Oslo we had Jack the Lad supporting us, an offshoot of the Lindisfarne band. After the Isle of Calves Festival in Oslo we did four more shows in Norway. Bergen is a port on the west coast from where the car ferry sailed to Newcastle in England and was the capital of the Norwegian oil industry, many British workers could be found working here on the oil rigs or working as divers for the oil companies, a beautiful town at the end of a fjord.

My friend Gary Doon on the road crew wanted to see some of the Norwegian countryside and asked Robin if he would swap places with him. Robin jumped at the chance to travel in the band's bus, so Gary and I did the rest of the Norwegian shows by truck. On to Mandal on the south coast and then a 385-mile drive north to Trondheim near the Arctic Circle. As you approach the Arctic Circle you notice the apparent newness of the buildings amidst a barren landscape, nothing appears older than 1945, this is the result of retreating German armies who laid waste to all of Northern Norway on their way back to Germany after realising they'd lost the war. Further north there is a large monument to all the Russian soldiers who died in Norway during the war either fighting the Nazis or who died as slave labourers.

As I was heading north during one of the overnight drives, the early morning mist was hovering low on the ground and the sun was just above the Artic skyline, it was a really beautiful morning and the scenery was outstanding. In the distance I saw a something sitting by the side of the road next to a pine forest. At first I thought it was a large dog, but as I drew closer I slowed down to see what it was as it seemed far too big for a dog, it was clear that the large dog was in fact a grey wolf. I slowed right down as I passed him. I was so close I could see his eyes follow me. That 20-second image has remained burnt in my memory ever since like a slow-motion video clip. I will never forget the look on that animal's face as he looked back at me, a wild but very beautiful animal. I was later told by a local that wolves often come across from Russia.

The one thing that I always noticed about Norwegian audiences when you stand on stage and look out over the audience, 90% of the crowd were blonde and all you see is a sea of blonde hair stretching all the way to the back of the hall.

The last show in Norway was in Alesund. As if I hadn't had enough of a nervous breakdown with the truck crash I was in for another near-death experience. On arrival in Alesund we had a night off before the show the next day. The promoter had already taken the band off to a party and left a couple of his staff to wait for us and bring us along when we arrived. We were told that they were waiting to take us to where the band were. So we checked into the hotel and then followed them down to the quayside which was just outside the hotel. Alesund is on the west coast of Norway on the edge of a beautiful fjord surrounded by small islands. We got into a small four-seater speedboat and headed out across the fjord. Gary and I thought this was great, speeding along admiring the beautiful scenery on a warm summer evening, this was midsummer's week in Northern Norway, the sun didn't set at all this time of year and we were looking forward to meeting up with the rest of the band.

About 30 minutes and a can of beer later, I was getting to wonder where we were, so I asked the driver, "How far is this island?," he said it wasn't far. Just then the engine cut out, he sai. "We have run out of petrol, but don't worry we have a reserve can in the back." Whilst the second Norwegian was filling the tank, the driver proceeded to get out a hash pipe and lit it, he passed it to his friend and then offered it to us, Gary and I both said, "No thanks, we'd rather get to the party." He then admitted he wasn't sure where we were, which was a bit worrying. As I looked around I realised that I couldn't see any land, none at all anywhere. The only thing I could see in the distance was a North Sea oil rig, "How far out are we?" I asked with horror.

After a ten-minute hash pipe break and another can of beer the driver set off and I was sure we had either been kidnapped or were about to die in the middle of the North Sea with two stoned and drunk Norwegians. After another ten minutes we started to worry that we only had half a tank of petrol left to get us where we were going. We then saw some lights on the horizon and headed straight for them; the lights were a private family party on an island, but not the party we were looking for. The driver asked directions but Gary said, "Forget the party, just take us back to the hotel." Which they did and as soon as we hit the dock we were off the boat like greased lightning.

After the Alesund show we took the E6 south, a 350-mile journey all the way from Dombas to Oslo following the winding Gudbrandsdalslagen River downhill all the way to the sea. It was a memorable drive, warm and sunny and the scenery was breathtaking, waterfalls, rapids, twisting roads and hairpin bends surrounded by Norwegian pine forests, steep mountains on one side and sharp drops down a ravine on the other as we followed the path of the river.

Then Gary came up with an idea: how about we set up our own sound company? I said, "That would be great but it costs money to fund a business like that." Gary said he had a wealthy grandfather who was also a business entrepreneur and he would ask him if he would consider investing. The idea was hatched and the rest of the plan was put into place over the next few weeks. It would involve my family moving to the United States and working primarily for Dr Hook but also taking the sound system on the road with other artistes when Dr Hook were not working. Gary wanted me to design, build and source all the parts from England and he wanted to call the company 'Limey Sound' because it would in fact be an English PA system with English parts operated by an Englishman. He just loved the Martin-Midas system I was using for the Dr Hook tours as did their FOH engineer John Draper, the best they had used and far superior to anything they had in the States, which really surprised me. But there were a few hurdles to jump over before the idea became real and I wasn't holding my breath.

From Oslo we drove into Sweden for shows in Stockholm and Malmo and that was the end of the fourth Dr Hook tour. Well not quite, as the next day I had to drive down to Copenhagen where Colac were supplying the sound and lights for a third Roskilde Festival where Dr Hook was headlining on the third and last day. The festival was over three days and we had 44 acts including

Ginger Baker's Gurvitz Army, Steeleye Span, Weather Report and a lively folk group from Scotland called Five Hand Reel who were rather good, along with a multitude of other local and European bands, and finally on the last day Dr Hook, their last European show before heading back to the States.

Scott was there in his truck with his half of the PA and together we put a 10,000-watt system up as we had in Oslo, it sounded good. Ginger Baker's band were OK and Steeleye Span were an excellent festival band getting everybody up dancing and it was good to see the band again as I knew them all by now. Maddie Prior is such a lovely lady and so friendly.

I was out the front doing my babysitting job on the front of house mixer whilst the stage crew were setting up for Weather Report to come on. I was doing a line check on the microphones and getting a rough balance before the band's own engineer turned up to take over mixing the show. I'd laid out the channels and marked up each channel with white tape and a marker pen, the mixing desk was ready to go. The band were just about to go on but there was no sign of their engineer, that didn't bother me as I would have done the mix anyway if there was no one to do it. The band walked on stage and started to play, I started mixing when suddenly their engineer rushes up to the mixer in a panic, rips off the tape with all the channels marked up, screws it up, throws it away, puts on a fresh strip of white tape then says to me, "Do you know what the channels are?" I calmly said, "Yes, I had the desk already marked up and you've just thrown it away." He was in a blind panic, trying to do a mix on a desk without knowing what channel was what, I of course knew what the channels were from memory so I had to tell him as he re-marked the desk, the band had already finished their first song. Moral of that story, 'Don't panic and trust your systems tech'.

One of the frustrating things about babysitting an engineer who is using your PA is that you're standing behind him thinking, what is he doing? I could do a better job than that. It's only natural, when it's your PA, you know it inside out, and you feel confident using it and know how to get the best sound from it. Out of the hundreds of knobs, you can instantly put your finger on the right button because you know where they are without looking. Many times I've felt like pushing the guy aside and taking over, but of course you can't do that because it's his job and he works for the band, I don't. It's just one of the things you have to deal with. Of course I will always help the guy if he asks me for assistance or if something is not working correctly I will fix it for him. Sometimes I have to re-patch plugs and cables to fix something that's stopped working.

The last night of the Festival was Dr Hook and in true Dr Hook style they pulled off a publicity stunt that got them splashed across the front pages of every national Danish newspaper with captions like 'Lock up your daughters Dr Hook's in town'. For the last song they stripped off stark naked in front of the 100,000-strong audience, thankfully it was before the days of video screen technology so there were no close-up shots. The crowd went wild and couldn't believe what they were seeing, thankfully the band's modesty was helped by holding their guitars in places to cover themselves.

THIN LIZZY

On 11th July 1976 Thin Lizzy hit London at the Hammersmith Odeon in front of the biggest and most excited rock audience I had ever seen. The atmosphere in the hall was electric, you could feel the static coming off the crowd. The band's single 'The Boys Are Back in Town' shot to No 8 in the singles chart and the album 'Jailbreak' went to No 10.

Although Phil Lynott was suffering from hepatitis, he played on against his doctor's advice. I don't think anybody in the audience realised how sick he was, I could see he was suffering, with sweat pouring off him and steam coming out the top of his head and his frizzy hair as the heat of the stage lights fried him. It was a one-off concert to take advantage of their chart success and capitalise on their growing popularity. With the Thin Lizzy logo in mirror glass and flashing lights hanging above drummer Brian Downey's head, together with the flash bombs and pyrotechnics, this was a show I will never forget, one of the most memorable of my career.

JULY WAKES FESTIVAL

1976 seemed to be another year of outdoor festivals and the following week I was up at Charnock Richard for the 'July Wakes Festival', this time I brought my wife Estelle, my six-year-old daughter Tamzin and my one-year-old son Alex along for the ride. The festival was in a show-jumping arena that took advantage of its natural amphitheatre in the grounds at Park Hall. On Friday we had eleven artistes including Mike Harding and Five Hand Reel. On Saturday we had sixteen artistes including Hedgehog Pie, Dave Cousins, and Magna Carta and from the disbanded Lindisfarne band we had both Alan Hull and Jack the Lad. On Sunday we had twelve artistes including Bob Pegg, Richard Digance, John Martyn & Danny Thompson, The Chieftains and Bert Jansch (with another ex-Lindisfarne Rod Clements). Very much a folk festival with some very well-known artistes. Apparently Chorley shops ran out of beer and Rizla cigarette papers over the weekend. I'm not sure what the owners thought when they saw skinny dipping in the pool on the Saturday night.

A few days later I received a very nice letter from Brian Adams, the organiser, thanking me for 'the superb job' and the 'perfect sound' at the event. It was nice of him to personally write to me.

BILZEN FESTIVAL

In August it was another festival, this time at Bilzen in Belgium near the Dutch border, two days of music featuring Rick Wakeman, Mott the Hoople, Steeleye Span, Sutherland Brothers & Quiver, Franky Miller, Status Quo, Black Oak Arkansas, Camel, Kevin Ayers and the Jess Rodand Band. As we approached the town of Bilzen with our monster PA system following us in a 40ft trailer it looked like the town was already in full festival mode. We had to queue to get through the heavy traffic with thousands of people mingling through the streets.

BILLY CONNELLY – COLOSSEUM – THIN LIZZY

In September I managed to squeeze in a mini tour of Scotland with Billy Connelly before doing six days of rehearsals at The Roxy in Harlesden with Thin Lizzy. Their next big tour starting with three shows in Sweden was weird, instead of having a tour bus we were travelling in two Austin Princess cars with a chauffeur, one for the band and one for the crew, I felt like we were going to a wedding. We were taken all the way to Sweden via a ferry from Harwich to Esbjerg in Denmark in these two cars while the equipment went by tractor-trailer, then another ferry crossing from Helsingor to Helsingborg in Sweden. We played Stockholm, Gothenburg and Malmo to very enthusiastic crowds.

The UK tour was a week away but between the Swedish dates and the UK tour I was asked if I would stand in and do three dates for Colosseum II mixing FOH sound. A reformed version of the original Colosseum band with John

Hiseman on drums and Gary Moore on guitar and vocals, we did universities at Warwick and Manchester and then the Oasis Ballroom in Ryde on the Isle of Wight. It was great working with Gary Moore, what a brilliant guitarist, I just had to tell Gary I was in the middle of a Thin Lizzy tour, a band he once played guitar for, he seemed amused at that. Also in the band were Don Airey and Neil Murray who had previously played in Cozy Powell's Hammer. Colosseum II released an album *Variations* featuring Andrew Lloyd Webber which included the theme to the TV show *The South Bank Show*.

The Thin Lizzy UK tour to promote the *Johnny the Fox* album started in Oxford and we did 26 shows through October and November. The way the show started was impressive, with an intro tape of police sirens and blue revolving police lights high up on the lighting truss, an easily recognisable guitar chord from twin lead guitars going straight into 'Jailbreak', three flash bombs, one in front of each microphone stand igniting into a huge plume of smoke with an audience-blinding light show; the crowd erupted.

There were some memorable nights from that tour like Leeds University where The Who recorded their *Live at Leeds* album. Charlie who was responsible for putting the flash powder into the three flash pots along the front of the stage didn't take into account the low ceiling, so when the pots were ignited the smoke went up and hit the ceiling like a nuclear mushroom cloud, then came straight back down blanketing the stage in a thick screen of smoke that nobody could see through. It could have been straight out of a Spinal Tap sketch, it took most of the show to clear the air and the audience probably didn't see a lot of the show through the fog.

Brian Robertson's moment was on 30th October when the Glaswegian boy played his home town at the Glasgow Apollo. He was on a high that night and played a brilliant set especially the guitar solo on 'Still in Love with You', a classic power ballad rock song with an unforgettable guitar solo, one of the best shows on the tour. It was one of the greatest guitar solos I've ever heard and will go down as one of the greatest, certainly the live version being far better than the studio version.

Not so good though was 9th November when Brian got drunk on stage. Not having played one of his best shows he decided to take his bottle and smash the wood panelling around the back of the Guildhall in Portsmouth which landed the band with an expensive repair bill. Scott Gorham the other guitar player didn't do any damage or get drunk but he did have a problem with his guitar not working one night. His guitar roadie was running around trying to figure out the problem without success, so I calmly walked out from behind the monitor mixer, unplugged his guitar from his pedalboard and plugged it straight into his amplifier, problem solved, his guitar worked. He didn't have any guitar pedals but he did have a guitar you could hear, he was so pleased he thanked me afterwards. There were three sell-out shows at Hammersmith Odeon which went down brilliantly of course.

The Paris show was cancelled because the equipment truck didn't arrive, for some strange reason Nigel, the truck driver, realising he had missed the load-in by a long way, decided to drive straight to the hotel and wait for us. So when we eventually gave up waiting and headed to our hotel, you can imagine the shock and outrage by the band and crew when they saw the truck and Nigel parked outside as if nothing had happened. We were not pleased.

One of the highlights of the show was the way they went straight from 'Cowboy Song' into 'The Boys Are Back in Town', the last chord of 'Cowboy' also being the first chord of 'Boys are Back', brilliantly done. Another track 'Dancing in the Moonlight' featured John Earle on saxophone from The Graham Parker band who supported Lizzy during the last tour in March and April 1976. Huey Lewis played harmonica on 'Baby Drives Me Crazy' from this tour's support band Clover. At the end of the finale on the last show during 'Me and the Boys' (not included on the live album) Phil decided to take his bass guitar off and throw it up in the air, turning around and walking off stage leaving his guitar to crash to the stage. Without being rehearsed at all, Charlie, his guitar tech leapt across the stage and just caught it as it was 3 inches from hitting the stage preventing the guitar being wrecked. Well done, Charlie.

The album *Johnny the Fox* was released in October to coincide with the tour, a single from the album 'Don't Believe a Word' went to No 12 in the charts and the album went to No 11.

The final show of the tour was in Phil Lynott's home town of Dublin at The Stadium. In Dublin we stayed at the Westbury Hotel as did most bands that visit that city. Outside the hotel today there is now a life-sized statue of Philip Lynott, complete with bass guitar, who died in 1986.

During this tour the *Live and Dangerous* album was recorded at Hammersmith Odeon on a mobile recording truck parked outside. Despite rumours of some tracks being overdubbed in the studio the band deny that was ever done. Even if they did tinker with the mix, so what, a few tweaks here and there are OK if it improves the overall sound or corrects an odd mistake,

I'd rather have that than spoil a great live album and I'm sure whatever went on in the studio was nothing that hasn't been done on every other live album. At the end of the day *Live and Dangerous* is a classic live record from one of the best live bands around at that time.

Live and Dangerous was released in July 1978 and had many critical reviews with many calling it 'One of the best live LPs', 'The best live sound on an album', NME ranked 'Live and Dangerous' at No 1 in its '50 Greatest Live Albums of All Time'. *Classic Rock* magazine voted it the best live album of all time. It was a pleasure and an honour to have taken part in this historic recording, one of the few live recordings where my name is credited on the back of the record cover. For some reason the credits are not included on the CD version, I suspect due to lack of space, one good reason to keep vinyl. Every song on the album blows away the studio version. The best thing about *Live and Dangerous* is the production, it is still raw enough to capture the power and energy of the show.

The support band on this tour was Clover fronted by vocalist Huey Lewis who later went on to have hit singles with 'Do You Believe in Love', 'If This Is It', 'The Power of Love' with his new band Huey Lewis and The News. He was a great guy, so was the band, Huey would often hang out with the crew and have a drink with us backstage or at the hotel.

The band were due to fly to the States in November for a tour but Brian Robertson got into a fight at the Speakeasy Club in London injuring his hand on a glass bottle whilst protecting his friend. This prevented him from playing guitar for a while, so the US tour was cancelled. Although I did hear that Robertson was allegedly fired and Gary Moore took time out from the band Colosseum II as a stand-in whilst supporting Queen on tour.

Drink was one thing, cocaine was another but heroin was the beginning of the end for Lizzy, Gary Moore had left twice already and was now lined up to return for the Black Rose album after Robertson's second time of being fired. Gary Moore joined Lizzy for the third time at the start of 1979. Lizzy's tour manager Frank Murray was a good bloke and had a difficult job on his hands trying to control the band. The last show I did with Thin Lizzy was on 18th November 1976 at the Dublin Stadium. Dublin was also the last show I did working for Colac (for now) as I had committed myself to moving to the States to set up Limey Sound.

That wasn't the last time I saw Phil Lynott though, I bumped into him a few times on tour in different cities. On one tour with Lindisfarne, Lizzy was in the same city and I nipped over to catch the first few songs from their album

'Renegade' and sat next to my friend Pete Eustace at the FOH mixer before rushing back to mix my own show which started an hour later. Another time Phil was staying in the same hotel as me and came over to say hello, he was always very friendly but he was in such a mess, you could tell that heroin had got a hold of him. In January 1986 Phil Lynott died from heart failure and pneumonia after 11 days in hospital, he was admitted with a serious kidney and liver infection after collapsing from a drink and drugs binge at his home. It was heroin that eventually killed him. Not long after that, Charlie who was Phil's guitar tech also died of a heroin overdose, what a waste. My time with Thin Lizzy was one of the most memorable and enjoyable times on the road.

LIMEY SOUND

The rest of the year was spent setting up Limey Sound which Gary Doon had started to put together after asking his entrepreneur grandfather to invest. Gary's idea was to create a sound company in the United States to service the American market, but primarily to supply Dr Hook with a touring sound system. Gary wanted the name to be Limey Sound as it would be a mainly English system, designed and built in England and operated by a Limey engineer (me).

Gary's grandfather had agreed to finance the deal and sent over a sum of money to secure the initial purchase of the equipment with the condition he held a 2% share of the company leaving Gary and me with 49% each. Gary had sent funds direct to Midas for the purchase of a 24-channel front of house mixer and a 16-channel on-stage monitor mixer together with funds to purchase Martin speaker cabinets. Gary also sent enough money for me to put together the rest of the equipment like stage boxes, microphone and loudspeaker cables and all the components needed to finish the job.

We put our house up for sale and I went to the American Embassy in Grosvenor Square in London armed with all the relevant paperwork from America to get a green card and permission to work there. That's when my problems started.

16

LIMEY SOUND IN THE USA & PINK FLOYD'S QUAD MIXER

During the first two months of 1977 I spent the time building the equipment ready to ship over to America whilst I waited for my green card work permit. When I approached Geoff Byers at Midas about buying the two mixers I asked him if I could build the mixers myself as if I was still working there, he was busy and to my surprise he welcomed the offer.

Now that Midas had moved into new premises in Stanhope Street he also had a range of new channels made to fit into the new mixers. The new PR004 channels were pre-built by outside manufacturers so we didn't have to hand assemble each component onto the printed circuit boards as I used to do, this made it a simple job of putting the frame together, fitting in and wiring up the motherboard and plugging in the modular channels.

It was handy that Martin Audio and Midas Audio were neighbours to each other in Stanhope Street because I could call in to see them both when I was in the area. I managed to do a deal with Dave Martin, but only because he knew me so well, I told him I wanted the speaker cabinets supplied empty and I would fit the speakers and drivers in America when I arrived. He wasn't keen on the idea at first as he had never done that before, but I persuaded him that it was daft to buy American JBL speakers from America, pay the import tax and then re-export them back to America with all the extra weight and shipping costs. He reluctantly agreed and the deal was done. It saved me a packet in freight costs, I purchased eight Martin bass bins, four Martin mid-range cabinets and eight high-frequency horns. In America I had plans to add two RCA W cabinets for the sub bass.

Having had experience of assembling and wiring electronic circuits, I built three stage boxes with all the microphone sockets, along with the 32-way multicore cable that connects all the stage boxes with the two mixers, it took some hours wiring up that lot. Each of the two cables had 27 pairs of screened wires, the three stage boxes had connectors for the on-stage monitor mixer, the front of house mixer and an additional output for mobile recording if ever a show was to be recorded. I purchased a front of house effects rack and fitted it with a BSS four-way crossover. I phoned my friend Chas Brooke who I worked with the first time I was at Midas, he left Midas shortly after I did to set up his own company Brooke Siren Systems (BSS) with his partner Stan Gould. I told him what I was doing and got a good deal on the crossover.

The equipment was completed, the money had been transferred over from America and everyone was paid. On the immigration front it was not going so well.

Limey Sound's Midas FOH mixer and monitor mixer

On my visit to the American Embassy I was basically told that I had to prove to the Immigration Department that I could do a job that an American couldn't do, it was not like me doing an American tour with a British band. This was an American band using an American registered sound company and I was an alien director.

I was declined a work permit on my first attempt so Gary got an American immigration lawyer working on my behalf to pull the right strings. Dr Hook's management did all they could as well, writing letters in an attempt to get me over there, the band were looking forward to me working for them in America as I was. I tried again, this time with all the letters and paperwork that was sent from the American immigration lawyer.

While I waited for a decision from the Embassy we managed to get a buyer for our house and the day came to exchange contracts, but no work permit had arrived, so not wanting to be made homeless I cancelled the sale and took the house off the market, the next day I received a rejection in the post from the American Embassy for the second time. I was devastated.

When I was turned down a second time it was suggested I apply for a tourist visa initially and then reapply once I had settled in. That was a mistake and bad advice from the American lawyer. As to be expected the Immigration Department saw right through that plan and banned me from applying to work there for ten years on the grounds of attempting to work on a tourist visa. I'm pleased to say that it didn't affect my ability to enter or tour America with British bands.

All the legal documents had been completed to form the incorporated company and I was still a co-director of an American registered company 'Limey Sound Inc' but I wasn't allowed into the United States to work. The sound equipment arrived in America and Gary went away to decide what to do next, he had a sound system and no one to operate it.

BLACK SABBATH & AC/DC

I hadn't spoken to Scott Thompson at Colac since the last Thin Lizzy tour and not knowing what was going on with my immigration, he called to ask when I would be going to the USA. I told him the problems I was having with immigration and that it didn't look like I was going. He asked if I would do another Black Sabbath tour starting next month. I said I would, so in March

1977 we were back out on the road with Black Sabbath with AC/DC as the support act, this time to promote their latest album 'Technical Ecstasy', back into Shepperton Studios for two days of technical rehearsals followed by ten nights in the UK including four nights at Hammersmith Odeon.

SHEPPERTON STUDIOS

Shepperton Studios was starting to feel like a second home having spent so much time there, and as Shepperton has played such an important part in the history of Rock'n'Roll, I feel it deserves a mention in more detail. It's a really fascinating place, it's not open to the public but I had almost free access to walk around the site, huge doors are left open and you could see inside studios the size of aircraft hangers where film sets were being constructed or scenes were being filmed. Over the years many famous films have been made there, *2001 A Space Odyssey*, *Star Wars*, *Alien*, *Blade Runner*, *Superman*, *Robin Hood*, *Evita*, *Gosford Park*, *Harry Potter*, *Da Vinci Code* and thousands more, too numerous to mention. The site is huge and as well as making films, there were many small workshops hired by small individual firms specialising in various businesses connected to the film industry, like special effects, model making, set construction, film editing, sound editing, post production editing and costume warehouses where you could hire just about any piece of clothing for whatever period in history you need, if they didn't have it they would make it for you.

As you walked around you couldn't help but notice old discarded sets or pieces of equipment dumped or just left abandoned in the open parking area. There was an old submarine from a war movie, some old World War II armoured vehicles, a giant *Pink Panther* puppet, a full-sized castle, although on closer inspection the castle was actually made of polystyrene, buildings that were just a front façade with nothing behind except supports to keep the front up, whole streets sometimes. Shepperton had 15 stages in all, ranging from a small 3,000 square feet to a massive 30,000 square feet, even a complete water world tank the size of a small ocean. They were called stages but were actually large warehouses and some outdoor areas the size of fields big enough to build a city, and they have been used for this in films.

There were also other companies based there, The Who had a warehouse where they stored their stage equipment and set up a sound and lighting hire company called ML Executives to hire out their equipment. I did hear from the locals at Shepperton that ML Executives was set up as a tax avoidance company, but who knows if that was true, quite possibly. Also Entec had their sound and lighting warehouse there. Since then both ML and Entec have moved out of Shepperton and relocated elsewhere. There was also a very good canteen which did excellent subsidised food.

On one occasion I had to deliver some equipment to one of the studios, as I walked in Elton John was there playing a grand piano on the stage floor rehearsing for his next tour. Because the acoustics in the studio were absolutely perfect, the sound coming off the piano miked up through his PA system was mind boggling and I just stood there in total awe listening to the sound of the piano. I hadn't heard a piano sound that good through a PA before. The quality was true hi-fi. But I couldn't help thinking as I stood behind the sound engineer at the mixer, with all the outboard effects and equalisers he was using that once you get on the road mate, you won't have the luxury of acoustics as good as this.

This time along for the ride on the Black Sabbath tour was a new Australian rock band AC/DC. They would pay a heavy price to be on the road with Sabbath but ultimately ended up bigger than the headliner they supported. I recognised the bass player, Cliff Williams, as he'd played in a band I once worked with called Sugar with Laurie Wisfield who later went on to play with Wishbone Ash. I did a gig with Sugar in Colchester on 12th July 1969, that's a co-incidence, and Jamie Litherland who was playing with Colosseum (that name again) at the time suggested to Cliff he audition for the job of bass player, small world in the music business. The band were polite but not very friendly, I had to babysit the engineer whilst he mixed the FOH sound and they were loud.

When a band supports or opens a show for a headliner you might expect the artiste to get paid for performing, that was the case years ago. That is until managers were being approached by so many bands asking if they could open the show for them, they got to thinking that these guys would actually pay to be on the same bill as us. So it became known as a concert 'Buy In', where a band actually pays the main act for the 'privilege' to play on the same stage as them. This has three benefits for the support act, it gives the band access to a guaranteed audience, it introduces the band to a new set of potential fans and you get to learn some useful tips from a professional headliner. The benefit to the headliner is that they generate more income. I worked with many support acts who eventually went on to become the main act, sometimes ending up even bigger than the band they once supported.

From the first time I saw AC/DC I realised they would be a powerful band,

I'll never forget they always started the set with 'Livewire', a killer track. For a band to be successful you need three things basically, talent of course, a hard work ethic and a commitment to succeed. Not what some bands do, go out on stage, run through a few songs and expect to be a hit without working for it. I was sure AC/DC would be successful because they really worked hard on stage, it showed and they worked the audience, they certainly went down well at each show and deserved their success.

Starting off on a 10-date UK tour at Glasgow Apollo, a horrible place to do a show, not so bad with previous acts I'd been there with like Ralph McTell and Billy Connelly who had relatively little in the way of equipment. Sabbath had a monster production (for its day) with three 40-foot articulated trailers. One for sound, one for lights and one for staging and backline, all fully loaded all the way to the back doors. The stage was about 10 feet off the ground and the equipment had to be loaded into the building at the back of the stalls, wheeled down the long aisles to the front and then hand-lifted on to stage or fork lifted up, as you can imagine, it took hours to unload the trucks and set up the stage. It wasn't until a few years later that someone had the bright idea of knocking a hole in the wall and ramping the gear from the street directly onto the stage. The stage happened to be on street level so it was relatively easy to load in after that. Down the road to Newcastle City Hall, which is basically a town hall theatre with a wraparound balcony and choir steps at the back of the stage. Not much room to put the equipment on the stage so some of it went on the choir steps at the back, most of it was left in the truck so a scaled-down production was loaded in.

On to the 10,000 capacity New Bingley Hall in Stafford, an exhibition hall, the first thing that hits you when you go into this hall is the smell, no one told us that during the week it was used as a cattle market. Although the cow poo and straw had been cleaned away you could still smell it. If it looked like a barn, smelt like a barn and sounded like a barn, it was a barn.

Next Liverpool Empire, another old cinema but with a very large stage, a pleasure to work in, except for the load-in and load-out which is 20 feet above stage level, again it takes hours to load in and load out. The sound in there is a bit rough, OK in the stalls where the majority of the speakers are pointing but go into the balcony and it's so high above the stage that all you hear is a mumble from the stage below. In 1977 we didn't fly speakers in the air, it just wasn't done and we didn't have the gear to do it anyway, at best you would just point some horns upward in the direction of the balcony. After Cardiff and Southampton we went on to do four nights at Hammersmith Odeon. What a difference, I've always liked Hammersmith, it's easy to load in having the stage directly at ground level and the sound is always good in there, always a pleasure.

One bad memory of the Hammersmith Odeon show I did with Thin Lizzy was during load-out. I took off my Thin Lizzy sweatshirt with the words 'Crew' printed on the back and placed it on the side of the stage. 99% of the time your personal belongings are safe on stage, but on this occasion someone decided they would steal my sweatshirt. This was no ordinary sweatshirt and not one you could buy from the merchandising stand, it was a limited edition and only given out to the immediate Thin Lizzy road crew. So it came as a surprise when I did Hammersmith with Black Sabbath only four months later to see one of the stage crew wearing my Thin Lizzy 'Crew' shirt. I didn't say anything during the day but waited until the load-out was almost completed by which time I was pumped up on adrenaline. I then confronted the wearer in front of all his crew mates by asking, "Where did you get that sweatshirt?" He said he was given it by Thin Lizzy. Knowing that none of the Lizzy crew had given their sweatshirt away, I accused him of being a liar, a thief and a disgrace to the Hammersmith crew and told him he stole it from this very stage only four months previously. He looked shocked and ashamed and I left him in the hands of his crew mates. I never saw him at Hammersmith again. I wasn't especially attached to the sweatshirt, in fact I had forgotten all about it, it was the fact he stole it from the stage and then had the nerve to wear it in the same venue, he should have realised that we worked these venues on a regular basis.

The Black Sabbath backline crew played a cruel joke on the only American on the crew, they convinced him he needed a work permit visa to work in Scotland as it was a different country to England, he fell for it so they told him they'd have to 'smuggle' him through customs in the back of the truck hidden behind the equipment. They waited until they saw the toll booths at the Forth Road Bridge which at night resembled a customs post with all the lights on and told him to climb in the back, he spent the rest of the journey in the back of the truck totally unaware he was already in Scotland and just going over a toll bridge. I'm not sure to this day if he ever realised what actually happened.

At the beginning of April after the UK tour, we headed off on our European leg with 17 dates over 22 days through 9 countries, Germany, Holland, Belgium, France, Switzerland, Denmark, Norway, Sweden and Finland. The first night was in Paris at the Pavilion.

Black Sabbath are credited as having invented the term 'heavy metal' with Tony's down-tuned guitar sound that gave what can only be described as very dark chords. Tony lost the tips of 2 fingers on his right hand in an industrial accident at work when he was younger whilst working in a factory. He thought he'd never play guitar again, but he adapted his guitar playing by fitting false tips to the ends of his fingers, you wouldn't know by listening to him play.

Jezz the keyboard player doesn't get much of a mention, not many people knew that Sabbath had a keyboard player unless you accidently saw him through a gap in the curtains. He would have his keyboards set up off stage in the wings or if the stage was not big enough he would be on the floor next to the stage, I gave him a monitor speaker so he could hear the rest of the band. If you're sitting in the audience and you listen close enough you can just hear keyboards in the background mix. I was speaking to Jezz backstage one night and it used to annoy him that he was not part of the band or even recognised as a part of the show. He was on a weekly salary and considered only one level higher than the road crew. Jezz told me how sometimes backstage after the show or in a hotel bar people would ask what job he did with the band, he would say, "Keyboard player" and they would answer, "What keyboards? Sabbath don't have keyboards." But of course Sabbath did both live and on record.

Our truck driver James Atkinson got us into trouble one night in Germany by shouting and screaming at the stage crew, they were doing a good job as far as I could see but James who was driving the sound truck was having a bad day and was not in the mood to be dealing with idiots as he called them. The job of local stage crew is to push the cases from the stage up the ramp and onto the truck, where another team would be waiting to pack the truck under the supervision of the truck driver. Sometimes if we got the stage cleared early, we the road crew would help pack the truck, as we knew where each box had to go and in which order, this is critical for three reasons. If the equipment isn't loaded and packed in exactly the right order it may not all go in, secondly by seeing an empty hole you immediately know that something is left behind, and thirdly the pack has to fit tight so that no damage is done to the equipment whilst in transit with it sliding and banging about. On this day he was shouting and screaming at the stage crew for some reason when the crew boss called the crew out on strike and said they would not load that truck and continued with the other two trucks. The rest of the road crew including me had to load the truck that night. James can be a hothead sometimes but I worked with him many times both before and after this tour and we got on really well. I'd always request James first if I booked a truck and driver, he had his own transport business called Atkinson-Sanders, one of the best.

At Easter there was a third band on the bill, Gillan, who opened the show in front of AC/DC. Ian Gillan left Deep Purple in 1973 and started his own band Gillan, he was easy to work with and didn't ask for much.

In Gothenburg the Scandinavium is a huge indoor ice hockey arena where the ice is covered over with wooden boards. It was cold, my bones were frozen, even though I was on the go all day I just couldn't get warm with having to walk on top of a frozen ice rink all day. The show went well but after the show there were rumours that there had been a fight between Geezer Butler from Sabbath and Angus Young from AC/DC. Geezer allegedly pulled a knife on Angus, I don't know what it was about but Angus ended up punching Geezer in the face, that caused a huge row with the others and ended up having AC/DC thrown off the tour. I knew of course that Sabbath didn't like AC/DC much, their style of rock was more aggressive.

Their vocalist Bon Scott could sing better than Ozzy and was going down a storm with the audience. I think a bit of jealousy was going on there. The following shows in Oslo, Stockholm and Helsinki were cancelled and we all went home via the Esbjerg-to-Harwich ferry.

UFO

I got home expecting a bit of time off and to sort out the problems I had with Limey Sound Inc in America when I had an unexpected phone call from a rival sound company Entec saying I had been recommended to them by someone, I don't know who but they wanted to know if I could fly out to Karlsruhe in Germany tomorrow and help the crew out with some problems they were having with their PA system.

I went to Heathrow and got on the next flight out picking up my ticket from the airline help desk. The flight was at 7pm to Frankfurt changing planes to Stuttgart arriving at 10pm. When I arrived at the hotel there was no sign of the crew, they were driving down from Gothenburg. I waited around in the bar for a while and eventually went to bed knowing that I would see them in the morning. I knew the venue was only ten minutes away so I walked over and found the crew had just arrived and started to unload the truck. It was a 1,500 capacity sports hall and the band was UFO. They had already been out on tour for a week and I was instantly confronted by a hostile attitude from the crew. The crew boss Bruno was the only one talking to me and I got the impression they didn't really want another crew member along, they certainly didn't want an 'outsider' as they saw me. The Entec crew must have thought they were quite capable of doing the job without me and I think they saw me arriving as a failure on their part. I don't know whose idea it was to send me out, but the Entec management must have felt they wanted me there to fix the problems they were having. Not having the co-operation of the crew made my life difficult both on a professional level and a personal level.

The problems were mainly in the mixer, being a Midas mixer I was confident working on it and went about stripping it down and doing some minor repairs, some of it was just bad contact joints, some dirt on the connectors and a general tidy up. I also found a Martin bass bin speaker was wired up backwards reducing the power of the system. I had to do this work over the period of a few days as the FOH engineer wouldn't give me access to the mixer until he was ready. I also tidied up the wiring on the system, which was a complete mess. I can't stand to see untidy wiring and it doesn't do any good having your wires in a mess when you're trying to find a fault. It wasn't my job to tidy their cables up for them but I just wanted to do something constructive, meanwhile the crew were watching me go through all the cables in the cable trunk sorting them out, repairing broken ones and tidying up the mess. Later they said they were grateful for what I had done but they didn't want to admit to it.

We did eight shows in Germany, one each in Switzerland and Holland and two in France, the largest hall was the 2,500-capacity Parc Des Expositions in Colmar. I had not heard of the band before but apparently they were very big in Europe, Japan and America. The band consisted of Phil Moog on vocals who embarrassingly carried a set of body building weights into hotels in a shopping trolley, he looked really silly, Andy Parker on drums, Paul Raymond on keyboards and guitar, Pete Way on bass and Michael Schenker on guitar who was formally with the German rock band The Scorpions. He later returned to The Scorpions after leaving UFO a few months later.

I discovered years later that Bernie Marsden from Cozy Powell's Hammer and Whitesnake played in the band as did Don Airey of Deep Purple, Rainbow and Whitesnake and Aynsley Dunbar of Whitesnake and Journey, also Jason Bonham, son of Led Zeppelin's John Bonham. There have been some well-respected musicians going through the ranks of this band. I would say they were a typical rock band for their time, reasonably good but not that good, they were hardly even heard of in Britain. The best thing I remember about UFO was Michael Schenker playing guitar.

As we arrived in Hamburg in the crew bus for a day off, the band had already checked in. The tour manager grabbed one of the crew in a panic and told him to get up to Michael's room, who had a girl with him, to warn him his wife had just arrived in reception and was trying to find his room. I think the girl was smuggled out just in time.

Around this time, in Germany there was a terrorist cell called The Baader-Meinhof Gang, also known as The Red Army Faction who were doing a lot of terrorist activity, bombings, kidnapping, assassinations and robberies, they'd killed a lot of people. The German police were on the lookout for these people big time. As we drove around the autobahns every day we would see the police crouched down with machine guns hiding behind road signs and bridges ready to stop vehicles.

One day, coming out of our hotel, three members of the crew and myself were walking towards our 15-seater transit mini-bus when two police cars who must have been waiting for us, suddenly screeched up and four German police officers jumped out with their guns pointed at us and shouted something in German I didn't understand. When you have four armed police pointing guns at you, you don't argue. I immediately dropped my bag as did the others and we put our hands in the air, once we said we were English, they relaxed a little and asked for our ID, we all had our passports to hand and readily handed them over, the officer was very apologetic and polite and told us they had a tip-off that we might be members of Baader-Meinhof and let us go. Not a very pleasant experience.

By this time the crew had accepted me into the team and we got along ok, I felt I was as much a part of the crew as any of them except for one little jerk. A 20-year-old kid who was new to the game and thought he knew it all, he didn't like me, kept making sarcastic comments like, "Here comes the bloody troubleshooter," (his job description not mine) and he probably saw me as a threat to his job, which I wasn't as I had no intention of working for Entec, at least I wasn't intending to at the time, later on was a different story. The UFO tour finished in Hannover on 14th May and the rest of May and June were quiet so I was pleased to have some time off although I was not without things to do.

LIMEY SOUND UK LTD

After consulting his accountant, my partner Gary Doon decided that as I was unable to join him in America with Limey Sound Inc, he wanted to buy me out and offered me a very generous compensation package for my 49% share of the business. He was told that as I was an alien director of an American registered incorporated company it doubled the company's tax liability. I didn't have much choice really, there was no point me holding out and inconveniencing Gary or the business so I agreed to sell out and he sent me a handsome cheque.

I decided I would put the money to good use and went into Midas with the intention of purchasing my own Midas sound mixer. I also wanted to start my own sound company, but not having the entire funds to purchase all the equipment and the cost of warehousing it, I decided I would just put together the front of house mixer, FOH rack with sound processors, equalisers, stage boxes, multicore cables and power cables. In fact everything to do a show except the loudspeakers and amplifiers, which I could easily rent as and when I needed them and I wouldn't need a warehouse to store them.

Whilst I was in Midas, Geoff Byers had started building Pink Floyd's huge Quadrophonic mixer that was to be used on their next world tour. Never one to miss a trick and knowing my previous experience of working at Midas, Geoff asked if I would lend a hand in getting this beast assembled and wired up. I was happy to help. I saw Pink Floyd a few times over the years previously at Dagenham Roundhouse, a small pub in London where Pink Floyd had placed WEM speakers all around the room in a four stack array allowing the sound to be panned around the room in 270 degrees, that had never been done before. They were very innovative live and in the studio. I saw them again at Alexandra Palace for an all-nighter, also at London's Roundhouse UFO club and at Earl's Court Arena.

The mixer was based on the Midas PR004 channel and was split into three sections, the centre section contained the four quadraphonic outputs, six quadraphonic sub-groups plus quad and stereo master output groups. According to the technical specs given to me by Midas the mixers had 1182 push buttons, 447 rotary controls, 240 thumbwheel switches, 484 toggle switches, 67 rotary stud switches, 32 LED meter columns, 156 channel LEDs, 54 mono faders, 11 stereo faders, 5 quad faders, a total of 70 faders in all.

Each of the three boards were linked together via 36 pin cable connectors, these alone were no easy thing to wire up but I had done many in the past so it was no problem dealing with this fiddly job and it's the kind of job I enjoy.

When put together the desk was 12 feet long and had 40 input channels, 8 effects send and return groups routed via 8 stereo sub-groups or 6 quad sub-groups.

Put into simple language for sound techs, that's 40 into 8 into 2 into 4. Not considered large by today's standard but in 1977 this was a monster, some say the largest portable mixing console ever taken on the road at that time. It took three months to build the frame, wire it and assembly all the channels. It was something we were extremely proud to have built and to be invited to one of the shows and see it being used was a privilege and a real pleasure.

Although the name suggests Quadraphonic, this isn't strictly true in the same sense as a quadraphonic home hi-fi. Instead of the four-speaker system you would associate with quad, the Pink Floyd system uses a conventional left and right stereo front stack of speakers, a smaller left and right stack of speakers on the sides and a fifth centre stack at the rear, more like a 5:1 cinema system.

Strangely enough, whilst I was in Midas busily wiring away, two bosses from Entec called in to visit Geoff Byers and saw me in there much to their surprise and actually thanked me for what I had done on the UFO tour which I thought was nice of them.

17

NEVER SAY DIE – A BRIDGE TOO LOW

ROSKILDE FESTIVAL

July came around again and it was time for another Roskilde Festival in Denmark, the fourth one I had been asked to do. Not such a dramatic line-up this year but just as interesting, The main acts were The Jack Bruce Band, The Ian Gillan Band, John Miles, Dr Feelgood, The Chieftains, Tania Maria and a dozen or so local Danish and European acts. After checking into our hotel, which was like a cheap motel on the edge of Roskilde, we went down to the site to set up our sound and lighting rigs. After the first night I went back to the hotel, opened the door to my room and found four men sleeping in my room which was only a single room anyway. I had the right room and the right key but no sign of my suitcase, so unable to find the hotel manager who had gone home for the night, I helped myself to another room key and went to bed wondering what had happened to my suitcase. In the morning I challenged the hotel manager who could tell I was annoyed, and he admitted that he moved my case and put someone else in there, he wouldn't tell me why he did it, but he said he was pleased that I found another room key, I bet he was, otherwise he really would have known how mad I was.

Just before The Jack Bruce Band came on stage the crowd were getting restless. The band were late coming on and someone decided to throw a beer can onto the stage, whether by deliberate aim or just bad luck the can landed straight on top of one of the cymbals with a loud crashing noise. The crowd thought this was hugely funny and decided to join in with the fun, for the next five minutes the stage was raining beer cans, it was so bad it was unsafe to venture onto the stage and we all took cover until the can rain stopped.

DR HOOK

Despite what people thought of Dr Hook there was a strict no drugs rule, if anyone wanted to go for a smoke they did it on the band bus or crew bus, never in the venue or hotel. Hard drugs were banned outright, no-one was exempt, even the main guys, anyone caught would be sacked instantly. However there was a rather relaxed attitude towards smoking pot as long as it wasn't in the venue or the hotel rooms. In September a fifth Dr Hook tour was scheduled, titled 'Making Love and Music' after the new album. I was at home when their tour manager Nineyear Wooldridge (Nine to his friends) phoned to give me the tour dates and to tell me they wanted a bigger production this time.

This time we had a bigger budget, that meant a 40-foot lighting truss, a 40-foot trailer and a bigger PA. I chose to use the Black Sabbath PA but cut it down to just two of the six Vitavox 'W' cabinets. I just love the warm and powerful bass sound they produce and despite their size (6 feet x 3 feet x 2 feet) I found them easy to manoeuvre. With the aid of a four-wheeled dolly board, I was able to get them off the stage, out into the loading area and onto the truck on my own. I'm the only person I know who could ever do that.

I had to organise and book the sound and lighting equipment, find a crew, a 40-foot tractor trailer and a mini bus for the British crew as we needed to travel ahead of the band. I also had to hire a stage riser for the drums and a Hammond B3 organ, it's not worth shipping an American B3 organ over as they are really fragile and are not tuned to our 50Hz power, and 110 volt transformers to power the American equipment.

For the sound I went to Colac again but this time I was using my own 24-channel Midas mixer and control equipment. Colac supplied the rest, amps and speakers. I asked my friend Andi Banks to come along on the sound crew. As I had recently toured with Thin Lizzy, Black Sabbath and UFO, I knew what sound system I wanted and although Dr Hook were not a heavy rock band they did 'rock' and I wanted a sound system to handle the larger venues that Dr Hook were performing in; Dr Hook were huge in Scandinavia and so were the venues.

For the lights I went to Colac as well and asked them for a 40-foot front truss and some side frames and two follow spots, the truss also needed two wind-up Genie Superlift towers as some venues didn't have flying facilities, all these potential problems have to be catered for. I told them I wanted my friend Patrick Whitley (Paddy to his friends) and another lighting guy Happy Bray. For trucking I asked James Atkinson from Atkinson Sanders to drive the truck as I knew him well and despite upsetting the German stage crew one time with Black Sabbath he was a good driver and we got on well. During the show the bus and truck drivers like to earn some extra money operating follow spots so that was covered. The mini bus was a 15-seater transit so the four of us had enough room to spread out.

On the way to the first gig James had to swing by Copenhagen Airport and pick up Dr Hook's backline equipment which had been flown in from America, we joined him there to help load it onto the trailer.

The first two shows in Sweden were in 10,000 seater ice hockey stadiums, one in Gothenburg and one in Stockholm. From there we went into Norway for four shows. It was in Oslo that James kept telling me that he wasn't sure that the truck would make it to the next venue 310 miles through the mountains to Trondheim. I have to admit I wasn't listening to him at first as I thought the road was passable, I'd done it myself driving a 3-ton truck but I wasn't thinking that he was hauling a 4-metre-high trailer. It was at the crew meal before the show that he said, "The trailer won't go under the low bridges, there aren't any bridges high enough for me to drive under." This was a shock so we studied the map in great detail looking for bridges with a 4-metre height clearance. James said if we cut down these side roads and bypass some small towns we could get through but there was no guarantee we could pass under all the bridges. This could have ended up a serious *Spinal Tap* moment.

The crew's mini bus. Dr Hook tour 1977 with Andi Banks

A Bridge too low

Measuring another low bridge

For the drive to Trondheim we decided to travel in convoy with me driving the mini bus ahead of James; the first part of the journey was OK. It was when we got up into the north of Norway we encountered our first hurdle, we had to divert from the main road and go down a gravel track, through what looked like a farmyard and back onto a side road where we stopped to check the bridge ahead. With James edging through slowly, he just made it with a few inches to spare, on to the next bridge and this time Paddy got a tape measure and climbed up the steel structure to measure the clearance of the bridge as it looked lower than the last one. It didn't have a height restriction sign on it as the other bridges had, this looked very close but again James just scraped under, across another farmer's field and along a dirt track then two more low bridges and we were clear, back on the main highway to Trondheim. When we got there the stage crew told us it was the first time a trailer that size had done a gig in Trondheim and a *Spinal Tap* moment was avoided.

The rest of the tour went uneventfully, four shows in Denmark and three in Germany. First we had to stop off at the WDR radio station in Cologne and do a radio show. We set up, did a sound check and rehearsal in the afternoon and did the show at 6pm for a one-hour live broadcast to an estimated 20 million listeners.

There was another *Musikladen* television show in Bremen, but the studio was providing all the equipment so we drove straight to Ostend for the ferry. The show wasn't even going out live, it was a 'lip sync' show, that's when they sing into a dead microphone and the TV viewers hear a pre-recorded track, so it looks like the singer is actually singing live but isn't, it's done all the time. Some singers are better at it than others, sometimes it's so badly done it's embarrassing.

That ended three weeks in Europe and we headed back to England for eleven UK shows with three sell-out shows at The Rainbow in London. The next day we had a day at the BBC doing another *Old Grey Whistle Test* TV show with Bob Harris, the last time Dr Hook did the *OGWT* was in 1975. The morning was spent setting the stage equipment and I put in a stage monitor system for the band to hear themselves as there was no PA in the studio. Then soundchecks, camera checks and dress rehearsals in the afternoon, which seemed to go on forever. BBC staff were never ones to rush anything. In the evening we recorded the show straight through just like it was live. In true BBC style the unions were running the show and only allowed us to do the minimum, if we wanted to plug something in we had to get a BBC electrician to do it and only into one of their own sockets. For some strange reason the BBC had produced 13 Amp sockets with sideways facing earth pins so you couldn't plug a normal 13 Amp plug into a BBC 13 Amp socket, how bizarre, only the BBC could think of that.

Dr Hook being as crazy as they were, decided to come on stage all connected together with a massive 8-foot-long safety pin, it was a joke towards the punk fashion at the time.

After the show, we went back to our hotel at the Kensington Hilton. Whilst sitting in the bar enjoying a beer with a few of the crew, we couldn't help but notice what was obviously a transvestite hooker attempting to pick up a very drunk middle-aged businessman, we all found it very entertaining and I dread to think what he woke up to the next morning. One more show at the Brighton Centre and then back over to Germany for four more shows.

In Nuremburg we had time to go sightseeing before the show and I particularly wanted to visit the Zeppelinfeld (Zeppelin Field) where Adolf Hitler held his Nuremburg rallies for the Reich Party Congress. I'd seen pictures of it in films but was not prepared for the huge scale of the place. The Zeppelin Field could accommodate up to 200,000 people and covered 11 sq km. As a soundman I was interested because legend has it that Hitler had the largest PA system in the world ever to be installed. The PA would not have been huge mountains of speakers stacked up like a rock concert, but smaller line drive speakers linked around the field on a loop. He was also the first person to ever use three vocal mics, something which has been copied by world leaders up to the present day. As you look around this massive stadium you get an earie feeling of what went on there, on the towers that surround the field you can still see the outline of the Nazi eagles that have since been chiselled off.

THE RUNAWAYS

Two weeks after the Dr Hook tour finished I was asked to do the front of house sound for an American all-girl rock band The Runaways on a European tour. The band consisted of Joan Jett lead guitar and vocals, Lita Ford lead guitar and vocals, Vicki Blue bass guitar and vocals, Sandy West drums and vocals. They had recorded one album in 1976 called *The Runaways*, a second album in 1977 *Queens of Noise* and their latest album which they were promoting on this tour was *Waitin' for the Night*.

I'd never worked for an all-girl group before and I was surprised how good they were, not because they were female musicians but because they were an all-female group and very young, easily as good as any male rock band and very proficient musicians as well with a professional attitude. Their music was raw rock with blinding guitar solos and a heavy drum sound driving the band along. The only downside was they were loud, very loud.

The first gig was at Sheffield University and they went down really well and I was impressed. We did five more shows in the UK, Birmingham, Newcastle, Glasgow and Manchester ending up at Hammersmith Odeon.

The support band on the UK leg of the tour, 999, thought it would be a good part of their act to kick the monitor speaker off the front of the stage. I told him straight, "If you do that again, you'll have to find yourself another sound company." He couldn't apologise enough and the hard-nut punk rocker suddenly became a very meek and mild individual. We got on OK after that.

The European leg got off to a bad start, we had two 7-ton trucks from a rental company. Andi Banks and I were in one truck with the sound system and Paddy, Geoff and Rick in the other truck carrying the lights and the backline equipment. The trucks came from a rental company and the problem we had was they only did a top speed of 50 mph, so journeys were long and boring. We had one overnight drive which was a game changer in that we didn't make it in time for the show, arriving at 10pm. This was caused by the trucks only doing 50 mph. The next day a mini bus and a 40-foot tractor-trailer with James Atkinson driving came out to meet us, and the two rental trucks went back to England. The tour was a headache; almost every night, the promoters booked us into tiny venues and small clubs. Rick sarcastically asked where the stage was and when the stage was pointed out he said, "I won't even get the drum kit on there," but we had to manage.

Two shows in Finland, Seinajoki and Helsinki both heavily covered in snow at that time of year then on to Norway. The rider which went with the contract was completely ignored by the promoters and we just went around going through the motions of setting up, doing the show and getting out as fast as possible.

Another problem we had was en route to the Chateau Neuf Club in Oslo. Norway in November can be very cold, icy and covered in snow, we made it through the mountainous roads OK but James jackknifed his trailer coming down a mountain road and almost wrecked his truck. Also the band had not arrived as their flight was delayed and they were supposed to do a television interview before the show. The TV producer asked if they could interview the crew instead, I wasn't keen on the idea but went ahead with it anyway leaving the questions up to the other guys to answer. Isn't it strange how radio and TV reporters ask the dumbest of questions sometimes? From there we went to Stockholm, Copenhagen, Svenborg, Malmo, Hamburg and the Paradiso Club in Amsterdam where the girls tried out the smoking products on sale in the venue, another one of Holland's legal drug clubs. Like all American visitors they couldn't believe it was actually legal to smoke pot in public in Holland with shops openly selling the products. Then three shows in Belgium and we headed back home.

Coming back into England via the Dover cross-channel ferry we were all pulled over by customs and they decided to give us the going over, knowing that we were a Rock'n'Roll band and knowing we had just come from Holland, they opened up our suitcases probably hoping to find some illegal drugs but instead discovered something they weren't expecting. I won't say which of the girls it was, but one of them had their suitcase emptied out on to the table and a number of sex toys fell out. I tried not to notice and once I had been cleared to go I quickly walked through to the exit.

A real life biographical film was made about the group in 2010 called 'The Runaways' with actors playing the parts of the band. Having known the girls personally, I found the actors in the film weren't anything like I remembered the girls to be, but that's movie makers for you.

STEELEYE SPAN

In February 1978 I was asked to do another Steeleye Span tour, they were promoting their album Storm Force Ten, Scott Thompson and Clive Davis from Colac worked the FOH sound and lighting desks while Andi Banks and myself looked after the PA, 'Paddy' Patrick Whitley was the lighting guy.

The band went through a number of personnel changes but on this tour the band were Maddy Prior vocals, John Kirkpatrick accordion, Martin Carthy guitar, Tim Hart guitar, Rick Kemp bass, Nigel Pegrum drums.

32 shows in five weeks and for a support band the Tannahill Weavers came along, a Scottish folk group I had the pleasure of mixing FOH sound for. After the tour they gave me a copy of their album which I thought was nice of them.

In Bournemouth at the Winter Gardens Mike Thompson turned up with the Maison Rouge mobile recording truck and they recorded their *Live at Last* album which even gives me a credit on the back sleeve cover. I was impressed with their live sound especially Rick's bass guitar sound, so clean and punchy, plays it like a lead guitar and the vocal harmonies and the tight rhythm section well-rehearsed.

Two sell-out shows at Hammersmith Odeon, the first night was a definite *Spinal Tap* moment, the soundcheck went OK and I was on the side of the stage by the monitor mixer waiting for the show to start. The one thing about Hammersmith is the fire curtain: before a show can start, the fire marshal must see the fire curtain come down and go up again to prove that it works. I've seen this work numerous times without any problems but on this occasion the fire curtain came down, gently touched the stage and somehow on the way up it caught the outrigger on the lighting support tower. When it started to go up the curtain, which weighs a good 4 tons, started to lift the lighting tower with it. I could see the overhead truss starting to move and there was nothing anybody could do to stop it, the truss started to tip and with it sparks and flashes were raining down on to the stage as the cables were ripped apart revealing live wires. The truss came crashing down onto the stage with an almighty bang, luckily just missing the backline equipment. We all ran for cover to get out of its way and you could hear the cries of horror coming from the audience who had just started to enter the venue. The fire curtain came down again this time for real, the electricity supply was turned off and we all helped to get the truss up in the air again, the show started an hour late which is not bad considering the damage done. One of the scariest moments I ever encountered on a stage. The rest of the tour was a real pleasure, the band were really nice people to work with.

PERE UBU

In April I was asked to go along to Shepperton Studio K to set up a sound system for the rehearsals of a rock band from Cleveland, Ohio called Pere Ubu and to mix the FOH sound for their European tour. A rather strange band having a very large singer with a little too much blubber around the mid-riff, a most unusual looking rock star. Singer David Thomas came on stage with a metal claw hammer and started banging the hell out of a piece of metal in front of the microphone. I wondered what I was in for, their music was a little avant-garde, somewhat punkish but quite musical. I did six shows in the UK including two nights at the Roundhouse supporting Graham Parker and another three in Amsterdam, Brussels and Paris before returning to do two shows at London's Marquee Club. It seemed that a full-page cover story on the front of *Melody Maker* ensured that the Marquee was packed out and finished the tour off nicely.

BLACK SABBATH & VAN HALEN

I was scheduled to start a third Black Sabbath tour again in a few days but Ozzy Osbourne had left the band or been sacked depending on who you ask. The tour wasn't selling well and with only half-filled halls it looked like the tour would be cancelled. So Ozzy was asked to come back and as soon as it was reported that he was back in the band within hours the tour was a sell-out, much to the annoyance of Tony who had a new singer lined up to take over from Ozzy. But Ozzy was only there for the beer or should I say for the coke and I don't mean the drink. Ozzy was back in the band and we started off at Sheffield City Hall for what would be two months of heavy rock overkill for the 'Never Say Die' tour.

The support band on this tour was Van Halen, well known in America but unknown in Britain at that time, but as soon as Eddie Van Halen cranked up his guitar the crowds leapt from their seats and stormed the stage. It was like that for the rest of the tour, this young kid Eddie on guitar with his brother Alex Van Halen on drums, Michael Anthony on bass guitar and lead singer David Lee Roth, they blew Sabbath off stage big time.

Eddie Van Halen's guitar acrobatics and showmanship were brilliant, David Lee Roth was a far better singer than Ozzy as well. By the time Sabbath came on stage all was forgotten and the loyal Sabbath fans forgot about the support band.

Setting up for Van Halen on the first night, the band hired their backline equipment in England, but Eddie's guitar amplifier didn't have a 13-amp plug on the mains lead. He came up to me and asked if I knew how to wire a plug, I said I did and offered to do it for him, this lad was in England for the first time and had never seen a British plug before so I didn't mind helping him out, he was really appreciative and couldn't thank me enough for doing it for him, besides I wanted to make sure it was wired correctly.

It was a hectic tour with 29 shows in 35 days. This time I decided I didn't want to put up with doing the monitor mix for Sabbath, standing next to Tony Iommi's guitar stack every night, so we brought in my old mate Andi Banks to join the road crew. Andi was a good worker and he knew how to run a monitor desk which left me more time to look after the main system.

As normally happens on these tours, through road crew chat and backstage gossip, we heard the band were falling apart. First Geezer was sacked and brought back in again, then Ozzy walked out, not for the last time either and there was a bad vibe backstage, they never did a soundcheck on the whole tour. None of the band were talking to each other, they all arrived at the gigs in separate cars, wherever possible had separate dressing rooms and left in separate cars after the show. It was well known amongst the crew that the one thing keeping them going was their drug dealer coming along to each show to 'sort them out'. Tony would be shouting at Bill or Ozzy backstage, I don't know what about and I don't want to know but you could hear it along the backstage corridors. Having been on the road for months after their long American tours they were tired and hungover on the drugs that were keeping them going.

In Ipswich Tony punched a music reporter in the face for something that the reporter had said in his paper about the band some years earlier, it was all a bit vague but we heard all about it from the guys backstage, you get to hear a lot of gossip on stage and backstage.

Black Sabbath's single 'Never Say Die' from the album of the same name peaked at No 12 in the charts, we did Top Of The Pops and was the first hit single for the band since 'Paranoid' reached No 4 in 1970.

Bill Ward the drummer of Black Sabbath was suffering with some health problems, between every song or almost every song he would turn around and grab his oxygen mask and take some deep breaths. No one in the audience could see, but from the side of the stage you could see a lot more than the audience could. Ozzy and Tony would exchange looks and surprisingly the odd joke.

During the song 'Snow Blind', a song that was not about cocaine, we had an artificial snow machine above the front lighting truss which would produce small white flakes of polystyrene that would flutter down onto the stage like a scene from a Christmas card. Ozzy, not one to miss a trick, would turn his back to the audience, put one finger to his nose and pretend to snort some of the snowflakes, much to the amusement of Tony and everyone else standing in the wings. Geezer didn't take much notice of what was going on and just got stuck into playing his bass guitar.

Dry ice was used extensively throughout the show and when used in a subtle way had an eerie effect that looked quite effective especially with the right lighting. Dry ice is a solid form of carbon dioxide. It is used primarily as a cooling agent and when delivered to the venues in a solid block it's frozen at around –80°C. This is then stored backstage until show time when the dry ice is placed in a basket suspended above a tank of very hot water. Once lowered into the hot tank the ice melts rapidly and dense clouds of smoke-like fog are created which is then pumped onto the stage through pipes. Unlike fog machines, in which the fog rises like smoke, fog from dry ice is heavier than air and hovers near the ground and looks like early morning mist. Once the dry ice smoke reaches the edge of the stage it overflows off the stage into the audience like a waterfall. It can look really effective but not so much fun for those in the first few rows. But in a *Spinal Tap* moment when too much was dropped into the tank for too long, the whole stage would get smothered and looked like a dense fog, sometimes you couldn't see the band or the audience it was so thick.

A very strange thing happened at the end of the last show in England at the Hammersmith Odeon. The crew started breaking down the equipment as usual ready to load on to the trucks, but after 20 minutes or so we noticed that none of the backline equipment had been touched nor was there any sign of the backline crew, the lights were coming down, the microphones and speaker cables were put away, speakers were being stripped out and the backline was still in its place. After a while we found out that the backline crew had gone on strike and refused to pack the equipment away, they were in the dressing room discussing their grievances with the band for quite a while. We didn't know what it was about at first but speculation was that either they had not been paid or they were not being paid enough, but why wait until the last show of the tour and wait until the show was over? I would have said something before the last show. Eventually the crew emerged and started packing their gear away not looking too happy, could have been another *Spinal Tap* moment.

There was a break from Black Sabbath between the UK tour and the start of the European leg in October so I filled the time doing other things.

LINDISFARNE – RUN FOR HOME

In June I was asked to rig a sound system in Hammersmith Odeon for a one-off show for Lindisfarne, the Newcastle folk-rock band who had hits in the early seventies with 'Meet Me on the Corner', 'Lady Eleanor' and 'Fog on the Tyne'. The band had broken up in 1973 and had now re-formed for a comeback with their new album *Back and Fourth* they released a single 'Run For Home' which peaked at No 10 in the charts. The engineer Ian Leak was mixing FOH on this day but I did the monitor mix and really enjoyed the show, what a band. The re-formed band from the original line-up was Alan Hull on guitars, keyboards & vocals, Ray Jackson on mandolin, harmonica & vocals, Rod Clements bass & electric violin, Simon Cowe lead guitars & vocals, Ray Laidlaw on drums. I knew Rod Clements of course because he was playing bass in the Ralph McTell band in 1975.

JOHN McLAUGHLIN

Another artiste I hadn't worked with before, but was to come across many times over the next few years, was jazz-rock guitarist John McLaughlin. In August I took a truckload of sound equipment over to Scandinavia to mix FOH sound for John at the Concert House in Turku, Finland and the House of Culture in Helsinki, and again doing the Isle of Calves Festival in Oslo, Norway for the second year. The last time I did this festival was in June 1976 with Dr Hook after that truck crash. Also on the bill in Oslo was American folk legend Joan Baez who did an interesting set. From there I went to the Concert House in Stockholm and the Falkoner Theatre in Copenhagen. Scandinavia at that time of year is remarkable and really enjoyable, the weather is great, the sun shines most of the day and night and the people are really friendly.

I wasn't away from Scandinavia for long because in October I was asked if I wanted to mix front of house sound for Lindisfarne in Norway, just two shows, Chateau Neuf in Oslo and Grieg Hall in Bergen, it was a basic PA rig and as much as I could fit into a 3-ton truck. Unfortunately that's what it comes down to much of the time, not what size PA do I need for that venue but how much gear can I fit into the truck I'm taking. The shows turned out so well that their manager Barry McKay asked if I wanted to do their Christmas show in Newcastle, of course I said yes and that was the start of a twelve year run doing their Christmas shows.

Van Halen supporting on a Black Sabbath tour 1978.

No rest for the wicked, no sooner had I returned from Lindisfarne than I was back with Black Sabbath and Van Halen to resume the European leg of their tour. Eight shows in Germany and one in France, it would have been two in France, except the Paris gig was cancelled when the band heard the show was in a tent. The Pavilion where we were supposed to play was a 10,000 seater arena used by lots of rock and pop acts including Black Sabbath when we were there with AC/DC just a year before. But for some unknown reason the promoter changed the venue and moved it to a circus tent, probably because he could get more people in this gigantic marquee.

When the band heard about the change of venue they refused to play 'in a tent' albeit a very large circus tent, so as soon as we got the word that the show was off we started dismantling the stage and loading it all back into the three trucks. Lucky for us we could drive the trucks right into the circus tent under cover and away from the eyes of all the fans outside patiently waiting for the security gates to open. When they realized that the show was off and the gates were not going to be opened the mood turned nasty and we could hear shouting, whistling and missiles being thrown. So an escape plan was hatched by the tour manager. The plan was that all the trucks would be loaded up and we would drive through the gates in convoy including the two tour buses as fast as possible. When all five vehicles were ready with everyone on board and engines revved up, the gates were opened and three trucks and two buses flew through the open gates as fast as we could, unfortunately we were met by a rioting mob who didn't realise that we were only the crew doing our job. We didn't want to cancel the show and didn't have much choice in the matter, but they took their anger out on us and bombarded us with all kinds of missiles including bricks, bottles and security barriers, luckily we got away without any injuries but it was a scary incident and not to be forgotten. Van Halen were furious over the cancelled show and never forgave Sabbath for pulling the gig. Van Halen promptly went on French TV and radio to promise the Paris fans that they would be back, something that Sabbath should have done.

This wasn't the last time the band would miss a show either: with the band having checked into a hotel, Ozzy complained to reception that there was a strong smell in his room, the hotel were pleased to help and quickly gave Ozzy another room. Ozzy went into his new room and promptly fell asleep without telling his road manager that he had changed rooms. When it came to show time no one could find him and he wasn't in the room he was first registered in; it wasn't until the next morning he woke up to discover he had missed the show.

Luckily I wasn't with the band when he bit the head off a bat that had been thrown on stage, Ozzy thinking that the bat was a plastic toy picked it up and bit his head off just for fun, but then realised that the bat was in fact a real animal, he had to go to hospital for anti-rabies injections straight after the show. Ozzy left the band again in April 1979.

During a press conference to launch his solo career some years later Ozzy decided to bite the head off a white dove, the record company were so shocked and disgusted that he was banned from the building, but the publicity rocketed his career through the roof more than any record sales could have done.

When you think of the *Spinal Tap* movie you think of the Stonehenge incident where someone got the measurements wrong, where a 30-foot Stonehenge was supposed to be lowered onto stage, a four foot model appeared instead. It's incidents like that, that are inspired by fact, fiction or myth and they usually come from real life events. So it was that Black Sabbath had the idea of bringing in a replica Stonehenge arch onto stage, during the 1983 tour, only the error was not that it was too small like the *Spinal Tap* film, it was actually too big to get into the halls they were playing. It's incidents like this that went on to inspire the *Spinal Tap* movie.

I can't mention Stonehenge without mentioning the infamous incident which has gone down in Rock'n'Roll folklore. The story of Don Arden who wanted to replicate the cover of the latest Black Sabbath album 'Born Again' which featured a baby coloured red and made to look like a demon with fangs and horns. Don Arden hired a dwarf actor dressed up as a baby with horns just like the album cover.

For the opening of the show, with a single spotlight on him and a backing track of a crying baby the dwarf was told to crawl along the top of Stonehenge pretending to cry, then fall off the end. During rehearsals the stunt went OK with the dwarf falling off and landing on a specially placed mattress, unfortunately on the first night of the opening show of the tour the dwarf crawled along the top of Stonehenge and fell off the end as planned, the only problem was that someone forgot to replace the mattress for the dwarf to land on which resulted in the actor sustaining serious injuries. He was taken to hospital and wasn't seen again and the stunt was dropped permanently.

Whatever you think of Black Sabbath they invented the genre 'Heavy Metal' with that eerie guitar sound, they are without doubt one of the biggest rock bands of all time along with Led Zeppelin, The Who and The Rolling Stones.

Van Halen meanwhile having blown Sabbath off stage a few times had built up a strong following; after the UK and European tour ended they came back to London and headlined their own show at The Rainbow using all the sound and lights that were used on the Sabbath show. The thinking was that we had the trucks, we had the crew and we had the equipment, it only added two days onto the tour, it goes without saying that was a mind-blowing concert that allowed Van Halen to show what they could do when they had headline status and were not being restricted to using support band equipment.

LINDISFARNE

The Lindisfarne tour started in early November with rehearsals at The Roxy Theatre in Harlesden, a small theatre which used to be an Odeon cinema up until 1972. It eventually became a rock concert venue with all the seats taken out to allow more people in, ideal for a rehearsal room. Also along for the tour was Chris Rea with his band as the support act, a nice guy and a great band to tour with, they came down to our rehearsal room for a production rehearsal and bought along a studio engineer to mix the live sound, he worked for Gus Dudgeon in the studio. I tried to help him out as he was having problems with feedback. Feedback is when a microphone picks up the sound coming from the speakers, amplifies the sound again back into the speakers, which then gets picked up by the mic again. Around and around it goes until the system takes off and you get a loud squealing or whistling sound. Of course you don't get feedback in a studio because you are in a controlled environment and there is a thick glass wall between you and the artiste.

If Chris Rea had asked me to mix his sound I would have willingly done his sound as well as Lindisfarne's, because I was there anyway. I ended up spending my time helping Shwep. One of the most annoying aspects of babysitting as it's called (that's when you rig the sound system, set it all up then hand over controls to someone else who works for the band) is having to sit there with him in case he needs any help. You are sitting behind him and you're thinking that sounds awful, or why doesn't he do something about this or that, and you know you could do a better job, it can be so annoying and frustrating. I will always help someone out if they need help but some engineers just don't like to ask and I don't have the time to give them lessons on how to set up a mixing console. I know what it's like from both sides. When I'm employed by a band to do their mix and you turn up at a venue to use someone else's sound system, there will be a systems tech there who has rigged the system and set the system up for you. Being used to operating any sound system I'm given I'm used to jumping on a new mixer and just getting on with it because I know how mixers work and what they do but not all engineers have that knowledge or experience.

For the next two months we did 28 shows around the country in various universities, colleges, city halls, town halls, theatres and ballrooms and at the end of that we did five nights at Newcastle City Hall, home of the Geordie band. Lindisfarne have become well known for their unique brand of folk-rock, with a definite left-wing political message in the lyrics of their songs which has made them a legend and an institution in the North-East of England. Even though I didn't agree with some of their political views I got on really well with the band. I wasn't that interested in politics and tried to keep my views to myself. Alan Hull in particular would try and wind me up and try to convert me to some of his left-wing views, but they still employed me to do their sound and I remained good friends with them for many years.

The first show at the Colchester University of Essex was a BBC Rock Goes to College, which was recorded live by the BBC for a live radio broadcast. The show was introduced by DJ Pete Drummond and it turned out to be not too bad. (It's still on YouTube.) The next day we had to sit through a video recording session for the band's latest single, not just a straightforward video recording of the band, but lip syncing to the track take after take, after take, with multiple camera angles and re-shots and edited in-fills, it went on all night.

Also included on the tour was Wembley Empire Pool (now renamed Wembley Arena) as part of a multi-act show. I couldn't use my own PA as the promoter had hired a PA from Britannia Row. I was very disappointed when I walked into the venue, as the system was just not up to it and I wished I could have dragged my own system in from the truck parked outside, but I couldn't do that nor did I have the time to replace it so I had to make do with what was provided.

The tour ended up with four nights at Newcastle City Hall for what was billed as the Lindisfarne Christmas Party, and believe me it was a party, on stage and in the audience. A Christmas tree on stage with decorations and lights and the audience were given a party hat as they entered the venue, party poppers rained down from the balcony and everyone seemed in a party mood. Something I will never forget and it went on for four sold-out nights until I went home on Christmas Eve.

A Midas mixer and the outboard effects racks on the balcony at Newcastle City Hall for the Lindisfarne Christmas shows. 1978

18

TOP OF THE POPS

TOTP (*Top of the Pops*) was broadcast weekly between 1964 and 2006. The show started off in Manchester, then moved to the BBC Studio Centre at White City in London as it was easier for bands to get to. It was recorded on a Wednesday and transmitted on a Thursday and had around 15 million viewers each week.

It makes me laugh when they claim *Top of the Pops* to be 'live', it's not live and never has been except for an occasional show. Initially performers mimed to the record but The Musicians' Union put a stop to miming in 1966, insisting artistes play live in the studio and be paid to play live. The BBC got around that by pre-recoding the band before the show. What they call live is in fact a playback from a previous recording. They go through a pre-arranged ritual and both sides know what's going on.

What happens in real life is that the band record a live performance during the afternoon when they are doing camera checks, then when it comes to the transmission the tapes are switched so the audience in the studio hear the live sound, but the audience at home watching television hear the previously recorded version. The band may actually perform live in the studio in front of a live audience but that is not what you at home hear through your television sets, that is why sometimes the lip sync on the picture is not in time with what you are hearing. Sometimes the record company will supply a recorded version for playback which is switched for the BBC recorded track, which is why the song sometimes sounds just like the record, (how convenient). Bands take days or weeks to record a song in a recording studio, something that can't be replicated in a TV studio in one day. On some occasions the show uses a live vocal to a pre-recorded backing track which at least makes it sound a bit more live.

Some bands who didn't like the miming idea used to sabotage the performance by messing around and deliberately make mistakes, or play different instruments other than the real thing or pretend to play items that were not even musical instruments, like playing a child's toy instead of a real instrument. It made a mockery of the show.

The other illusion with *Top of the Pops* that you don't see on television at home is that it appears that the thirty-minutes show is done in real time, in actual fact it could take two hours to make the thirty minute show, with artistes working on alternate stages and cameras having to be moved from one place to another. Not to mention herding the audience into a new position so it looks good on camera, the audience is relatively small but with clever use of camera angles it makes the studio look full. The fade out of one performance is cut, then the introduction to the next performance is merged into the tail end of the previous performance to give the effect that it's continuous. It's all tricks and mirrors.

LINDISFARNE

1979 saw me going on a trip down under to New Zealand for three shows, a long way to go for three shows I thought but I'm not going to turn down the opportunity to go there. The band and crew met at Heathrow and we all went on a 33-hour flight via Muscat, Singapore and Perth, changing flights to Christchurch on the southern island of New Zealand. The road crew consisted of Yollow and Jim who looked after the backline, the same guys who did the last tour. This was the first time I had done a long-haul flight since the American tour in 1970; the time passed by with complimentary drinks from the hostess and constant meals being given to us as we flew east through different time zones. We arrived in New Zealand on a Sunday and the whole town was closed, absolutely nothing was open, not even a bus running.

Looking around the town was like going back in time, the cars were mostly British 1950s and 60s vehicles in immaculate condition due to the climate. Looking around the shops was an eye opener, what they called second-hand junk shops we would call antique shops, lots of old British furniture being sold off from what I suspect came from British immigrants who settled here in the 1950s and 60s as part of the £10 Pom scheme. As January was in the middle of their summer the weather was warm and sunny and we enjoyed a day off before the first show at the Town Hall in Christchurch. As you would expect, New Zealand is so like England you wouldn't believe, the architecture could be a replica of any English town, the Town Hall no exception.

I was provided with a not-so-bad sound system from a local sound company, but considering I was in New Zealand it was better than I expected. I went through the usual soundcheck and the band put on a decent show, the stage lights were typical for a town hall.

We had two days off before the next show and we all headed north across the Cook Straight into Fitzroy Bay to the northern island which is more heavily populated. Yollow, Jim and I hired a car and headed off into the hills for a bit of sightseeing, the scenery was breathtaking, like prehistoric rainforests, I wouldn't have been surprised to see a dinosaur around the next corner. We stopped at a mountain top cafe and enjoyed a sun-soaked lunch admiring the colourful birds that came to our table to share our crumbs. Later that evening the band and I were taken out to dinner by the promoter to a steak house and I had the best T-bone steak I'd ever tasted. I was amused to be offered a doggy bag after the meal to take home any uneaten food, the bag even had a picture of a dog on the outside, all part of the service.

After two days off it was back to work and another Town Hall, this time in Wellington on the southern tip of the north island. I was pleased to see we had the same sound company again, they had a basic 24-channel desk with a 5,000-watt system and it sounded quite good after tweaking the EQ a bit.

From Wellington we flew to the capital Auckland for an outdoor festival in a 20,000-capacity venue but not before another break of four days, although it was quite hot and sunny the promoter was getting worried about the weather forecast of a cyclone coming in from the Pacific Ocean,

The show was to be at the Western Springs Stadium, which is a natural amphitheatre and is normally used as a rugby pitch during the winter and a speedway track during the summer. Elton John played there in 1971, Led Zeppelin in 1972 and Deep Purple in 1975. I went down there to take a look, the crew were busy erecting the stage and had started to erect the control tower. I wasn't happy with where they were putting the control tower so I asked if they would move it closer to the stage, they were happy to oblige as they had only just started to put it together. The control tower is the place where the sound mixer is positioned along with the lighting mixer and above us on the top level were the follow spots.

The day before the show, the cyclone came on land from the Pacific and hit us hard, so hard in fact the concert was cancelled and we were confined to the hotel for 48 hours, we couldn't go out it was so bad. I'd never seen wind and rain like this ever before and we were told to stay away from any windows in case they blew in. We passed the time sitting in the hotel lounge just watching in awe the torrential rain and wind outside, palm trees almost doubled over, debris being flown around like matchsticks and all sorts of items flying through the air, it was good advice to stay away from the windows. That put an end to our Auckland show and we got ready to go home via Australia where some press and TV shows were being lined up. The promoter asked Frank our tour manager for the airline tickets so he could change the tickets to the new flights, unbeknown to Frank the promoter did the dirty on us and cashed in the tickets to try and recoup some of his losses.

I don't know if the promoter was insured but if he wasn't he certainly should have been. He must have lost a lot of money, not only refunding money to those who'd bought tickets, but having already paid out on all the expenses of booking the venue, building the stage and paying the band's fees. Not only were we stranded without a show to do we were also stranded without any return tickets to get home. Frank made some frantic phone calls to Barry McKay back in England and Barry made phone calls to the promoter with threats of legal proceedings if we didn't get our tickets back. Three days after the show was cancelled we were still stranded in the hotel. I don't know who was picking up that bill but Alan Hull was sick of waiting and bought his own ticket home with his credit card and went ahead without us.

The next day the dispute was resolved and we all headed to the airport and flew to Melbourne in Australia where we stayed for another three days with a suggestion that a concert, a TV show or interviews could be arranged. Whilst we were there the band and I were invited to the local concert hall for a Joe Cocker concert, the second time I was to come across Joe and not for the last time either. He put on a brilliant show of course. Melbourne was a very pleasant town, again very English in its culture and architecture. Unfortunately no shows or TV interviews were organised, so the next day we headed home to England where I had the rest of February off.

JOURNEY

At home I received a phone call from Pat Morrow (Bubba as he was known) a roadie who used to work for Dr Hook, he now had a job as tour manager with an American rock band called Journey made up of former members of Santana. I had never heard of them but apparently they were very big in America; whilst I was away with Lindisfarne they came over to England to support Santana on tour. Bubba very kindly invited my wife Estelle and our two children to come to the show at Wembley, which they did. He left me the new album and a tour jacket and phoned to give me the tour dates for the Journey tour which was 21 shows throughout March and April going to Germany, Switzerland, France, Holland, Denmark, Sweden and the UK.

The band were Steve Perry on vocals, Neil Schon on guitar, Greg Rolie on keyboards, Steve Smith on drums, and Ross Valory on bass; the tour was to promote their latest album *Evolution* which had just been released. The first thing I had to do was organise some sound equipment for the tour, I went back to Colac who rented me some equipment. For this tour I decided to use the now familiar Black Sabbath PA. I used my own Midas mixer and front of house control equipment. The effects were quite basic, a space echo, a harmoniser, a phaser and the band's own engineer Kevin brought his own Aural Exciter for vocals which give Journey that distinct vocal sound. Kevin was a good soundman so I had no problems with that, although I still had the job of babysitting. Zenith were the lighting company and Edwin Shirley were supplying the truck and tour buses.

The Brixton Astoria was the venue and we loaded in for two days of production rehearsals with full stage sound and lights. After rehearsals all the gear was loaded into the trailer for the overnight drive to Hamburg. Whilst the equipment went overland by truck and ferry the crew flew from London to Hamburg where we were met by the tour bus which turned out to be a bit of a shock. We were expecting one of Edwin Shirley's luxury tour buses, but what we had was a ski holiday sleeper bus with 16 bunks and nothing else, no seats, no catering area and no lounge, so we had nowhere to sit except on our bunks. Luckily we were told this was only for a few days before an Edwin Shirley bus came out to do a changeover much to our relief.

The first venue at the Audimax in Hamburg is a well-known venue I'd worked in before; the venue has tiered seating with a capacity of 1,800 going up at quite a steep angle so the back row is quite high above the stage. After I set up the mixer at the back of the stalls I was thinking the venue looked a lot smaller than I remembered it from the last time I was here but couldn't put my finger on why. After checking the system out and doing a line check, I heard this low frequency rumble and the floor started shaking, I looked around behind me to see this huge wall moving sideways to reveal another bank of seats at the back doubling the size of the venue, that's where the extra space was I was missing. The first show went well and we then went off to do another six shows in Germany to full houses.

The road crew were a weird bunch, after getting on really well with the American Dr Hook crew who I regarded as brothers, this lot were very insular and not very friendly. One of them took exception the day I wore a Van Halen T-shirt, calling Van Halen all sorts of insulting words and putting them and their music down, I didn't argue with him. I later found out that in America there is a rivalry between the two bands with one supporting the other on various shows, I didn't see why the crew had to take it so personally, I usually get on with the crews from other bands I tour with. I can only think it's like football fans disliking fans from rival teams, a bit pointless. T-shirts are one of the perks of the job and with every tour you do you are given a bunch of T-shirts, sweatshirts, even tour jackets, so it doesn't take long to accumulate a hundred or more T-shirts in your wardrobe.

During one of the bus journeys I was talking to the American crew, one of them told me that in the early days of the band when they weren't making much money or selling many records the band didn't have any money to pay the road crew, and without a crew they couldn't do the shows, so the band made them an offer, to keep working for no wages now and receive ¼ of 1% of everything the band earnt in the future or wait for their wages when they got some money. Half the crew walked away saying they needed a regular weekly wage, the other half got their calculators out and decided to take the gamble. The next three albums *Infinity*, *Evolution* and *Departure* went triple platinum. *Escape* went 9x platinum, which meant there were some very well-off roadies working for the band. I've been in similar positions with other bands but not having faith in the artiste I walked away and that was the right decision. The half of Journey's crew that walked away on this occasion made the wrong decision, but you never know how successful a band will be, short-term or long-term.

The support band on this tour was the Pat Travers Band, a Canadian guitarist based in London with an English band and road crew. One of the Pat Travers crew got into an argument on the bus with a Journey crew member when he was accused of moving his stuff and taking his bunk. Lesson one on a tour bus, don't take someone else's bunk. After seven shows in Germany we did shows in Zurich and Paris and headed off to the UK for seven shows in England including Hammersmith Odeon.

After Birmingham Odeon we headed over the Channel again for two shows in Holland, one in Copenhagen and one in Stockholm. At the end of the European tour the band and American crew were scheduled to take an overnight flight from Stockholm to Tokyo for a Japanese tour, where they would pick up a Japanese sound and lighting company. The band would take their own backline equipment of guitars, keyboards and drums which is normal, but not sound and lights as the freight would be too expensive, this is why we service American bands touring in Europe. After the show we dropped the crew off at the band's hotel ready for their flight to Japan, and we headed off to catch our ferry from Esbjerg in Denmark back to Harwich.

The British crew and I were all sitting up front on the bus doing our usual after-show social chat satisfied that we did a good tour and looking forward to going home. After twenty minutes we heard someone shouting from the bunks at the back of the bus calling out "Where are we?" someone replied, "Twenty minutes out of Stockholm and you should be going to Japan." It was one of the American crew who had crawled into his bunk and fallen asleep, no one knew he was there, so the driver Bob stopped the bus and threw him off saying, "I'm not driving back to Stockholm, you'll have to find your own way back." So he did, life can be hard for those who don't get their act together on the road and it's often the case that no prisoners are taken with those who don't pull their weight.

A shock travelled through the music business in April when Kate Bush's lighting man Bill Duffield died after a fall at Poole Arts Centre, I know that venue well, he apparently went back into the theatre when the lights were turned off and fell through an unprotected trap door in the stage, he fell 20 feet and died later. It just shows how dangerous stages can be. Kate later did a tribute concert for his family.

THE DAMNED

Two weeks off and I had two shows with a punk-rock band The Damned, one was a small venue in a club and the other was at The Greyhound in Croydon, the same venue where I was denied access to the stage by Atomic Rooster when working for Renaissance. I didn't react the same way with my support band as Rooster did to me and I allowed them as much room as they needed on stage. It was a typical punk audience with some weird looking people coming in, from vampires to ghouls, fancy-dress outfits from tartan-clad, safety-pinned, parrot-headed haircuts to those in Nazi uniforms, not my type of music but I did the best for the band mixing their sound as I would for anyone else. The thing with working freelance is you don't always get to choose who you work with. If you want to work you take whatever jobs come along. I would rather work freelance and have the variety than work for one band all the time which means listening to the same songs day in, day out and year after year, which can happen with some acts.

To show the variety of different genres of music styles I get to work with, I go from a punk band one day to doing a show with cabaret artiste Alan Price at The Piccadilly Hotel in London. Alan once played keyboards with The Animals and later had his own TV show with Georgie Fame, he has now gone middle of the road doing the cabaret circuit and performing at corporate events.

DENNIS BROWN, RUDY THOMAS & BROWN SUGAR

The variety of working with a sound company is noticeable when you go from folk to rock to punk, cabaret and reggae all in four months. After The Damned tour I was asked to put a sound system together for a tour with Jamaican reggae star Dennis Brown who had a hit single with 'Money In My Pocket', also on the tour were Rudy Thomas, a Jamaican reggae singer and Brown Sugar, a three-piece female reggae act from London. Whenever you get a three-act show it usually means a recipe for disaster, throw in Jamaican reggae artistes and that doubles the disaster ratio. Not something I was looking forward to as I knew the tour would be totally chaotic. I like listening to some reggae but I was not a big reggae fan, it was work and it was something different to add to my experience.

Straight in at the deep end we were booked into the 3,000-capacity Rainbow Theatre in London for three days, one day's rehearsal and then two nights with both shows sold out. The organisation was at best disorganised and at worst non-existent. There was the usual backstage catering for the crew but this time the band had bought their own Jamaican cook over to prepare food for the band in one of the other dressing rooms, whilst Angie, who luckily I knew from previous tours, prepared English food for the English crew. There was some friction between the English and Jamaican cooks with the smell of cooked goat and who knows what else coming from the Jamaican catering area. Backstage was filled with thick smoke from the burning of marijuana, every room and every corridor was filled with thick smoke, it was so bad I needed a gas mask to walk through the area. In Rasta culture marijuana is used like a religion and they paid no attention to the fact it was illegal in this country.

The band seem to pay no attention to time slots either, they did their own thing in their own time. In Jamaica they just keep playing until they decide to stop. Here we have time curfews to keep to, stipulated by council licensing laws, it seemed like it was going on all night until they were told to end it.

Having said that, the band had a great sound with a four-piece brass section and a full band, seemed like a lot of people on stage as you would expect from a reggae show. Dennis Brown performed well. Rudy Thomas also did a good show but once you hear one reggae song the others seem to blend into each another. Brown Sugar I suspect were a last-minute addition to add another act on to an already busy show. Reverb was a prominent part of the sound mix with their Jamaican sound producer giving loads of reverb effect, too much sometimes but that's his choice and his trademark sound.

After the Rainbow shows we did nine other shows around the UK mainly in Top Rank-type nightclubs and theatres ending up on the last day at the BBC doing a *Top of The Pops* where Dennis played his hit single 'Money In My Pocket'.

My friend Andi Banks had been helping me with the PA system on tour with many bands, but I forgot that all along he is a very good bass guitar player. I first met him when he was playing bass in KA and Reign with Robin Le Mesurier. He'd put a new group together and they were rehearsing in a room above a pub in London. He called me one day asking if I'd go down to the rehearsals and have a look at the PA system they were using, something was wrong and it didn't sound very good he said, so I went down there with my toolbox to have a look.

I sent the band off to the pub whilst I started to check it out. The best way to find a problem was to go back to basics and ignore whatever settings were on the mixer, so starting from scratch and putting all the knobs back to zero I found that indeed it didn't sound right.

The first thing I could hear were speakers out of phase, I took the backs off the speaker cabinets and found that the left stereo speaker was wired in reverse to the right stereo speaker therefore cancelling each other out. As well as that, one of the two speakers within the cabinet was wired out of phase with the other. Having put that right I started to reset the mixer. As this PA was being used as a rehearsal PA for the band, I panned the four microphones slightly off-centre depending on where the microphones were positioned across the stage, added a touch of reverb, only slightly though, just enough to give an edge to the vocal sound and just enough so you *can't* hear it, too much reverb and it will sound mushy.

When I'd finished Andi and the band came back from their pub break and couldn't believe the difference, it was loud, it was clear and they were impressed. I was pleased with the result myself and happy just to be able to help out an old friend.

STIFF LITTLE FINGERS

Whilst I was away on tour with Journey and Lindisfarne Andi Banks had got himself a job as tour manager with a new punk band Stiff Little Fingers from Belfast. Stiff Little Fingers were at the forefront of the punk movement, along with The Sex Pistols, The Clash, Sham 69, The Damned and The Undertones. In 1979 they became the first band ever to hit the UK top 20 album charts on an independent label with their debut album *Inflammable Material.* Initially they wrote about their lives, growing up in Belfast at the height of the Troubles, songs like 'Suspect Device' and 'Wasted Life'. Andi needed a sound system and engineer for the tour and I was his first choice to do their sound, I was happy to oblige and help him out. The first show was at the Lyceum Ballroom in London and then straight over to Dublin for a show at Bellfield University, before crossing the notorious border into Ulster. As we drove along the road from the Republic we knew when we'd reached the border, we saw the remains of a blown-up customs post at the side of the road left in ruins and blackened with smoke, there was no border police or customs officials, they were long gone so we drove straight through. When we reached the Ulster Hall in Belfast the neighbourhood was like a bombsite, as was most of Belfast at that time during the Troubles. Shops were boarded up with wire mesh grills and the doors were locked. If you wanted to buy anything you would have to press the doorbell and wait to see if the shopkeeper wanted to let you in. Army and Police Land Rovers looking like armoured tanks patrolled the streets.

It wasn't long after the load-in when halfway through setting up the stage the British Army came in dressed in combat uniforms and asked us to leave the building so they could search it, they had a tip-off there was a bomb in the building, I guess they got that all the time. Thankfully they found nothing and after an hour we went back in and carried on setting up.

After the show we checked into the most heavily bombed hotel in the world second only to the Beirut Hilton, the Europa Hotel. First we had to walk through a barbed wire security fence topped with razor wire before reaching the checkpoint booth; if you were a legitimate visitor the guard allowed you through the gate into the hotel grounds where you were tracked by cameras and watched by security. Once inside it was like any other hotel and you wouldn't know where you were, but first thing in the morning I was awoken by a bomb blast across the road in an Insurance Company building where black smoke was billowing out of the windows, everybody seemed to be going about their activities as if it was normal to them, oh look another bomb.

Back in England we did nineteen other shows around the country. I was approached backstage after the show at the Lyceum in London by a young lady dressed in full punk gear and a hairstyle looking like a multi-coloured parrot, she told me she worked for Malcolm McLaren and asked if I would do the sound and put a quote in for the next Sex Pistols tour. I politely declined the offer, I dare say a number of soundmen would have jumped at the chance of working with the best known punk band in the world, but I had other plans and it didn't involve The Sex Pistols, she looked at me shocked that I had declined, she even tried to talk me into it but I politely left.

The audiences would turn up dressed in typical punk uniforms, tartan trousers, safety pins through their noses, and brightly coloured hair all spiked up looking like parrots. The crowd at the front of stage, mostly comprising young teenage males ,would pogo dance all night trying to out-pogo their neighbours, but ending up falling over each other, the end result was a mass of bodies resembling a sack of snakes, girls would be wise to avoid this area for fear of injury. Worst of all a disgustingly synchronised volley of phlegm would rain onto the stage at various times during the songs.

The demise of the punk era was not an era I missed, although a few good bands did survive, evolved and became mainstream, bands like The Police, The Stranglers, The Clash and The Jam. The sound reminded me of my time with

Third World War who were doing punk in 1970 long before these guys were doing it. The punk era didn't last that long although remnants did survive in some form through the 1970s, the Sex Pistols being the best known band and defining the punk era. The anti-establishment anarchists eventually grew up and became normal, even Johnny Rotten did some TV commercials.

I believe the punk era happened because the young kids growing up saw middle-aged millionaire rock stars on arena-sized stages, performing long drawn out solos, relying on huge lighting rigs, video screens and pyrotechnic special effects to supplement their show. Then along came kids their own age with beaten-up guitars and second-hand amps, thrashing out two-minute songs with lyrics they could understand, in small pubs and clubs. That's why punk happened.

VAN HALEN – LINDISFARNE

A week later I was back out for my third tour with Van Halen, one show in Belgium, one in Holland, three in Germany, three in France and five in England ending up with two sell-out shows at the Rainbow. Thirteen shows in all.

In June Lindisfarne were booked to play the Roskilde Festival in Copenhagen, this time I wasn't working for Colac but for Lindisfarne so it was a busman's holiday for me. I flew out the day before the show, did the sound for the show and flew back the next day, what many call a white glove job, which means you don't get your hands dirty, although I was helping out on stage before heading out to the mixing tower in the middle of the field. Entec were supplying the sound this year and they were using the familiar Martin-Midas PA.

Whilst I was at Copenhagen Airport waiting to board the flight home I ran into Ralph McTell who I'd toured with in 1975, he had just performed at a folk club in Copenhagen and he was waiting to board the same plane as me back to Heathrow. We agreed to go off for a drink in the bar and have a chat about what we had both been doing since the 'Streets of London' tour. He didn't tour with a band again preferring to do just solo gigs on his own so he didn't need a soundman to travel with him. As we sat there enjoying our drink we suddenly noticed that they hadn't called our flight to the gate, although we had been listening out for it, many other flights had been called and had departed. We decided to check, and discovered that the flight had gone on time without us; after complaining that our flight wasn't called we were booked onto the next flight. I guess we were too busy chatting and drinking to notice.

Stiff Little Fingers had three European festivals in July. Oulu and Helsinki, both in Finland, and Bilzen in Belgium, more white glove jobs, turn up, mix and go, easy money, that's the beauty of working for a band instead of a sound company. Someone else sets up the equipment and you do the mix and yes, someone else babysits me while I mix and they stand and watch, it works both ways, but unlike some engineers I don't need a babysitter.

Another one-off gig with Stiff Little Fingers this time at the 'Rock Against Racism' free festival at Brockwell Park in Brixton supporting Aswad. It was chaos, the place was packed, I tried to get onto the mixing platform halfway down the field but thirty or more people were crowded on to it and hanging off the scaffolding all around it. With no security I had to fight my way to the front so I could get my hands on the mixer. I called up the stage on the intercom to get some security out there. I had no room to move and could hardly reach each end of the mixer without pushing someone out of the way. Those at the back of the platform were just pushing those in front into my back and either side, they were all around me, I couldn't move. No security ever arrived and as a result I wasn't very happy with the sound that day, I just couldn't do my job in those conditions and I was disappointed I couldn't achieve what I wanted. Lead singer Jake Burns had to ask the crowd to step back from the front and not push forward, people were getting crushed by the security barriers. At the front were mostly young white skinheads doing a pogo dance while a mostly black Rasta crowd were watching from the back waiting to see Aswad.

LINDISFARNE

For the rest of July and August I had a long break and took the family on a holiday to Tenerife before starting a 44-date tour with Lindisfarne, which included seven sold-out shows at the Newcastle City Hall. The band had released their new album *The News*. The support band on this tour were Chas and Dave who play a kind of music they called 'Rockney Pop' a cross between rock and cockney pub sing-a-long songs, they were great fun to tour with and Dave especially was a good laugh off stage. Also along was compere Mick Elliott as himself.

19

INVASION AND DEFECTOR TOURS

DEF LEPPARD

At the start of January 1980 I was back in Shepperton Studios again for production rehearsals with a new young rock band called Def Leppard, never heard of them but they did have a big management company behind them and in the same stable as AC/DC. My first impression was that they had potential but were still very green and inexperienced, but I thought they would become a big-name band one day. They played their guitars too loud but that might be a sign that I was getting old, but there is a limit to how much your ears can take night after night without going permanently deaf. Their road crew were a bunch of young lads as well, I think they were their mates from school as they didn't have the attitude that goes with working for a professional rock band and didn't show they had that much experience. They also thought it was a bit of a laugh going on tour with a band and treated it like a holiday. They were in for a shock, and one of them didn't even survive the rehearsals and was sent home.

It was quite a long tour, 38 shows going from January through to March, most of the shows were in small clubs, colleges, universities and town halls. London's Marquee Club was packed out and we did two nights where I bumped into Jess, a roadie who I'd given a job to in 1970 to work with me with Renaissance. The only problem with Jess was he didn't turn up for the first show preferring to accept a job with Led Zeppelin instead. I can't blame him for that, except he could have at least let me know he wasn't coming. He went on to brag about how he had such a good time with Zeppelin in America and how the band had their cash stolen from the hotel safe, except it wasn't really stolen, Jess told me it was a set-up between someone working for the band and someone working for the hotel to have the night safe broken into and the cash from the show stolen. I was thinking he had too much to drink and was talking too much for his own good, I don't know if that story was true, if it was he shouldn't have been blabbing about it and I didn't really want to know if it was true or not.

Some of the Def Leppard gigs were ridiculously small, like Retford Porterhouse, which only held about 100 people. I had trouble cutting the PA down to size to fit the room which wasn't much bigger than my lounge at home. Then the Fford Green Hotel in Leeds where the truck took up the whole car park. It was my policy to put as much PA sound equipment in a venue as would fit, so even if the venues were small it appeared like a big rock concert. It was a bit silly really as the band were carrying a full-size PA and lighting rig for a concert hall tour with a 40-foot trailer but only doing small rooms, so most nights we left some of the equipment in the trailer. It's all about image. I later heard that when Whitesnake were starting out they cancelled their gig at the Fford Green because they couldn't get all their gear in. I have never cancelled a gig because the venue was too small, you just have to adapt and get on with it.

The drummer's brother Robert was road manager and mixing the sound but he only wanted to be road manager and asked me if I wanted the job of mixing their sound. On a few occasions he told me to take over the controls while he went walkabout or sneaked backstage, leaving me to do the mix, I made a few changes when he wasn't looking, he never knew.

The last show was equally small, the Cricket Club in Northampton where the promoter decided we didn't need a stage crew to unload the trailer. Even though it clearly states on the contract rider that the promoter must provide six stage crew to unload, assist with set-up, breakdown and reload after the show. As he was adamant that he wasn't going to provide a crew to assist us, we eventually put some equipment in but only a minimal amount. A few weeks after the tour I heard a single on the radio from Def Leppard's new album, it's amazing what you can do in a studio these days, I couldn't believe it was the same band. The record producer Mutt Lange transformed Def Leppard's sound sending them from small venues into stadiums just as he had with AC/DC. My predictions that they would be big were right.

DR HOOK

A few weeks later Dr Hook flew over to London for a special one-off *Old Grey Whistle Test* at the BBC Studio. Nineyear Wooldridge phoned to ask if I could put a monitor system together and take it into the BBC Studios for the show. It all had to be done in one day, set up, soundcheck, camera check and dress rehearsal before the show. It was recorded as if it was a live show, so although it was recorded live it was not transmitted live, the show went out on another day. This time Kate Bush was on the show and the band had to interview Kate, or rather Dennis and Ray did whilst the others stood looking on.

A month later Dr Hook were over for another tour in the UK, Ireland and Europe. The first show at the National Stadium in Dublin started with a disaster, all was going well during the day, the band came on stage at the start of their set and went into the first number, almost immediately some idiot on the balcony above decided to knock over a glass of orange juice which crashed down from the balcony above right on top of the sound mixer SPLAT! The juice went everywhere and started to seep into the slots between the channels and master faders, then one by one the channels started to cut out and the sub-groups stopped working altogether resulting in half of the band's microphones not working, John Draper panicked and asked me to do something. I went through the sub-groups to see which ones were working and it turned out no sub-groups worked at all and only one stereo master was working. I went along the desk and routed all the channels to the master output faders, I repatched the crossover to mono and that got us through the show.

After the show I told the guys to leave the mixer on the back of the truck and I would take it into the hotel with me to give it a total strip down, clean and test before the orange dried. The problem with orange juice is that it's acidic and can eat through gold-plated contacts, destroying a PC board. I had to clean it off quickly before it did any permanent damage. At the hotel with the help of the road crew, we got the mixer into the lift and up to my hotel room. Once in the hotel room, I spent most of the night stripping the whole mixer down, and cleaning the gold-plated contacts on every plug and every socket inside the mixer. There were 36 plug-in modules and each module had a 32 pin connector, so each pin and socket had to be cleaned with a cotton bud and switch cleaner. Luckily it didn't do any permanent damage and the next night everything worked OK. After that episode I swore I would never place a sound mixer directly under a balcony again. We did a further nine shows in the UK with the last show being in the Rainbow Theatre before heading off to Europe.

During the two Hammersmith Odeon shows we had a mobile recording truck parked outside to record the shows and they released a live album in 1981 entitled 'Dr Hook Live in the UK'.

Whilst setting up for the last show at London's Rainbow Theatre the new bus driver sent to do the European leg of the tour walked in to the Rainbow and before introducing himself he said to me, "Who's got the coke then?" I could tell he wasn't asking for a drink. I told him, "No one does coke in this band and if they ever did, they would be out." I straight away phoned the bus company and told them to replace the driver immediately. As production manager I didn't want a coke-head driving our bus and I wasn't going to employ anyone who was sticking white powder up their nose.

The European tour was due to start straight after the London show, but just before the band went on stage we heard the European dates were cancelled. I don't know what happened but that was it. The following day we unloaded the PA into Colac's warehouse and went home.

TOUR BUSES

Len Wright Nightliner Tour Bus. 1980.

Tour buses can vary so much depending on where you get them from and who is paying for them, they are always called 'a bus', whether it's a 12-seater van or a luxury coach. At worst you can get a ski coach with two rows of bunks three high with accommodation for thirty people, no seats just bunks, the idea of that is to transport you to your ski holiday as quickly and as cheaply as possible, not ideal for living on for more than a day. At the other end of the scale you can have a double-decker luxury coach with twelve bunks upstairs complete with back-of-the-bus lounges with TV and music systems and seating downstairs with kitchen and a matching entertainment system. That's just the crew buses, for the artiste they could hire a private apartment on wheels with double bedrooms. Toilet rules on buses are quite strict and universal amongst all bus and coach operators. That is they are only used for liquid waste and not to be used for solid waste, some say except in an emergency, but it is up to you to make sure you don't have an emergency whilst you're in transit or you face being moaned at by everyone on board. The loo is situated next to the emergency exit and many people have nearly died mistaking the exit door for the loo.

The kitchen area is usually well equipped with a decent-sized fridge, microwave, kettle and a sink for washing your dishes. The bunks usually have headphone sockets to plug headphones in for the bus entertainment system and a power socket to plug in your music player, a reading light and a pair of curtains to pull across your compartment. The bus driver will normally clean up the bus during the day whilst you are working on stage and you are expected to keep his bus reasonably clean and tidy. One tour I was on with a really inconsiderate bunch of idiots ignored this rule, and had an entire bin full of rubbish dumped on the stage in the middle of the band's soundcheck. The driver said ,"You treat my workspace like a pig sty I'll treat yours like one," and walked off to the stunned silence of everybody on stage. No one ever messed in his bus again.

DAVID GATES

In May I had the pleasure of being asked to fly over to Cork in Ireland for a one-off concert with David Gates, the American singer-songwriter famous for being with the band Bread. Now performing solo, he did a show including all his hits with Bread. A local sound company in Ireland supplied a decent system for me to use, after tweaking it a bit here and there it sounded all right, my biggest problem was the acoustics in the City Hall in Cork.

What I remember about this show was after the soundcheck I ventured down the road to a local pub for a drink and something to eat before the show and I was amazed how friendly the locals were to me.

VAN HALEN – INVASION

A week later I was back on another Van Halen tour. This one was called the Van Halen Invasion tour but we called it the white tour because everything onstage was white, even the monitor speakers had to be painted with a white gloss paint, it looked horrible but that's what the band wanted so we had to oblige if we wanted the tour. Lead singer David Lee Roth even wore white gloves, he said it was to prevent getting dirty hands from the microphone cable, he even hired a roadie to clean his mic and mic cable before every show. This of course was before radio mics were commonly used.

The tour bus picked us up in London and we travelled to Harwich for the cross-channel journey to Holland for the Pink Pop Festival which is held in Maastricht each year. The Invasion tour was massive as far as equipment goes, when we arrived the trucks were still on their way, when I say trucks I mean eight 40-foot trailers packed with all the equipment, one was just for PA speakers, one for backline, two for staging, three for lights (apparently the biggest lighting rig in the world), one for merchandising and assorted bits and one was a spare just in case one broke down which eventually got used for spare parts and junk equipment. Over the top? Yes, but it was meant to be, over the top and in your face and full on Rock'n'Roll, that's how the band wanted it. There were 32 road crew for this production, all travelling in two 16-berth buses.

My old friend Patrick Whitley who I worked with on many other tours was production manager and he booked Edwin Shirley Trucking for the tour. Edwin Shirley is a trucking company that specialises in the music business and only hauls band equipment around; their trucks are top of the range and impressive looking with their maroon and yellow colour matched tractors and trailers, drivers queue up to be able to work for Edwin Shirley. The condition to drive with the company is that each driver owns his own tractor and must have it sprayed in Edwin Shirley colours so it matches the trailers. The trailers are owned by Edwin which are low-loaders with air-ride suspension to reduce damage to the electronic equipment carried. The drivers are very good and all work in a professional way. Edwin passed away in 2013 but his company rolls on. At the funeral his coffin was rolled in on a flight case, a perfect Rock'n'Roll way for a Rock'n'Roll trucker to go.

The Pink Pop Festival was held in an Olympic-sized stadium with a race track around the outside. As we stood with the stage crew waiting for the trucks to arrive, we saw the first truck pull into the arena and drive around the track towards the stage, then the next one pulled in and followed the first, after the third truck pulled into the stadium one of the stage crew asks, how many trucks do you have? As the first truck pulled up to the stage we now had the fourth, fifth and sixth trucks pulling in with a lot of moaning and groaning coming from the stage crew, by the time the eighth truck had pulled into the stadium the crew were busy discussing amongst themselves in their own language how they planned to unload the trailers.

I have to say that seeing eight tractor trailers all lined up one behind the other with matching colours did look very impressive, very Rock'n'Roll.

Thirteen shows followed in Holland, Germany and France, which all went well, I was babysitting the support band's engineer working for a German band, Geoff, who spoke such good English I thought he was English; it turned out his mother was English and had married a German, he was born and raised in Germany and spoke perfect English with no accent at all.

One of eight Edwin Shirley trucks outside a Van Halen concert

There must have been a NATO exercise on as all the shows in Germany were 90% filled with American GIs in full combat uniforms like they had just walked straight off the battlefield, Van Halen being a very popular band in the US especially amongst the rock music fans.

Just for fun I thought I would wear a Journey T-shirt to see what reaction I would get from the Van Halen crew, I'm pleased to say I didn't get the same negative reaction I received from the Journey crew when I wore a Van Halen T-shirt, they were more curious about when I had worked with Journey and how the tour went. One amusing moment on the tour was, the band always checked into hotels under false names to prevent fans from contacting them, one band member called himself 'Hugh Jazz'. They all found it highly amusing when the hotel staff would call out 'Mr Huge Ass'.

The lighting rig was allegedly the biggest in the world at that time and was designed to be, the whole thing was flown on twelve Demag motors hung from the roof. When there were no flying facilities in the building the whole thing balanced on twelve Genie Superlifts, each one manned by a stage tech and cranked up 6 inches at a time, each time it was moved it was left to settle before the next six-inch lift, it took some 30 minutes to raise it to its full height; meanwhile the sound and backline crew were waiting to get their gear on stage.

David Lee Roth was very athletic on stage and did his usual stage acrobatics, but one TV show they did in a studio in Italy had a low ceiling, he jumped into the air and smashed his nose on the lighting bars, he looked really funny when he came in the next day with a white bandage across his nose, nobody was laughing in front of him but plenty were doing so behind his back. That was definitely a *Spinal Tap* moment. Davis Lee Roth was a big show-off and really liked himself. He was too obnoxious for some fans, some even called him an egomaniac, but despite being that he always put on a good show and worked really hard on stage. One of the highlights of the show apart from Eddy Van Halen's guitar solos was Alex banging the gong behind the drum kit whilst it was on fire.

The disappointing aspect as far as the German support band was concerned was when we arrived in England for the UK leg of the tour. The European venues were all large stadiums, sports arenas and sports halls with 10,000 to 20,000 capacity. Our first show in England was at Newcastle City Hall which is only a 2,100-capacity town hall and all I heard from the German crew was how rubbish English venues were compared to Europe, at that time I had to agree with them, there were not arenas in the UK except for Wembley.

Apart from that, Newcastle ended up being a Spinal Tap gig of monumental cock-ups. Production manager Patrick Whitley decided to put the full lighting rig in or as much as would physically fit and it spanned 30 feet out over the audience. Van Halen's lighting rig had by this time become world famous as being the biggest light show in the world, it doesn't matter that they didn't need all the lights, it was a Rock'n'Roll image thing that they had to have the biggest lighting rig in Rock'n'Roll history.

The load-in started at 8am, the road outside the City Hall was coned off for the trailers to unload but due to the limited space only two could park at any one time coming and going in rotation. As well as that, a power generator had to be brought in to power the massive lighting rig and PA system as the mains power in the building wasn't big enough to handle it, we would have blown half of Newcastle. By midday the crew were still unloading and trying to fit a stadium lighting rig into a small city hall stage; because the stage size was restricted the rig had to be cut down and modified to fit, that took time, by late afternoon the rig was finally up in the air. I started to bring the PA system in, putting in as many speakers as would physically fit on the stage and a scaffold tower was erected for more speakers to cover the audience on the balcony.

Things were running so late that it wasn't until 5pm that the backline and stage risers were put on stage and the band didn't get a soundcheck that day. We were still plugging in cables as the audience was let into the hall. The support band went on late and the changeover ran over time so the show started late, by the end of the day we were all shattered but despite that it was a brilliant show. A light show I will never forget as the trusses reached out over the stage and over the heads of the audience like a space ship, the audience must have felt the heat from the lamps, it was blinding.

Once the show was over the load-out started and everything had to be loaded back in the trucks in reverse order, the only problem was congestion, bits of equipment from eight trucks had to be loaded and waiting for the right truck to arrive took all night. The backline went out first, then the sound, finally the lights which took forever, thankfully by 3am I was on one of the crew buses asleep, it took until 6am to fully load all the trucks.

The next problem was we were due to load in at Glasgow at 8am in two hours' time and it would take the trucks four hours to drive there. Patrick was criticised by management for overdoing the production in Newcastle.

Although he meant well, it was over-ambitious to put such a big production into such a small venue, as a result the load-in at the Glasgow Apollo was late starting, putting everything back by two hours and it was another difficult stage to set up on. Unfortunately the last truck to leave had to be the first to arrive. The support band was told not to bother turning up, it would take too long to set up. This event went down in rock folklore as one of those Rock'n'Roll moments, and was talked about on every tour bus for some time. After Glasgow, Manchester and Leicester I left to fly straight off to Canada to start a Dr Hook tour.

DR HOOK – CANADA

The day I left also clashed with a Lindisfarne show at Knebworth, I would have liked to have been there but Canada called. On the bill at Knebworth with Lindisfarne were The Beach Boys, Santana, Mike Oldfield and Elkie Brooks, but I couldn't be in two places at once and I couldn't turn down 6 weeks with Dr Hook. I was going to see my Limey sound system that I had built and shipped to the USA. I flew from London to Halifax, Nova Scotia and by the time I got there the truck had made its journey from Nashville, Tennessee across the border into Canada and had arrived in Nova Scotia. This was an 18 date tour over 33 days, a lot of travelling and some days off in between. East coast to west coast almost like a holiday for me and more relaxing than any European tour.

The venues were generally ice hockey stadiums and arenas holding around 10,000 people, not the best venues for acoustics but Dr Hook were as big in Canada as they were in the UK, Australia and Scandinavia. For some reason they didn't enjoy the same commercial success in their native USA as they did in other parts of the world. The tour started on the east coast of Nova Scotia on the Atlantic and we just headed west until we hit the Pacific Ocean in British Columbia, stopping on the way in places like St Johns, Toronto, Thunder Bay, Regina, Saskatoon, Calgary and Vancouver. In Edmonton we played the 10,000 seater Concert Bowl.

My partner in Limey Sound, Gary Doon, asked me to come over and do some upgrading to the sound system and complete a few things that were left unfinished, due to me not being able to get a work permit for the USA.

As well as the normal Dr Hook crew we also had along for the ride a young lad of about 16 who was the nephew of the band's manager Ron Haffkine. The crew were not pleased to have had this guy thrust upon them getting in the way. He didn't have any experience of working with a band and basically didn't even want to learn. If someone was keen to learn and was willing to pull his weight then that was different and people would help them out, but he only came along for a holiday with no intention of being part of the crew. I slapped him down once when he sarcastically asked why I was here with the band, he asked, "Was it because I didn't have any work in England?" I told him on the contrary, I had just finished a Van Halen tour, missed a Knebworth concert and I was due to start a European tour with Journey when I got back home. That shut him up.

Halfway through the tour, disaster struck, I don't know to this day what happened but it might have been a fault in the AC supply, half the amplifiers blew when they were switched on, which meant that about half the PA was out of use. I did manage to get enough power together by cheating a bit and doubling up some speakers and there was enough headroom to get by.

After I had stripped down the amplifiers and did an examination backstage I discovered the output transistors had gone short circuit and blown, I didn't have any spares but Gary phoned around and found a local electrical repair shop and asked if they had any in stock, as it happened they did.

The next day was a day off until show time, not for me though, Gary had arranged for me to go in to the repair shop with my tools and amplifiers and borrow their bench to do the repairs. I managed to change around twenty power output transistors and get the modules back up and working, it took me most of the day but I did it. I walked into the venue with the amplifiers to a round of applause, I didn't need that, I just wanted to plug them in and try them, and they all worked. Why they blew was a mystery but luckily they never blew again. I have to say, I was only able to do the repairs because the amplifiers were Midas which I was familiar with having worked at Midas.

One glitch in the itinery was a one-off show across the border at Duluth Arena in the USA for which I didn't have a visa or work permit to enter. A plan was hatched for me to enter as a hitchhiker travelling around Canada who was going to visit friends in Minnesota, all evidence of Dr Hook and even Rock'n'Roll connections were removed from my suitcase including tour T-shirts especially Dr Hook T-shirts. I wasn't alone, Rick the merchandising salesman who was selling all the band's T-shirts, sweaters and programmes on the merchandising stall was a Canadian citizen and didn't have the papers to enter the USA either.

Dr Hook PA Stack in Canada

At the border crossing the border police gave me a grilling and wanted to know why I was travelling with this American band and where I was going. I managed to convince them of my story, received a 3-month visa and was allowed to enter. After the show Rick and I were dropped off near the border and we took a taxi across while the bus took a longer route and picked us up later after we sat in this one-horse town for two hours waiting for the bus to arrive.

Most nights we had hotels, they were mostly Holiday Inns or Howard Johnsons and we only slept on the bus for long journeys. After the show at The Corral in Calgary, an ice hockey and rodeo arena, we had a few days off before the next show. So the band and crew were booked into the Fairmont Hot Springs Spa Resort Hotel, a ski resort in the winter but this was July and there was no snow, but it was still an amazing place to have a week off, with beautiful views across the Rocky mountains, this resort had three swimming pools, one was normal temperature, one was warm and one was very hot, all heated naturally by an underground volcano and the pools had to be artificially cooled as the water came straight from underground, the weather was hot and sunny and we had a good few days relaxing.

On the bus, which was hired from a company called Rolling Rock Leasing, we went through some beautiful scenery through miles of pine forests and across the Rocky Mountain range. The last show was at the Memorial Hall in Victoria, British Columbia and whilst the band and crew all took different flights to their respective homes, I took a flight from Vancouver back to London. A very successful and enjoyable tour.

JOURNEY – THREE DEGREES – THE HIT MEN

The opening show with Journey was back at the Audimax in Hamburg, this was not a big tour but it did have nine shows in Germany plus one in Switzerland, then two sell-out shows at the Rainbow Theatre in London. Again I was babysitting the band's engineer, which does get a bit boring, having to sit and watch someone else doing the mix. Kevin their engineer was a good soundman so I had no problems with him and the band sounded great.

When I got back I had some one-off shows with different artistes, this time I was doing the front of house mix for a band called Praying Mantis at the Marquee Club, a British heavy rock band.

Some shows with the Three Degrees followed, including the Congress

Theatre in Eastbourne, part of a tour to promote their *Gold* album. That was a real privilege and a delight to work with these ladies and they were really friendly and helpful during the soundcheck. The line-up included Shelia Ferguson, Valerie Holiday and Helen Scott. They performed their hits 'When Will I See You Again', 'Take Good Care Of Yourself', 'Woman in Love' and some lesser known songs. Then a show with The Hit Men, an Australian hard rock band at the Embassy club in London.

Andi Banks called to tell me Hattie Jacques had died on 6 Oct 1980, she had been ill for a while. As requested by the family in place of flowers I sent a donation to her favourite charity, I really respected the lady as she was so nice to me and my family.

STEVE HACKETT – DEFECTOR TOUR

Andi Banks got me a tour with Steve Hackett, the ex-guitarist from Genesis. Also on the crew were Billy Budis doing FOH and Steve Rayment on monitors, I already knew Steve from when he worked as a roadie with the pop group Mud. Steve Hackett's brother John Hackett was on flute and guitar, Dik Cadbury on bass, Nick Magnus on keyboards, John Shearer on drums and Pete Hicks on vocals. There was a 10 man crew, 3 on sound, 3 on backline and 4 on lights plus a tour manager.

We were using 37 of the available 40 channels on the desk, including a staggering 21 mics on the drums and percussion and all the shows were recorded on a cassette player so Steve could listen to the show later.

We started off in Oslo Norway at the Chateau Neuf, going on through Sweden, Holland, Belgium, Switzerland, France and Italy. It was quite an eye opener, I've always been a Genesis fan and was looking forward to touring with this guitar legend.

The first part of the tour in northern Europe was pretty normal. When we got to Italy it was a cultural shock, not because I'd never been there, I had, but because the attention that Steve Hackett got was gigantic. I hadn't realised how big Genesis were in Italy.

The first day in Italy the truck had a problem at the French-Italian border when it was held up by customs officials. We were at the venue in Turin waiting for the truck to arrive. As the day went on and it got to 6pm we started to hope that the truck wouldn't arrive, because we wouldn't have enough time to set the equipment up properly as the show was due to start at 8pm. Eventually the truck turned up at 7.45pm, there was not enough time to unload, set up all the equipment and sound check, but being Rock'n'Roll, the show must go on.

After a full day of sitting on a hot bus with only light refreshments to keep us from being bored we were not in a fit condition to start working. When the tour manager came on the bus the lighting guy told him that "We are all completely shattered and don't have enough time to set up the gear." As I looked out of the window I could see the truck had reversed up to the loading dock, flight cases and speaker cabinets were rolling down the ramp, I said to him, "Speak for yourself, mate, I've got a show to do." I knew that if we pulled the show we'd have 10,000 fans starting a riot, so we jumped off the bus and made our way inside to rig the sound.

I can tell you that this was the fastest set-up I had ever done with a 40-foot trailer load of equipment; in less than 45 minutes of the truck arriving, the band walked on stage with guitars and started playing, just 30 minutes late. We didn't put in the full production but it wasn't far off. With lights in the air, speakers stacked up on stage and the backline in place, everybody was still plugging in cables when the band started playing. Some things never got plugged in, we just let the show roll on. It was a case of 'plug-and-go'.

I hate it when a truck arrives late, it gets to the stage where you are thinking, please arrive in the next half an hour or don't arrive at all, as it's so much hassle to load in when the audience is sitting there and you don't have time to do things properly, and are not able to check that everything is working before the show starts.

All the venues in Italy were Palasports which are sports arenas with 360-degree seating and they were all sold out; venues that were supposed to hold 10,000 were letting in double that amount despite the fire regulations. It was estimated that 20,000 people were in some of the venues that were built for just half that. This caused some problems. The back of the stage had black drapes hanging, which is normal on most shows to enhance the visual effect of the stage. Some backdrops had the band's logo on it, some had an album cover and some were just plain black.

The problem started when thousands of extra fans had been allowed in, in part thanks to the Italian police, who instructed the promoter to open the gates as there were so many people outside without tickets trying to get in and a riot was close to starting. The promoter had no choice but to open the gates and allow the mass of people in whether they had tickets or not. Unfortunately 20,000 into 10,000 doesn't go and there was a seating shortage, so they took the only seats that were available; these were behind the stage, but they'd been blocked off due to sightline restrictions.

The fans could hear the band but not see them; this was bound to cause problems and it wasn't long before a disgruntled fan decided to climb up the lighting tower and cut down the drapes. This brought more fans from their seats onto the stage and they were pulling and tugging at the drapes until they came down ripped to shreds. The rest of the show went on without any back drapes.

Further south the crew tour bus came across a narrow street with parked cars either side; the driver was slowly making his way down when an irate Italian motorist decided to come up the other way. In England the car driver would have given way to the bus, but the car driver was determined he was not moving. After a lot of shouting and arm waving he went back to his car and came out with a handgun and started waving it at our driver who decided it was safer to back up and let him through, all of us were sitting low in our seats just in case he started having some target practice at the bus.

One of the weirdest things about an Italian audience is that they seem to think it's their right to record the show. I've never seen so many microphones in one place, at most venues you might see someone with a portable cassette player discreetly trying to record a show and you could always pick them out because of a red recording light reflecting off their face. But in Italy they didn't even bother to hide anything, they came in with a case full of equipment, setting up two large studio microphones on long stands to record in stereo. They would sit there with a mini mixer and headphones monitoring the sound and I don't just mean the odd person, I mean almost everyone in the 10,000 seater arena were at it, never seen anything like it, it looked like a free-for-all recording session.

After Italy we did three more shows in France, which was less stressful, before returning home to England.

It was a day after I got home on 8th December that the world was shocked by the death of John Lennon. Shot four times on the steps of the Dakota, where he lived in New York, he was pronounced dead on arrival at the Roosevelt Hospital. This was a great loss and we will never know how many more great songs he would have written if he were still alive today.

Crew bus and equipment trucks.

Steve Hackett (centre) on The Defector Tour 1980.

LINDISFARNE

On 20th December I headed north to Newcastle for eleven shows in ten nights at Newcastle City Hall, a record for any artiste at that venue, even Rod Stewart only did two nights there although I'm sure he could have done more. Five shows running up to Christmas Eve then two nights at home with the family for Christmas Day and Boxing Day and then five more nights up to New Year's Eve. This time I brought the family back to Newcastle for the last five shows, my wife Estelle my daughter Tamzin and my son Alex all came with me and I booked a family room in the Swallow Hotel in Newcastle. For the children it was a holiday and a chance to play in the City Hall, exploring the corridors and running around the balcony, during the day when I was not soundchecking we would go out and do some sightseeing or shopping. During the shows I reserved some seats for the family next to me at the front of house sound mixer which was placed at the front of the balcony, not my choice but something the promoter Barry McKay had reserved ever since promoting the City Hall shows. That was OK by me as I got a good view of the stage and I didn't like mixing under the balcony anyway. After the New Year's Eve show we headed home.

Photo: Lindisfarne Musical Productions
Lindisfarne at Newcastle City Hall for eleven sold-out shows.

Photo: Lindisfarne Musical Productions
Lindisfarne at Newcastle City Hall for eleven sold-out shows. 1981

20

MOVE TO CONCERT SOUND

LINDISFARNE

In 1981, unlike the previous two years, Lindisfarne decided to tour the rest of the country after Christmas instead of before, so we ended up doing 55 shows in ten weeks to the end of February. I was touring with a full-size concert system including my favourite Vitavox W bass bins but not all the venues could take them. The first show in January was at Friars in Aylesbury, then we did 8 shows in and around London in small venues including the Marquee in Wardour Street, the Greyhound in Fulham, Dingwalls in Camden Town, the Tramshed in Woolwich, the Half Moon in Herne Hill, the Crystal Palace Hotel and the Venue in the West End.

After that it was non-stop around the country back-to-back in true Lindisfarne tradition, there was no time for days off, it costs too much money to keep a band and its crew on the road, not to mention the production costs of hiring sound, lighting, trucking costs and hotels. So if there's a vacant hall, college or theatre, Barry will book it, the production costs are already paid for so some income is better than none. By the end of February we had done 55 shows.

ROSE ROYCE

Two weeks after the Lindisfarne tour I was asked to do front of house sound for Rose Royce, a five-piece R&B group from LA on a 17-date tour of the UK. This group were a real pleasure to work with, they were very friendly and helpful, and they were just pleased to be here, a really easy tour. Two sold-out shows at the Victoria Apollo Theatre and a return show there which was tagged on to the end of the tour. Whilst we were in Brighton at the Dome a lady came up to me at the mixer and asked, "Are you John from London?" It was an old friend I used to know from years back and who I hadn't seen for years, she happened to be in Brighton on a day out and on impulse decided to buy a ticket for the show, we sat and chatted for a while before the band came on stage. They performed their hits 'Car Wash', 'Wishing on a Star', 'Love Don't Live Here Anymore' and others.

Then I had three months off while there were no tours around so I took time out to spend with the family, something I wish I could do more often. I do get time off inbetween tours, it varies, sometimes a few days, sometimes a week or two or if it's quiet I might get a couple of months off, so I make the most of it when I can.

In July Lindisfarne headed across to Ireland for an unforgettable festival in Lisdoonvarna, an annual event that has been going on for hundreds of years where farmers from miles around meet once a year and do some match-making to find themselves a bride. This tradition has been kept up although there's not so much finding brides at the event these days, instead it's an excuse to get drunk and listen to live music which attracts over 50,000 people, that's a lot of people in a town which normally has a population of around 700.

On arrival in Lisdoonvarna we checked into the main hotel in town, a large pub hotel. When the time came we headed off to the festival site only to be held up in heavy traffic with cars trying to get to the festival site from all directions. One problem which could only happen in Ireland was the main road into the site, which was designated a temporary one-way road as it was only wide enough for one vehicle. Although the road was clearly signed as one-way at the entrance end, nobody put a sign up at the other end so cars were still trying to come up a one-way road the wrong way. Not very helpful when you're driving a 3-ton truck. The stage was in a large marquee, we set up and the show went really well, afterwards we headed back to the hotel. When we got there the village square was heaving with so many people we could hardly reach the hotel. The bar was packed and pints of beer were flowing out of there by the second. Someone was busy using a sledgehammer to knock a hole from the bar out to the street to sell beer to those who couldn't get into the hotel, after a while pints of beer were being handed out through the hole to people outside, when I decided to go to bed the stairs were completely full of people siting, lying or sleeping all the way up the stairs and along the corridors, I had to step over bodies everywhere and thought, *I'm not going to get much sleep tonight.* I'd never seen anything like it.

ROCK ON THE TYNE

In August Barry McKay was organising a concert at Gateshead International Stadium called 'Rock on the Tyne', an athletics stadium and football pitch with a capacity of 12,000 in the stands but more when the pitch is included. On the bill was Ian Dury, Elvis Costello, The Polecats, Rory Gallagher, Doctor Feelgood, a new group called U2 and special guest Lindisfarne.

Barry asked me to organise the sound for the event which was held over two days in August. The headliners Ian Dury and Elvis Costello normally use an American production company called TFL (Tom Fields Associates). I was told they would prefer to use them. I've known some of their crew for years so it wasn't a problem. I called them up and arranged a meeting to discuss what sound equipment they could supply for the event.

When I arrived at their warehouse some of their crew were loading a 40-foot trailer with sound equipment ready to take out on tour; being nosey I looked inside to see what was going in the trailer. I saw a man with a tape measure measuring the inside of the trailer. When I found out why he was measuring, my heart sank: the sound business had taken a downward step towards corporate insanity, he later told me that TFL were designing a new speaker cabinet and that he wanted to fit three across the inside of the trailer, his attitude was 'never mind what they sound like as long as they fit inside a trailer, that's all that matters'. Speaker cabinets follow a very complex formula in design and each cabinet has a resonant frequency tuned to the speaker, just like tuning a car engine to its exhaust, if it's not tuned right it won't perform as well as it should. A cello has a different size body to a violin for a very good reason, Baritone, Tenor and Alto saxophones all have different size bodies and are highly tuned to give the correct sound for that instrument, so it is with speaker cabinets, you don't just screw a speaker into a wooden box. The size, shape, even the internal baffles all matter.

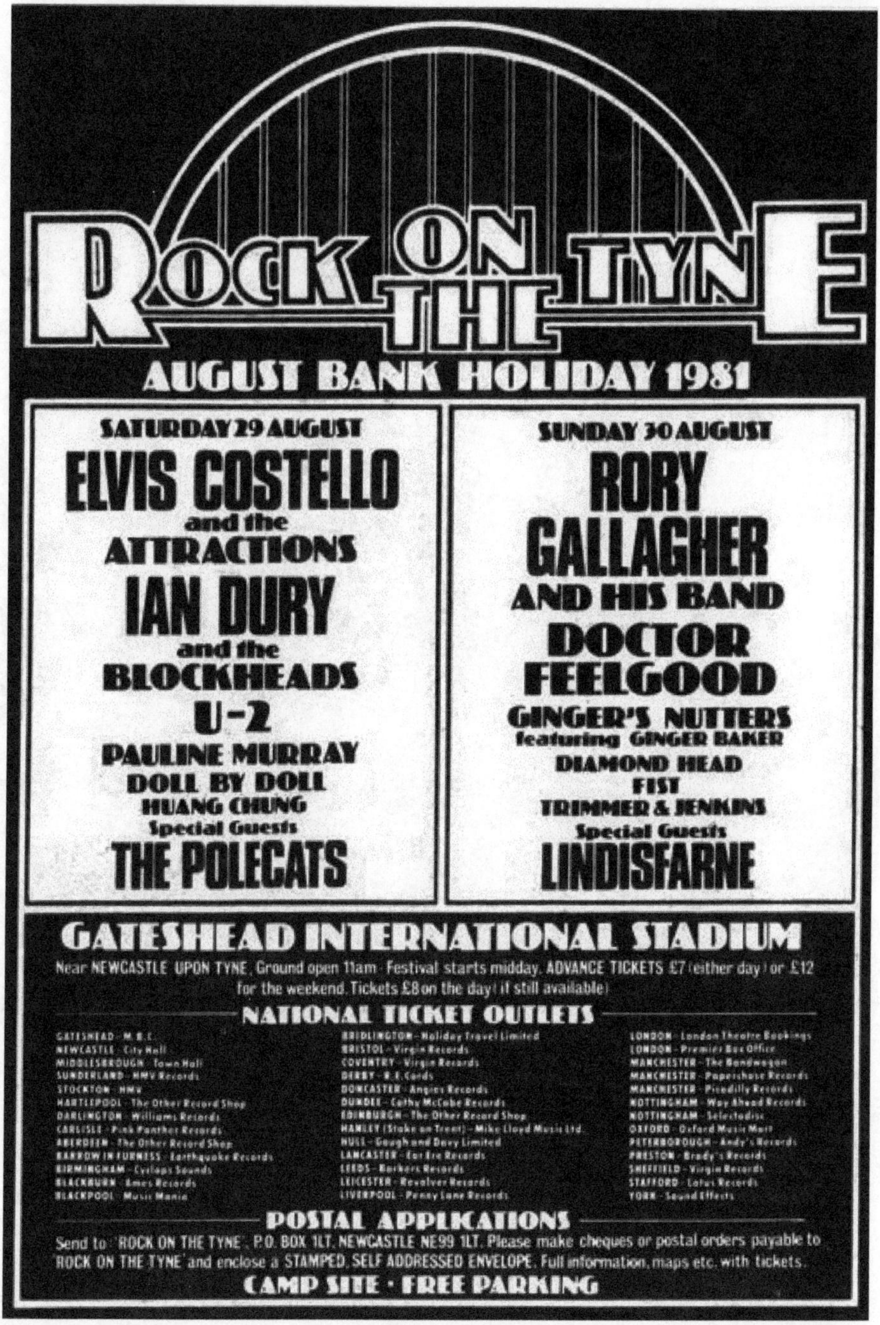

Image © Barry McKay
Rock on the Tyne Poster

Photo: Jonathan Brown
Mixing Lindisfarne at the 'Rock on the Tyne' festival 1981
Using a TFA sound system

Despite what was going on downstairs we worked out the size of the sound system, mixer and effects I wanted to put into Gateshead and said, "See you on the day." The TFL crew were busy rigging their system so I left them to it and set up the mixer ready for soundcheck. The day went well with Lindisfarne doing their usual set and getting a good local response from their home audience of Geordies.

In 1982 Lindisfarne released their *Sleepless Nights* album on their own LMP label. September to December was a Lindisfarne tour with a break in the middle so I could slot in a Dr Hook tour.

DR HOOK

This time Dr Hook had a support act called Sundance, with Mary Hopkins as the lead singer. I did the sound mix for them and they were a pleasant enough group with a folky kind of sound. A 19-date tour with two sold-out dates at Wembley Arena, the last show being at the RDS hall in Dublin.

Wembley was presenting a problem for the promoter, Danny Betesh of Kennedy Street Enterprises, a really nice guy and one of the best promoters to work with, he was one of the first promoters to book a Beatles tour in 1962. He wanted the sound to be flown above the stage to increase sightlines and sell more tickets. For this I went to Concert Sound because I knew they had some new cradles for flying speakers in the air, it was basically a platform made of scaffold bars with a motor for lifting them in the air. I had one each side and split the system with one third in the air, one third on the ground and one third on the stage.

This was before flying systems were the norm and before speakers were flown from the roof to the ground, what we take for granted now wasn't even invented then. Bands were just starting to fly their sound off the stage so audiences could get a better view of the stage. From the early 1960s the general method of installing a sound system in a venue was to place a speaker stack each side of the stage pointing forward towards the audience. As venues got bigger so did the sound systems required to fill them. We ended up with piles of speakers the size of a mountain each side of the stage, but with bands doing even larger and larger venues like arenas in Europe, hockey stadiums in America, ice rinks in Scandinavia and Canada, promoters had to block off huge swathes of seating each side because the public couldn't see the stage for the speakers. The promoters didn't like losing so many seats and pressure was starting to be put on us to reduce the size of the sound system or move the speakers somewhere else.

Of course delivering a good sound is always a compromise and you can never achieve what you want due to other factors like seats in non-visual areas, lighting rigs and their supporting towers on the stage and stage equipment all getting in the way.

This was when we started to fly the speakers from the roof. It happened in small steps, first conventional speaker cabinets were placed on a cradle and hung above the stage whilst still having a reasonably sized stack on the stage at each side. Slowly things evolved, EAW, Martin and others brought out speaker cabinets with flying hooks on them so we hung them directly from motors and we lost the cradle or platform which held the old type speakers. Then more and more speakers were being flown and fewer and fewer speakers were placed on the stage until all the sound was hanging above the stage.

Now of course, we see the familiar pencil-thin arrays, called 'line arrays' a line of very slim speakers hung in a vertical arc from the roof (or from cranes when used outdoors). This method creates a very clean and clear-looking stage with no speakers on stage at all except for maybe a few small speakers to fill in black spots around the front of the stage. Sub-bass speakers which do not need to be part of the line array, because bass frequencies are non-directional, can be placed anywhere and are usually situated under the stage out of sight giving an earthquake effect through the floor.

With the increased use of 'in-ear' monitors, those large wedge-shaped monitor speakers disappeared from the front of the stage entirely, again creating a very clean and clear-looking stage for the artiste to perform on. The sound now became 'invisible' and more space was created for the overall production. Looking back it must have been really ugly to see a mountain of black speaker cabinets each side of the stage. Promotors love it as now they can sell the entire venue out without losing seats with restricted vision, sightlines as they call them, some went even further and used a revolving stage in the middle of the venue and sold seats 360 degrees around the stage. This may have made more money for the promoter but only a quarter of the audience actually saw the show full on at any one time. Personally I wouldn't want to watch the back of someone's head and sides for three quarters of a performance.

Flying a PA system involved getting into the venue early with the riggers. The first job for the riggers was to hang the flying points for the lighting rig, this always goes in first; once the hanging positions have been chalked out on the stage or floor, the riggers will be in the roof hanging steel wire with shackles across whatever roof trusses are available, nice and easy in a theatre where hanging points have been built in for theatre productions, where props and backdrops are regularly used. But when you get into a multi-purpose venue or arena this is where the riggers skill comes in, a good rigger will drop your point dead on your mark within a sixpence, of course not all roof trusses are in the right place to hang a wire directly above where you want it, so a mish-mash spider's web of steel wires linked across various roof trusses are employed to get the hanging point just where you want it. A rope is then dropped and an electric motor chain is attached to the rope; the rigger pulls the chain up and attaches it to the rigging point. Once all hanging points are in place and motors are hooked onto the lighting rig, the lighting crew then proceed to raise the truss into the air.

Very slowly the motor starts to climb up the chain, the lighting rig attached to the motor also climbs up the chain, a simple lighting truss may only have two motors but could easily have several. In the case of Van Halen's lights they used twelve motors.

Whilst the lighting crew were doing that I would have the frame with a row of speakers ready to be raised into position above the stage. After the lights are up in the air and out of the way, the sound system goes through the same procedure. Using Socapex connectors for the speaker cables saved a lot of time as you could connect a whole block of speakers with just one plug and a few flying leads, but we were not alone in using Socapex connectors. In the early 1970s Showlites started using Socapex multi-pin connectors to speed up rigging the lights which seemed to take forever when plugging in each lamp individually one at a time, but instead of speeding up the lighting rig it just meant they had time to rig more lights, so the rigging time remained the same and lighting rigs just got bigger.

In 2013 seventy-six people were injured when the ceiling in London's Apollo Theatre in Shaftesbury Avenue collapsed onto the audience during a show, the ceiling also took part of the balcony down with it. In 2012, an hour before 40,000 fans were allowed into a park in Toronto, Canada, the roof of an outdoor stage collapsed; the drum technician with Radiohead was crushed to death by a section of the metal canopy when it crashed down onto the stage, and he was killed instantly. Life on the road can be dangerous. One tip when riggers are working overhead is always wear a safety helmet or keep well away, I have nearly been hit a few times by an odd shackle being dropped from the roof 100ft above, missing me by inches. If one of those hits you on the head you wouldn't wake up. I also had a couple of experiences with lighting rigs falling over.

Whilst travelling on crew buses, the crew generally tell stories, jokes and experiences are shared from previous tours. Greg, a lighting engineer, had just finished a tour with ELO (Electric Light Orchestra) with their famous flying saucer lighting rig, a monster of a rig he tells me, with the lights inside the roof of the saucer. The flying saucer at the start of the show would be closed on the stage, the house lights would go down and the saucer would slowly rise with flashing lights and jets of smoke shooting out from underneath to reveal the band inside the saucer playing the first song. The roof of the saucer lid would then become the overhead lighting rig. On one gig in America he tells me a nightmare occurred when one of the four motors raising the saucer decided to stop working, leaving the other three still lifting the saucer and lighting rig, which was going up lopsided, half of the first set was performed with the lighting rig hanging on its side while the techs got the motor working, it was something that could have come straight out of a *Spinal Tap* movie.

What happens a lot while you're on tour is you might have a day off in a European town and there may be another English act in town as well; they'd be doing the same venue as you the night before you're due to be in there, in which case you may get an invitation to attend the show. Sometimes tour managers contact each other to obtain some access passes or you may even know one of the crew working on the other tour. It's a very close-knit family of crew members as you often meet up with guys you have previously worked with on different tours. If there is no known contact, it's easy to get in and see a free show, all you need to do is show up at the front entrance or the backstage door looking like you're one the crew, wearing an English tour T-shirt and a laminate tour pass around your neck, you tell the security guard that you're working for the band and walk through with a confident look on your face, it's never failed.

In June Lindisfarne did a 19-date tour including a trip over to Austria for a couple of festivals in Graz and Vienna, a few nightclubs, universities and city halls and a quick trip over to Ireland to the Opera House in Cork, before going back to the Cambridge Folk Festival, where the truck got stuck in the mud and had to be towed out by a farm tractor. The tractor driver had a full-time job on his hands at this event as all the band's vehicles were slipping and sliding in the mud trying to get off the site after a torrential downpour. Then onto the Theakston music festival supporting Jethro Tull which was a much drier event.

LIMEY SOUND TO CONCERT SOUND

1982 was a particularly quiet year, not a lot of tours were going around and I hadn't heard from Colac in a while. I later discovered why: they had sold the business, Scott Thompson and Clive Davis got out and bought a hotel in Sri Lanka, good on them. The equipment, lock stock and barrel was bought by another sound company which I knew of called Concert Sound. I decided to take a few months off and didn't take any work until June. I also made the decision to sell off my sound equipment and placed an advisement in the music press, I had a few calls from interested people but the best offer I received was from a Swedish rock band who was working in England and wanted to buy the entire lot, cases, cables and everything. They called at my house and loaded their van with all the equipment I had in my garage. My wife was rather overwhelmed by these four guys in our house, six foot tall, blonde, tanned and good-looking Swedish men.

DR HOOK

October saw Dr Hook coming back for their ninth UK tour and this time I approached Concert Sound to supply the sound equipment. Concert Sound was a sound company which was originally the PA system for a band called Man with most of the crew coming from Wales. They had a warehouse in a railway arch in Watford.

I went to their warehouse to discuss the equipment I wanted. When I walked in I was surprised to see Colac's speakers stacked up, just like being in Colac's warehouse. I immediately said I wanted the Vitavox W cabinets for the bass end. That's OK, they said nobody else wants to use them as they are so big. At six feet tall and three feet wide I'm not surprised but what a beautiful sound they produced and worth all the hassle of lugging them around. I also approached ML executives, a company owned by The Who, but their quote was too high.

The first gig was in The Kings Hall, Belfast, and the same venue where the Army had previously called everybody out of the building to sweep it for a bomb that was supposed to have been left in the building. All part of a working day in Northern Ireland. I met the US crew at Heathrow and we flew over to Belfast the day before the gig but to my surprise the lighting crew didn't show up at the airport. When I checked into the Europa Hotel in Belfast I telephoned

London to see what had happened, only to discover that the crew had confused the first show day with the flight day and were not expecting to travel until the following morning, panic all round, the lighting company apologised and got the guys on the next flight out.

In Belfast I was confronted by an angry lighting crew who had just arrived and wanted to know how long I'd been with the band. Expecting me to say one day, they were visibly stunned when I said ten years. I also told them I'd never given out a wrong date or missed a first show in those ten years, but I wasn't blaming them, it was a mistake by their office. That got the tour off on the wrong foot, especially when John Draper (Dr Hook's sound engineer) went into a long lecture at the lighting crew about the band not tolerating any crew member doing drugs on the tour.

The same thing happened as the last visit to Belfast, the Army came in to evacuate the building while they sent in the sniffer dogs looking for a bomb supposedly planted somewhere. Twenty-four dates in and around the UK went really well including two more sold-out shows at Wembley Arena.

Our tour manager Jim Sullivan had a bad experience when he hid his briefcase behind some seats while he went off to do something, only to go back later and find someone had stolen it, if that wasn't bad enough he had all the night's cash from the concert in that briefcase, a silly thing to do. He was not in the promoter's good books after that, he lost quite a few thousand pounds. The case or its contents were never found and some lucky thief had a good Christmas.

21

GUITAR TRIO WORLD TOUR

After I rented a sound system from Concert Sound for the Dr Hook tour I was pleased to receive a phone call from Mick Anderson soon afterwards, asking if I'd like to take a system out for one of their tours. I said I'd be pleased to, who was it and where was it going? It was a European tour and the band were The Commodores. Unfortunately Lionel Richie had just left the band and this was their first tour without him, consequently the venues were going to be smaller than their previous tours when Lionel was with them.

I went down to the warehouse where Mick told me I was to be the crew boss and that Peter Grainger would be along in a few days to assist me. I was a bit surprised and a little anxious, I didn't want to appear as if I was taking his job as Peter was one of Concert Sound's most experienced engineers. I got to know Peter quite well when he was doing the sound for Dire Straits. Peter was cool about being second string and told me he was happy to have a more relaxing tour without the pressure of being in charge. Also along on the tour mixing monitors was Dave Catlin, a good bloke who I got to know really well over the next few years.

The band themselves were a bit nervous going on stage without Lionel and a few times a voice from the audience would call out "Where's Lionel?" It must have been hard for them but they put on a great show as they were all exceptionally good musicians in their own right. We did two shows in Germany, Munich and Boeblingen, two in Holland, Amsterdam and The Hague, and two nights at

Hammersmith Odeon. There was a day off after the two Hammersmith shows and the promoter asked if I'd leave the sound system in for a one-off show the following night for Bobby and The Midnites, (no, never heard of them either). They sounded like an American soul-funk band similar to the Commodores and were very good.

There were actually only five Commodores, they had a five-piece backing band called The Mean Machine and three vocalists so on stage there were twelve people. I had ten mics across two drum kits plus miscellaneous keyboards and pianos, congas, guitars and a three-piece brass section, 30 channels altogether. The tour went off really well.

In March I received an unexpected call from Entec who I'd worked for when I did the UFO tour, they asked if I'd travel up to Liverpool to mix the stage monitors for a BBC Radio One roadshow for Dexy's Midnight Runners. This was a live radio show and they needed someone to do the monitor mix. I was happy to do it of course but I was surprised when I got there to see my old friend from the UFO tour Bruno standing there. I think he was shocked to see me as well. I asked Bruno why they wanted me to do this, when they had their own crew who could have done the job just as well. He didn't know either just saying it was a management decision to get me in. I'm not going to argue with that especially with what they offered me as a fee for the day. Dexy and his band were easy to do and the show went off really well and everyone was happy, especially me and my bank balance.

STEVE HACKETT – 'HIGHLY STRUNG' TOUR

In April and May I was back on the road with ex-Genesis guitarist Steve Hackett for the second time for a 21-date UK tour. My old mate Andi Banks got a gig working for Steve Hackett as tour manager, and he got me the job of supplying the sound again; the job title I was given in the tour itinery was PA Boss, never had that one before.

The band were booked into Shepperton Studio M for seven days set-up and technical rehearsals, sounded like an easy week, another chance to wander around the studio sets and peer into the open studios to see what was going on and who was doing what.

One of the PA stacks on the Steve Hacket tour,1983.
Consisting of 2 Vitavox W Bass bins, 8 Martin Bass bins, 4 Martin Mid-range speakers, 10 Vitavox hi frequency horns.

This time I hired a sound system from Stage Audio Services for the PA and Billy Budis was the band's front of house engineer. We were using 32 channels, 12 of them were on the drum kit, and there were also Steve Hackett's many guitars plus keyboards, flute, pedals, bass guitar and backing vocals.

No Italian stadiums this time, we did all the usual Apollos, Odeons, City Halls and seaside pavilions with two nights at Hammersmith. Steve Hackett was a decent enough bloke but could be a bit grumpy if the show didn't go down as well as he wanted.

Billy Budis later became Steve's manager who apparently then went off and had an affair with Steve's wife, so much for loyalty and not what I'd call a great career move, he left shortly afterwards, I can't think why.

GUITAR TRIO

Then a change in direction and a new door opens. Whilst I was out with Steve Hackett I received a call from Marshall Arts asking if I'd call into their office to discuss a job which they'd like to offer me. Marshall Arts is a company owned by Barrie Marshall who is a well-respected concert promoter and part owner of Concert Sound. I had no idea what it was about but I went in anyway. I met a guy called Vance Anderson who happened to be the brother of Mick Anderson who was running Concert Sound so it was all in the family.

Vance said he'd asked his brother Mick at Concert Sound if he had anyone on his crew who could wire boxes together with wet string and gaffa tape and make it sound good. They called me.

I guess this was a job made for me and it's something I enjoy doing best, taking poor-quality equipment and trying to make it sound good. The job was not too difficult except some of the sound systems I had to deal with were at best demanding and at worst rubbish.

Vance told me Barrie Marshall was promoting this tour and he was taking a trio of acoustic guitarists on a world tour and we would be using an assortment of sound systems in various countries, he wanted someone along to get the sound systems kicked into shape and working to a reasonable standard.

Vance asked if I wanted to go on a world tour with 'The Trio' (as they unofficially became known) as stage manager, monitor engineer and general tech guy for the tour. I had to drive a car with three acoustic guitars and the band's baggage to each venue and hotel, set up three chairs, three microphones and get the guitars to sound as loud as I could. Vance had the job of tour manager and front of house sound engineer. It was just the two of us on the road along with the three musicians. It sounded like a nice trip.

The musicians involved were John McLaughlin from The Mahavishnu Orchestra who was a classically trained jazz guitarist from England; Al DiMeola, an American jazz-rock guitarist who had his own electric jazz-rock band and Paco DeLucia, a Spanish flamenco guitarist rated to be the best flamenco guitarist in the world and voted the world's best flamenco guitarist several years in a row, can't argue with that.

This sounds like an unlikely combination, a strange mixture of different guitar genres. Together their blended guitars created an acoustically brilliant sound. Releasing their album *Passion, Grace and Fire* in 1983, they wanted to tour the world to promote it, the world this time meant Europe, Australia,

America, the Far East and Asia and could take up to a year, although not all in one go.

I said I would be happy to accept the job and Vance told me we would leave on 11th March for our first TV show in Baden-Baden for SWF television which was to be broadcast throughout Germany.

I had met John McLaughlin before in Sweden and Finland in 1978 and he remembered me from those shows and we got on well. Meeting Al DiMeola and Paco DeLucia was difficult at first and it took some time to get to know them and for them to trust me. They seemed to eye me with suspicion and were not that friendly with me to start with but after a few shows we got on OK.

The tour continued in Europe, performing in concert halls, opera houses, jazz festivals, and some more TV shows. The first concert shows by coincidence were at the Concert House in Stockholm and House of Culture in Helsinki, both of which I did with John McLaughlin in 1978.

The equipment I was carrying was just three acoustic guitars, with no sound, lights or backline equipment to worry about, it was an easy gig for me. We flew between most cities but on short journeys we used two hire cars, one for me, the guitars and the baggage and one for Vance who drove the three musicians. Vance always insisted on top-of-the-range Mercedes hire cars which we would pick up at airports on arrival, he would drive down the autobahns in Germany at 180km per hour (120mph), I could hardly keep up with him, scared the life out of me sometimes, especially as the car would start to shake about when it got to 110mph; that sounds fast but on German autobahns the speed didn't seem very different to the other vehicles travelling alongside us.

My job upon arriving at the venue was to set the stage and inform the hall manager what the situation was with the stage set; they had never had to deal with a show like this before and I made sure it was going to be presented as a professional act not just what some thought were a bunch of folk guitarists.

I wanted three upright chairs placed in an arch centre stage with three guitar microphones and three vocal microphones. Although there was no singing in this show they all wanted a vocal mic to talk to the audience and introduce the tunes they were playing. I also needed two DI (direct injection) boxes for John and Al's guitars, Paco played a purely Spanish acoustic guitar and didn't have the luxury of being able to plug in. This caused a problem because the levels of John's and Al's guitars were limited to how loud we could get Paco's guitar. Microphones are prone to feedback if cranked up too loud so Paco's guitar was the benchmark level for the other two guitars. The two DIs were only used to give an extra fullness of sound, something that Paco didn't want, he was a purist flamenco player and didn't want anything extra added to his sound. Behind each guitarist I placed a monitor speaker for each of them so they could hear themselves and each other; after a couple of soundchecks I knew what they wanted and the rest was easy.

One of my other jobs was to announce a 20-minute intermission halfway through the show; this I did with some fun, sometimes putting on foreign accents or posh English accents to confuse the audience. Vance thought it was funny and highly amusing.

The next few shows were in Oslo, Copenhagen and Amsterdam where we did a live TV show for the *Sonja on Friday* TV show. Then on to Frankfurt and nine further shows in Germany, the venues were especially large for what I would have expected for an acoustic guitar trio, I was expecting small clubs and theatres but in fact we were selling out concert halls, large theatres, sports arenas and the type of venues normally used by big rock bands. Most of the venues I was familiar with as I had worked in them before and the stage crew were surprised at the non-existent equipment set-up on stage.

The instructions I gave to the lighting board operator was for one beam of light over each chair and a general wash across the stage, no fade-ins and no fade-outs during the show, and a black backdrop curtain across the back of the stage. The rider requested large quantities of potted plants to dress the stage and I took quite an interest in artistically positioning the plants, some of which were 6 feet tall and some palm trees as high as 10 feet.

For the next three weeks we flitted back and forth across the French-German border and eventually worked our way down to the south of France and into Spain where Paco was considered a god. Strangely enough the Spanish didn't like Al DiMeola so much and applauded Paco and John much louder, much to Al's annoyance, it might have been down to Al's Italian background. The songs were all instrumental, consisting of a blend of classical, jazz and flamenco, varying in style and dynamics, each would do a solo spot whilst the other two would accompany playing rhythm. They must have been quite popular as we were selling out large venues right across the continent and we didn't even have a support act; The Trio (as they became known) performed both halves of the show.

By the time we got down to the Mediterranean it was June and we were enjoying a warm summer. In Orange we performed in a Roman amphitheatre, then Nice, Lyon, Toulouse, Barcelona, Milan, Bologna and Rome making the most of the summer weather. Whilst in Rome we heard that Margaret Thatcher had won the second of her three elections in the UK.

Then it was north for a show in Brussels. In Den Haag, Holland I had a disagreement with the Dutch lighting guy Franz, he must have thought it was a heavy rock concert and spread the entire front of the stage with lighting frames on these ugly scaffold bars, they would have looked ugly even with a rock band and I wasn't going to have them on my stage. So I unplugged them and dragged them around the back of the potted plants and told him, you can plug them in here and illuminate the back of the plants. That was my mistake because Barrie Marshall came to the show and saw the effect of the plants illuminated from the rear and Franz got the credit for the lighting.

The next show was supposed to be at Hammersmith Odeon the following day but a promoter for an open-air festival called 'A Midsummer Night's Dream' had seen the show and wanted the trio to perform at his two festivals in Darmstadt on 18th June and in Augsburg on 19th June. He was told we couldn't do those shows because we were booked to do Hammersmith on the 18th. His solution, which spared no expense, was for us to perform at Darmstadt at 1pm and provide us with a private Learjet to fly us to London for our Hammersmith show that night, then fly us back by Learjet for his show in Augsburg on the 19th. So that's what we did.

We came off stage at Darmstadt and drove straight to Frankfurt Airport where we got priority clearance through customs and drove straight onto the tarmac and boarded our own private 8 seater Leah jet into Heathrow. We did the show at Hammersmith Odeon that night and the next day had a private hire car to Heathrow where we boarded the Leah jet back to Munich for the festival in Augsburg.

On the bill in Augsburg was Robert Palmer who had been in the Vinegar Joe band with Elkie Brooks from 1971 to 1973. I caught him backstage and we had a good chat about what we had both been doing since the Vinegar Joe days, he was in a good mood. Also on the bill were Crosby Stills and Nash, Mike Oldfield, Blue Oyster Cult, Peter Tosh and Van Morrison.

That show was the end of the European leg of the tour and I had some time off before flying to New York for the American leg of the tour, so I booked a fortnight's holiday for my wife and two children and headed off to Tenerife for a well-deserved rest.

The Guitar Trio stage in a Roman amphitheatre. France

Vance Anderson (centre) loading our baggage into a Learjet at Frankfurt Airport on our way to Hammersmith Odeon.

During the summer break I was asked if I could do a disco for a friend's birthday party, I said I'm a soundman not a disc jockey, but they wanted me to do it anyway. I didn't have any disco equipment but I did have an awesome sound system, all I needed to do was to add some more bass speakers for the large room they had hired. The disco mixing decks I didn't have but I thought it wouldn't be hard to knock up a console, so I purchased two turntables, a DJ mixer and built it into a wooden case, went down to the warehouse at Concert Sound and borrowed two 15-inch bass speaker cabinets, an electronic crossover and a power amplifier. I used my Tannoy studio speakers from home for the mid-range and top-end and away I went. I also purchased a light controller and built some lighting boxes with PAR 38 lamps. I had a fairly decent collection of albums that included dance tracks of the day so that was taken care of. It went really well and afterwards I gave the disco decks to my son Alex to play with, he kept them for quite a few years. It was just a fun thing to do that kept me busy at home whilst I was not working.

In September we were back on the road again this time in America, starting off in Buffalo at the Music Hall. Distances between cities were greater in the US so we flew most days, hanging around airports was getting to be like waiting for a bus. For this part of the tour we were joined by a support guitarist I hadn't heard of but would soon hear a lot of in later years, it was Steve Morse.

Steve Morse was voted best overall guitar player by *Guitar Player* magazine and held the title for five consecutive years. In 1986 he joined American rock band Kansas and in 1994 joined Deep Purple replacing Richie Blackmore. Steve performed the first half of the show as a solo artiste performing instrumental jazz tracks from some of his many albums which he recorded with his previous band The Dregs, a jazz-fusion guitar band. Steve was a really nice guy and easy to get along with, he seemed really humbled at the pleasure of sharing a stage with these three guitar greats, he confided with me once that he was nervous at playing with these guys as he had admired them enormously as professional guitarists. For the encore he was invited onstage to join the trio for a four-way battle of guitar solos which went down really well with the audience.

After Buffalo, Boston, Philadelphia and New Haven we crossed over into Canada playing in Toronto and Montreal. In Quebec, where most of the citizens are French-speaking, John McLaughlin embarrassingly asked the audience "Does anyone here speak English, this is Quebec yeah?" There was a deadly silence where nobody said a word, John promptly went straight into the next song and I thought to myself, what was that all about?

We carried on performing in Elizabeth, New York, Detroit, Baltimore, Washington DC, Cleveland, Milwaukee and Chicago. Occasionally Vance would disappear for a few days leaving me in charge of the band doing both the FOH sound and monitors. We did the famous Montreal Jazz Festival where Vance dropped me in it by leaving me on my own, we turned up and had no chance to check any mics, monitors or do a soundcheck, which is normal for a festival. I asked for three chairs, three guitar mics and three vocal mics and two DIs. I just had to go for it in front of 10,000 people with no sound check, but that's just something you have to do at these festivals and thankfully I think I got away with it.

America brought me into direct contact with the unions. Having to deal with the American union stage crews was exasperating, I never was a fan of union labour, they always seem to be under the impression that their job is there for their benefit rather than the people they are supposed to serve. The unloaders' job was to unload the vehicle and take the equipment from the vehicle to the loading door, from there the stage crew would take over and carry the equipment onto the stage. So when I turned up at the Front Row Theatre in Cleveland, Ohio with just three guitars in the boot of the car they were a bit surprised, they were expecting a truck full of equipment. The union crew behaved like a bunch of 1960s dockers who insisted I was not allowed onto the stage because I was not a union member, only they were allowed onto the stage until the equipment had been unloaded and set up, even though they didn't know where to place anything.

They asked where I wanted the guitar cases placed, so I told them in the dressing rooms and I made sure they were locked until the band arrived. The chairs, mics, DIs and 3 monitors were placed on stage in roughly the right place but I wasn't going to argue because I intended to make adjustments later when they weren't looking. I wasn't allowed on stage so after everything was set up and the stage crew went for their break I sneaked on stage and adjusted the mics and moved the monitor speakers to where I wanted them, I knew how the band wanted them.

Vance would arrive later with the band for a soundcheck and the trio expected everything to be in place and working as they liked it. The only other piece of equipment I was carrying was my tool box which was a box of tricks containing a variety of gadgets, plugs and adaptors and bits of wire which I used to bodge up any PA system and to get the sound systems working to a decent level, I usually got by pretty well.

The famous Beacon Theatre on Broadway in New York was a pleasure to do, a 3,000-seater venue built as a cinema in the days of silent movies, it had very good acoustics. Its two balconies and neo-Grecian design is very impressive with Greek god sculptures and paintings on the walls.

After two weeks touring the north-east USA we went south to Houston, Dallas, San Antonio, where I took time out to visit the Alamo, the famous fort where my childhood hero Davy Crockett tried to hold out but eventually lost against the Mexican army. In the 1960s film *The Alamo*, Fort Alamo was in the middle of a desert, which it probably was in Davey Crockett's time in 1836, so I was disappointed to see it overshadowed and dwarfed by skyscrapers and hotels with the Route 37 highway running just across the back of it. It was in the middle of a city so I suppose that's what they call progress.

Carrying on to Austin, New Orleans, Phoenix, Albuquerque, and Tucson we had a day off when the trio did the *Tonight* TV show with Johnny Carson at the NBC TV Studios. Then onto San Diego, San Francisco and Los Angeles where we did two nights at the Beverly Theatre.

In Albuquerque I met this incredibly beautiful lady backstage who in the language of my childhood cowboy films would have been described as a half-breed squaw, but in today's politically correct language would be described as a mixed-race native American Indian. This lady in her mid-teens was dressed in a modern style full traditional Indian costume and was probably the most attractive lady I had ever seen; why she wasn't in the movies I don't know, maybe she was. I instantly fell in love with her but she wasn't interested in me, she was after Al DiMeola, but even he declined to take the bait.

During a day's drive I came across an Indian reservation just out of town and I decided to stop off. I had mixed feelings really, disappointed that this once proud nation of Indians were relegated to living on the fringes of civilisation like gypsies on a travellers' site. They were very poor, some living in trailers, some in traditional teepees and a few wooden shacks. The main part of town (if you can call it that) was dominated with shops selling souvenirs and Indian cultural products like clothing, totem poles and some very fine artwork. The rest of the area was a dumping ground for old abandoned pickup trucks and cars, children ran around barefoot and stallholders lined the street selling a few items to the tourists who came to see how these folk lived. It wasn't my intention to visit here but I saw it as I was passing and have always been interested in Native American culture. Even as a young boy I had always

Guitar Trio tour from left:
Steve Morse (guest), Al DiMeola, John McLaughlin, and Paco DeLucia

Ritz Theatre, New York. Al DiMeola, John McLaughlin, Paco DeLucia

been disgusted by the way the invading Europeans pushed these Indians out of their homelands as if they had the right to do so' maybe I watched too many John Wayne films, whenever the cavalry charged I always rooted for the Indians.

America is so culturally and racially mixed, the new name for American Indians is now Native Americans. One thing that always puzzled me is that it seems the new politically correct term for black Americans is now African-Americans and those from China and Vietnam are Asian-Americans, why is it white settlers are not referred to as European-Americans?

In San Francisco I made contact with my old friends John Draper and Gary Doon from Dr Hook, they showed up at the venue during the afternoon, it was great to see them again and to meet them in a different environment other than a Dr Hook show. They couldn't stay for the show as they had prior commitments but I persuaded them to stay at least for a few numbers before they had to leave.

Then onto Vancouver, Seattle, Salt Lake City, with the last show at the Rainbow Theatre in Denver.

The good thing about this tour was that all the sound and lights were supplied by a local equipment rental company or by the venue itself with their own in-house equipment. Quality varied so much and some were better than others but we did OK.

From here the band had eight days off before doing a show in Hawaii. I said goodbye to Steve Morse and wished him well, Al DiMeola flew on ahead on his own and I travelled with John and Paco. Vance had to fly to New York for a business meeting and I was given the temporary job of tour manager, (that should read babysitter), to take the band on to Hawaii.

We took the flight via Los Angeles to Hawaii for a concert at the Waikiki Bowl just outside Honolulu. Let's make one thing clear, if the itineary says 'Day Off' it doesn't mean you're not working, it just means there's no show.

We booked into the Colony Surf Hotel right on the beach at Diamond Head with the extinct Waikiki volcano overlooking it from the mountain ridge behind; we arrived at night so I didn't see the full view until I woke up the next morning. My room had windows on three sides, one side looked straight up to the extinct volcano overlooking Honolulu, I opened another window facing some palm trees and immediately a white dove landed on the windowsill, the third side faced the beach looking out onto the Pacific Ocean. It was beautiful, just like you imagine a tropical island to be, with palm trees, sea and sunshine. The hotel was right on the beach with its own private sand going down to the sea and a restaurant right on the beach covered with tropical plants and palms. But beware of the restaurant, it has a very strict dress code, John McLaughlin, Paco DeLucia and myself attempted to walk in for a meal the first evening and the waiter ushered us to a wardrobe where we were discreetly 'invited' to try on some dinner jackets. It was a bit of a joke really because although our clothes underneath were not scruffy, they just didn't go with a formal dinner jacket. I didn't enjoy the meal as the jacket was too hot and heavy to wear, I couldn't wait to finish.

The hotel was a short walk to downtown Honolulu. During the day it's a very nice city with some good tourist attractions and souvenir shops, the shops are open all night 24 hours and I made sure I took a wide berth around the hookers hanging around the streets looking for business.

Amazingly within a day John and Paco got bored with their 5-star hotel on the beach, how I don't know, Oahu is such a beautiful island, I guess they'd seen it all before. They decided they wanted to fly to another island where Al was staying, the island of Maui, known to be the playground of the rich and famous. Houses there are millionaire prices and hotels rooms are a year's salary for guys like me, but as I wasn't paying I didn't argue.

We packed our cases and headed to Honolulu Airport to get on a small Cessna propeller plane with just 10 seats. There we took the one-hour flight past Molokai Island landing at Kaanapali in Maui, but not before taking a flypast over some volcanic cliffs and lava flows, amazing waterfalls and tropical rainforests.

The Colony Surf Hotel was nice, but nothing compared to the hotel in Maui; it was like something out of paradise. It was so warm the reception area was open-air and there were tame parrots flying around the hotel reception, which was a bit like being in a jungle. But I wasn't here to have a good time I had to look after the band, although I did have a whale of a time enjoying 5-star luxury.

I didn't realise but John had arranged for a friend to meet us and she gave us a lift from Kaanapali to the hotel. Al Dimeola was already checked into the hotel and lounging on a sunbed with two very attractive girls, oh how the famous live. Although we had a few days off before the show at the end of the week it was no holiday for me, I was about to find out what being a tour manager with these three was all about.

From left. Paco DeLucia, John's friend, Me, John McLaughlin.
Arriving on Maui Island, Hawaii. 1983

Vance was in telephone contact with me from New York and my main objective this week was to get immigration clearance into Australia. Not so hard you might think, the only problem I had was Al, he didn't want to get off his sunbed and go to the embassy for a visa. The office must have got us cleared for admittance as the shows were already sold out but we still needed the visas. An attempt to borrow a Polaroid camera to get some passport-type photos didn't work out as Al was pulling silly faces and not taking the whole thing seriously. In the end Vance called the band and said if the shows were cancelled it would cost them a lot of money in broken contracts. I did eventually get Al and the others on a plane back to Honolulu the day before our show although Al was doing his spoilt brat bit, faking an illness and had to be 'helped' on and off the plane. At the Australian embassy I arranged for a professional photographer to call by and take our visa photos.

The show at the Waikiki Shell in Honolulu was a great night, the sun was just setting over the stage as the band went on and the sunset was breathtaking. After the show we drove straight to the airport for our ten-hour flight to Australia, taking off Friday night travelling across the International Date Line and landing Sunday morning. Saturday just completely disappeared across the dateline, we flew from Friday into Sunday which was weird but I wasn't concerned as I knew I would have two Saturdays when I flew back the other way.

In Australia we performed 3 nights in Sydney, 2 in Melbourne, one each in Adelaide, Brisbane and Sydney and Perth, then back for a second show in Sydney.

In Adelaide I had the pleasure of meeting up with a long-lost cousin I hadn't seen for years and my elderly aunt who I hadn't seen since they left England as a '£10 Pom' in the 1950s, I invited them all to the show which they enjoyed.

(A £10 Pom is a British citizen who signed up to a government scheme which encouraged Britain's to emigrate to Australia, tickets only cost £10, and a Pom is an Australian slang word for a Brit. Hence a '£10 Pom'.)

After this stage of the tour we were supposed to have a break and go on to China, India and other far eastern countries, but boredom in the camp was growing and Al wanted to get back to America to do his own stuff with his own band. He was also under pressure from his record company to finish his new album that he started before the tour. The tour was cut short after Australia and we flew home via LA and New York and on to London, going the long way back across the International Date Line. We took off on Saturday morning and landed in LA on Friday night, a weird experience going back in time. Vance and I then stopped off in New York to take care of some business for a few days, arriving back in London early December.

22

THAT *SPINAL TAP* MOMENT

I've mentioned a few times in this book *Spinal Tap* and those *Spinal Tap* moments, it's worth mentioning here a bit more about that band and the film, especially for those not aware of *Spinal Tap*. When the film *Spinal Tap* initially came out, a lot of people thought it was a real band and the reason for that was it was so close to the real thing it could have been a real band, as a result of that the film found great success as a cult movie.

Spinal Tap the movie is a fake documentary film about a fictional British heavy rock band that make it big and go on to tour America. Take the ten biggest bands in the world, roll them into one and that's *Spinal Tap*, I'm sure the script writers must have been to a few Black Sabbath shows for some inspiration.

Along with a full host of promoters, managers, agents, record company executives, roadies, groupies, wags and hangers-on, those special backstage and behind-the-scenes moments makes it an interesting and entertaining movie, including the scandals, rumours, wives, girlfriends, breakups and arguments that plague every band not just rock bands. They even have a girlfriend who latches on to the lead singer and tries to manage them, ending up playing in the band, sound familiar?

The Stonehenge incident where a life-size replica is supposed to be lowered onto the stage is ruined by a miscalculation when the actual model comes in measuring 18 inches high instead of 18 feet high, this is an exact reversal of Black Sabbath's show piece where a Stonehenge replica was built so big it was too large to fit into the venues; even though it was carted halfway around America in the back of a truck it was only ever used once.

The incident where one of the pods fails to open at the start of the show is a typical malfunction on any tour, you can see roadies struggling to open the pod, smashing it with hammers to release the band member trapped inside. Reminiscent of U2's 40-foot fibreglass shell which failed to open, trapping them inside. Also ELO's flying saucer that got stuck at an angle halfway open at the start of one of their shows. On a tour I did, the drape at the back of the stage failed to unfold when released, the backline roadies were hilariously bashing it with brooms to release it, only succeeding when one of the crew climbed up the lighting tower.

One of the highlights of the film for me was when the guitarist was showing a reporter his new guitar amplifier, proudly explaining that all previous amplifiers had volume controls that only went up to ten on the dial, but this amplifier went up to eleven. Right across the board, eleven, eleven, eleven, therefore in his mind it was that much louder. The reporter quite rightly asks, "Is that louder then, why don't you make ten the top number and make that the loudest number?" The guitarist thinks for a while and says, "But this is one number louder because it goes up to eleven." By this time we had gathered that the guitarist was a bit thick not realising that the numbers on the front panel are just numbers and don't actually go any louder when turned up to maximum.

Interestingly enough before this film was made all volume controls did go up to ten as the maximum number, but Marshall Amplification based in Bletchley were approached by the film-makers and asked to manufacture a special front panel for the film where all the dials went up to eleven; to this day all Marshall amplifiers now go up to eleven.

Even the backstage food has its own sketch reminding me of some disgusting food I've had to sample on tours. As the tour starts, concert appearances are repeatedly cancelled due to low ticket sales and tensions increase when retailers refuse to sell their latest album because of its sexist cover.

As with most bands their popularity eventually dwindles. Where they were once booked into 15,000-seat arenas, on Spinal Tap's current tour they're being booked into 1,200-seat halls, claiming "Our appeal is becoming more selective."

Like a lot of bands I could mention, Spinal Tap also got lost in a labyrinth of backstage corridors, trying to make their way from the dressing room to the stage, including myself, I've often got myself lost backstage.

Spinal Tap may be a fictional band but anyone in the music business can see their own band in the film in one way or another. The characters could easily be a band member of so many bands and what they do is fairly typical of a British rock band making it big in America.

One band member leaves the group in the middle of a show because he is upset by an equipment malfunction. This reminds me of one band I once worked for. Then the guitarist slides a violin against the guitar during a solo in a direct take off of Led Zeppelin guitarist Jimmy Page who uses a violin bow to do the same thing on his guitar. When the members of Spinal Tap talk about their drummer suffocating on vomit, it's a direct reference to a number of musicians who have died, or who are rumoured to have died, the same way, including Jimi Hendrix, Led Zeppelin drummer John Bonham, AC/DC vocalist Bon Scott and Big Band-leader Tommy Dorsey.

It then became a common insult or joke on the road for a band to be told they were 'Worse than Spinal Tap' or 'Funnier than Spinal Tap'. One magazine ranked *Spinal Tap* number 48 on its list of The Greatest Movies of All Time. *Time Out London* named it the best comedy film of all time and it was ranked No 1 on *Entertainment Weekly*'s Top 50 Cult Films.

MIDEM, CANNES

January 1984 started off with a trip down to Cannes in France for the International Midem Festival, a showcase exhibition and music market for the music industry. Cannes Midem is a marketplace where new audio products are launched and music technology shown off. It's a two-way street where European, American and Asian companies can present their products to distributors and potential customers, promote music, make connections, meet people and sign contracts. People come from all over the world. It's the same venue that hosts the Cannes Film Festival each year.

As far as audio products go it's always hard to establish where products actually come from these days. In the old days you knew that Sennheiser was German, Shure was American, Tannoy was English and so on, even with known manufacturers the parts inside could be built or assembled in another country. The same applies to car manufactures, Japanese-owned Nissan and Toyota build cars in England, Indian-owned Land Rover cars are built in China and American Ford builds cars across Europe. This also applies to audio products and probably everything else we see in the shops.

With three days of concerts, conferences and meetings, I was there to mix front of house sound in the main theatre in the Nouveau Palace which had an amazing line-up of international stars there to entertain the public, festival goers and the exhibitors. All the big companies were there, from recording studios, equipment manufacturers and record labels. They had their stalls laid out trying to make sales or promote their products.

Whilst I was there I took some time out to wander around the exhibition arena and saw some familiar faces including Dave Martin from Martin Audio who I talked to for a while mentioning that I was using Martin speakers in the theatre next door.

At this year's event we had Tina Turner, Herbie Hancock, Spandau Ballet, Joan Baez, Paul Young, Bananarama, Van Morrison, Richard Thompson and Break Machine. When I arrived with my team from Concert Sound we had Midas mixers and a Martin speaker PA system supplied by a French sound company which was already set up, which I was happy to use. The mixer was placed on the balcony so I could look down onto the stage and see all that was going on. The show was not actually live although the vocals were live. Each act performed or sang to their own backing track, this is because the whole thing was being recorded for French television and they didn't want to deal with mixing live sound for numerous acts one after the other. Run of the mill stuff for us soundmen but television culture is totally different, and I expect they didn't have the experience or confidence to go for a totally live show. We had just vocal mics and backing tracks to work with, that makes my life easier. The biggest problem I had to deal with was, each backing track came in at different levels, each were equalised differently as well so I had to add or subtract bass or treble just to get them sounding the same.

The shows went pretty well, Tina was happy to see Rory Madden there looking after the monitor mix, Rory always did the monitors for the Tina Turner tours and did so for many years. Herbie Handcock came on and did his latest chart hit 'Rockit', a move from his traditional jazz roots to an electronic dance track popular with the latest break dance craze. This fitted in well with the next act Break Machine who performed another dance track 'Street Dance' with break dancers on the stage, Spandau Ballet and Joan Baez did a song each.

The second day Paul Young was on, my daughter Tamzin aged 14 at the time had a crush on Paul, I managed to get his autograph and gave it to her, which she was thrilled about. Typical of some of her school friends they didn't believe the autograph was real or that her dad worked with Paul Young, but those friends who knew me personally did believe her.

Bananarama I found out were having problems with their manager; although the microphones were not switched on in the PA, they didn't realise I was listening to the stage mics on my headphones and they were giving him some outrageous mouthfuls of bad language you wouldn't expect to hear from four young ladies, I couldn't believe what I was hearing, I should have recorded it.

On the third day Van Morrison, who was the only act on that day, did actually perform totally live, but insisted that the backstage area was cleared between the dressing room and the stage so he didn't have to see anybody on the route. The lighting crew had instructions not to put any lights directly on him. I don't know what his problem was, he hardly spoke to the audience all night and he didn't even speak to his band, he was passing on instructions to the band via his keyboard player, Georgie Fame. Van Morrison is a boring old fart. I don't know anyone who has met him and actually likes him, he may write great music and record some stunning albums but that's where his talent ends, even the musicians I've met who'd worked with him don't have anything nice to say about him.

This reminds me of a story I heard when he headlined a tour with Lindisfarne and Genesis. Whereas some artistes employ a stunt double to divert attention away from the star after a concert, Van Morrison employed someone as a stunt double that didn't look anything like him, the only qualification he had to get the job was he had the same name as the artiste. I'm not sure how that worked.

We had an enjoyable few days and it was time to head back to England. By coincidence I happened to be sitting next to Dave Martin from Martin Audio on the plane back, we had a good chat about music, sound systems, the exhibition and the way the music industry was going. He said he'd had a good exhibition with some good sales making the trip worthwhile. I tried to talk to him about speaker designs but Dave being Dave had too much to drink and was a bit out of his head, that's not unusual for Dave Martin. Halfway into the flight he fell asleep waking up just as we descended into Heathrow.

DR HOOK

Yet another Dr Hook tour and this time John Draper, who had been the band's road manager and FOH soundman since the beginning, wasn't there. He had left the band and got himself a job as road manager for Madonna. He'd even got himself on screen in the Madonna film *In Bed with Madonna.* I was asked if I would step in and do the front of house sound mix, there wasn't anybody else who knew the band as I did. I had sat with John for the last nine tours and knew every song, they offered me a generous payment for mixing each show and this was on top of the fee I was charging for production managing the tour and supplying the sound system. Thirty-seven shows over seven weeks including three nights at Hammersmith Odeon and unusually six nights at Bailey's Night Club in Watford. They must have been offered a big fee to play that venue. The tour was a sell-out again, the band's popularity seemed to be getting bigger on each tour. This time it was a UK-only tour without going into Europe.

I went back to Concert Sound to hire a sound system, I had Rory Madden as my sound tech this time, and he ended up working as monitor engineer for Tina Turner throughout her solo career.

Two days later I was asked to do a show at the Dominion Theatre in London for Paco DeLucia and his band, the Spanish flamenco king. It goes without saying the whole theatre was packed with Spanish fans living in the UK.

DR HOOK – AUSTRALIA

Before the end of the last Dr Hook tour the guitarist Rod Smarr asked me if I wanted to go to Australia with the band for their tour down under. I was under the impression that the job of soundman for that tour was Richie, the American guy who did all their American shows. When I mentioned this to Rod I was told that he preferred that I did the sound and that he could fix it for me. I said I didn't want to put anybody out of a job but I would be willing to do the tour if that's what the band wanted. It turned out that was what the band wanted, so a month later I was on a long-haul flight to Australia via Muscat in Oman and Singapore.

Twenty-seven shows around the coast of Australia, I didn't know there were so many venues in that country. Bands normally do the big cities of Perth, Melbourne, Sydney and Adelaide then fly out again. We started off doing two TV shows, *The Bert Newton Show* and *Hey It's Saturday Night*, a kind of variety show. Then it was on the road, three nights in Melbourne and another TV show, Brisbane, Sydney and Perth and up around the coast doing some really weird locations. An oval cricket ground in Port Hedland, a racecourse in Broome, an amphitheatre in Darwin, a rugby park in Rockhampton, a city park in Townsville, a showground in Toowoomba. Then a few more showgrounds, some conventional nightclubs and theatres around Tweedhead and Adelaide, across the sea to Hobart in Tasmania then back to finish up in Newcastle on the east coast. Strangely enough just like its English namesake, Newcastle is a coal-mining town.

Most of the time we flew between venues because of the distances involved and by tour bus if the venues were close by. The equipment usually went by truck overnight or the backline went as excess baggage on the same flight, sound and lights were supplied locally.

Me backstage at one of the outdoor Australian shows

In the northern towns there were a large number of aboriginal people in the audience. I'm sure they just came along out of curiosity to see what was going on and spent most of the show sitting on the ground huddled around in small groups.

There were some unexpected disasters on the tour. On one of the band's days off whilst Dennis was doing radio station interviews in Darwin a few of the crew and band chartered a 60ft sailing yacht for the day. They went off sailing around the harbour, bays and inlets. Gary Doon was knocked off the deck by the sail as it swung around, breaking his leg; for the rest of the tour he hobbled around on a crutch with his leg in plaster.

The sound and lighting equipment for most of the shows was supplied by Jands, a well-known Australian production company. I got on well with the sound crew and they did a good job, but I didn't get on so well with the Aussie lighting crew. They were a bit full of themselves, loud-mouthed, arrogant and thought they knew it all. Turns out they weren't that smart after all. At one of the outdoor shows I was standing on the stage doing some last-minute checks on the microphones when there was a sudden gust of wind, which blew one of the 20-foot-high lighting towers over. It was like watching something in slow motion, I could see it about to go over, and it was heading straight for the keyboard set-up, a stand with three keyboards on. Without thinking of the implications I ran across the stage and put my arms up to catch the tower with a steel frame of 16 lamps as it came crashing towards me. I don't know how I did it, I managed to catch the tower just inches away from the keyboards, which would have completely demolished the keyboard set-up and put an end to the show. I was struggling to hold the weight when two of Hook's road crew rushed over and took some of the weight while another helped push the tower up again. After that the band couldn't thank me enough for saving the day and Billy's keyboards.

I had a right go at the lighting crew for being a bunch of incompetent idiots for allowing a lighting tower to be unsecured and not tied down to the stage with such high winds about, they ate humble pie for the rest of the tour and kept out of my way. Just as well.

I also managed to meet up with another long-lost cousin from England I hadn't seen for over thirty years, he had emigrated with his family and started a new life there like so many other Poms.

JOHN McLAUGHLIN & PACO DELUCIA

Back in England I did a show with the Mahavishnu Orchestra at Hammersmith Odeon, great to see the guitarist John McLaughlin again and a pleasure to be working with him in this venue once again.

An unusual gig next was a trip to Tel Aviv in Israel for two shows with Paco DeLucia at the Israeli Jazz Festival. One show at the Mann Auditorium in Tel Aviv, home of the Israel Philharmonic Orchestra, and a concert the following day in the Hassenfeld Amphitheatre in King Sultan's Pool in Jerusalem. An 8,000-capacity outdoor venue, this was a magnificent setting, a valley just below the walls of the old city of Jerusalem, a biblical site, across from the tomb of King David and the Church of the Last Supper. On the way to Jerusalem the tour bus stopped in Bethlehem and we visited the church that is said to have been built at the spot where the stable was when Jesus was born, I couldn't see any trace of a stable so I have to take their word for it, but it was a memorable experience all the same. It's a shame the site has turned into a tourist area with advertising boards and tacky souvenir shops.

I flew out from Heathrow with Barrie Marshall from Marshall Arts, while the band flew from Madrid. At Tel Aviv airport we were met by Nitza Danieli, a representative from the local promoter, who became my personal tour guide throughout the weekend, showing me around the sights of Tel Aviv and Jerusalem. It's such a great country and the weather was beautiful, warm and sunny. A trip I will never forget.

Also on the bill were BB King, Freddy Hubbard and Brazilian artiste Tania Maria, I was looking forward to seeing Tania as I was a big fan.

Paco had his Spanish band with him, a six-piece including three of his brothers, all playing Spanish acoustic guitars with congas, percussion, flute and saxophone. Of course Paco was the band leader and the others just accompanied him with rhythm and handclaps. This was a bit different from the Guitar Trio gigs I had done. At the Hilton Hotel where we were staying, they had some other jazz festival events going on in the King Solomon room with other artists, which was like having an after-show party which went on quite late.

WHAM & STYLE COUNCIL

In September I got a call from another sound company, Lindsey Audio, who asked me to do a show at the Royal Festival Hall in London, a benefit in aid of the miners' families. Amongst the people who came on stage was Arthur Scargill, leader of the National Union of Mineworkers, who gave a speech to the audience criticising the government. The audience were not interested, some yawned, one heckled, "Nice tan, Arthur," another heckled, "Enjoy your holiday Arthur?" Others booed him off, the audience were only there for the music and the main act was Wham supported by The Style Council. I don't believe you should mix music and politics. The Style Council did a great set and sounded good.

Whilst the stage crew were changing over the set for Wham, their soundman turned on his backing track to check the tape was working, unknown to him I had the channel switched on, which meant that the whole audience got a two-second clip of Wham's opening song. Once he realised his mistake he muted the channel but it was too late, the crowd heard it and erupted, realising that the band were going to use a backing track. George Michael came on, did the first song and apologised to the audience but it was always going to be obvious that the band were not playing live. The vocals were live but even they were singing on top of a recorded vocal track.

TOM ROBINSON

After the Wham show the same sound company, Lindsey Audio, asked if I would do a tour with Tom Robinson, known for his hits '2468 Motorway', 'Glad To Be Gay' and 'War Baby'. I had a tour lined up with Shirley Bassey so I said I'd do the first four shows to help them out until they could get someone else in. I knew Tom Robinson from previous shows but the organisation of the tour was terrible and I was not sad the leave them early. Utter chaos is the term I'd use, the hotels were cheap and there was no food supplied to the crew, but as the tour was organised by Asgard Agency that's no surprise, they were not known for efficient planning or spending money.

SHIRLEY BASSEY

I had the pleasure of working on my first Shirley Bassey tour, not mixing this time but working on the sound crew setting up the speakers, stage equipment and looking after the microphones for a 32-piece orchestra. Quite a challenge putting the mics in place, especially as there was not a lot of room to move in between the musicians squeezed into some small stages and at the same time trying not to knock over an expensive violin or tuba.

Across the back of the stage on risers we had on stage left four trumpets, four trombones and five woodwind, in the centre we had a drum kit with seven mics and a percussion section which included vibes, timpanis and assorted toys which percussionists like to play with, stage right we had eight violins, two violas and two cellos, on the stage floor in front we had an electric piano and a grand piano, bass guitar, lead guitar and the conductor. Shirley had the rest of the stage in front to herself. A total of fifty-eight microphones in all.

Load-in was at 8am every day and we had to be ready by 2pm for the piano tuner who arrived to tune the grand piano which was supplied by the venue, we didn't carry our own piano on this tour although I have toured with a grand piano in the past with Pat Metheny complete with flight case. Sound check was at 4pm, crew meal was at 6pm, show time at 8pm.

We also had a lot of posh gits in the touring personnel apart from the technical crew, we had a secretary, hairdresser, limousine chauffer, baggage van driver and a tour executive, whatever the hell he did I don't know as we already had a tour manager. Eleven technical crew, two truck drivers and two caterers. I had the pleasure of working with Peter Grainger and Rory Madden from Concert Sound again. At this stage we were still using the traditional Martin speaker stack and whenever possible flying the speakers on a scaffolding cradle hoisted up by electric motors.

Rehearsals started in Dublin at the RDS Hall, the same day as the first show. A further ten shows followed, ending up doing three nights at the Royal Albert Hall, always a pleasure working at the Albert even if it is a pain loading in and rigging the speakers. I flew three cradles in the air, a small speaker stack on stage and a stereo stack up in the gods near the follow spots, a lot of cable runs were required and a long day rigging.

The shows were as spectacular as you would expect from Shirley Bassey. Shirley did a costume change every 4 songs and it was usually impossible for her to get to the dressing room to change, as they were generally too far away from the stage for her to be able to do a quick change and be back on stage for the next song. So a black-curtained quick-change area was constructed back stage or in the wings, wherever the crew could find room to erect it. Shirley was promoting her new album 'I Am What I Am', which had been recorded a few weeks earlier at Olympic Studios. Her show of course included all her big hits, 'Big Spender', 'Goldfinger' and 'Diamonds are Forever' etc. Although we were told by management not to talk to her unless she addressed you first, she was alright backstage and she didn't mind having a chat with the crew. The management told us not to call her Shirl, so we would call her Shirl just to wind up the management, as we knew that really annoyed them, I'm sure it didn't bother Dame Shirley.

LINDISFARNE

In November I was back on the road with Lindisfarne, using a sound system that I'd hired from Soundplant in London. I don't believe they are still in business but I was happy with the equipment they supplied. Lindisfarne started off as a folk group but don't be deceived by their wishy-washy records that were under-produced, their live shows rocked and they could give any well-known rock band a run for their money. If in doubt I suggest you check out one of the Lindisfarne live shows on 'YouTube'. I needed a system that would deliver the SPL (sound pressure levels) required for large halls and theatres whilst delivering a quality sound for the more subtle tracks and vocal harmonies. This tour was short by comparison to other Lindisfarne tours, mainly because they didn't have a new album to promote but they still had eight albums to take tracks from. Twenty-eight shows over thirty-one days including eleven shows at Newcastle City Hall, home of the Geordie band.

Another difference this time was the addition of a sixth member to the band with ex-Harcourt Heroes saxophone and flute player Marty Craggs. Marty also had a great singing voice adding another dimension to the harmonies. Another great Christmas set of shows. A time in my life that I'll never forget and a memorable venue that's probably got one of the best crowd atmospheres in the country.

At Hammersmith Odeon I was approached by Queen's drummer Roger Taylor, he told me he was impressed by the drum sound and wanted to know what mics I used on the cymbals. I told him I was using AKG C451 microphones, he wrote the number down and thanked me. I have no doubt that Queen's engineer was already familiar with this mic, but it was nice of him to compliment me on the drum sound, I thought it sounded pretty good myself.

During the show on 11th December in Portsmouth at the Guildhall, Barry McKay caught the band's bus driver drinking from the dressing room bar and quite rightly sacked him on the spot, as he was in no state to drive a bus. Barry phoned Berryhurst Coaches and asked for a replacement driver. This couldn't have come at a worse time for Berryhurst, as that very same night another Berryhurst driver crashed his bus after leaving Newcastle carrying Bucks Fizz and their band. The driver was involved in a collision with a lorry throwing Mike Nolan and Cheryl Baker through the windscreen almost killing the two of them and injuring other members of the band.

Once again I was given a cassette tape of organ music recorded from the actual pipe organ at Newcastle City Hall, the organ music of Christmas songs and carols were played to get the audience into the Christmas mood. I was instructed to play the music at a high volume whilst the audience walked in and during the interval. At the end of the show I played John Lennon's 'So This Is Christmas' over the PA whilst the audience left the hall, this was traditional for all the years I did Lindisfarne Christmas shows.

23

BEHIND THE IRON CURTAIN

PAT METHENY GROUP

After touring with the Guitar Trio, Vance Anderson, the tour manager who I was getting on with really well, asked if I wanted the job of production manager for a tour with The Pat Metheny Group. Pat Metheny was an American jazz guitarist; I seemed to be falling into a jazz circle with the last few acts I'd been working with, I like some types of jazz but didn't see my career going in that direction. For one thing, you can easily get categorised into a certain genre or linked to certain types of artistes and then not selected for others, whereas I wanted to be more flexible and work with various artistes of different styles. I didn't always get to choose who I worked with, and if the chance of work was offered to me then I'd be a fool to turn it down. The opportunity of working with Vance again was good enough for me and becoming production manager was a good gig and a good direction to go in.

The group was called The Pat Metheny Group rather than just Pat Metheny, even though Pat was the star and the main man. The band comprised five musicians, Lyle Mays on keyboards who insisted he was part of the PM 'group' rather than just a backing musician for Pat, Steve Rodby on bass, Paul Wertico on drums and Pedro Aznar on vocals and percussion. When I say vocals I mean he just did vocal accompaniment in a jazz style as there weren't many actual vocals on the instrumental tracks. It was also the first time I'd taken a concert grand piano on tour, it's remarkable how easily it takes apart and fits inside a flight case and how easy it is to reassemble the next day.

Concert Sound supplied the sound equipment and Vance was mixing FOH, Paul Boothroyd (aka Pab) was his assistant on the PA crew, he was a good guy. The lighting crew Eddie and Jeff were part of Pat's American crew and the rest of the backline road crew were all Pat's own crew from America. It was their first time outside of America and boy did it show, these guys were the most unusual bunch I've ever come across, culturally ignorant and totally unaware of anything outside of America.

David Oakes was their monitor engineer and electronics wizard, Leo the guitar tech was a young lad of about 17. I don't think he'd ever left his one-horse town before working with Pat. He seemed to think that America was the centre of the universe, he was in for a huge cultural shock to find there was life outside America. He eventually married Vance's daughter, how that happened I'll never know.

Niki was the only female on the crew and she had her work cut out looking after Pat Metheny's computers, which seemed to be breaking down every day; she was good at her job but she wasn't the most sociable member of the crew. Pat's guitars went through a computer network of effects which was way ahead of its time, hooked up by MIDI (Musical Instrument Digital Interface). Unfortunately the computers of 1985 were not as reliable or robust as they are today, each one had to be shipped around in a double flight case lined with foam. Niki was spending most of her time changing PCB boards and fixing them, she also had a spare computer on standby just in case one of the others packed up.

Pat programmed the computers himself with a range of sampled instruments, so he could play his guitar and what came out would be literally any instrument he wanted. That enabled him to do duets with a keyboard or a saxophone and you wouldn't know who was playing what, confusing sometimes.

On our first meeting with the crew, Vance was driving a 15-seater minibus. We picked them up at Heathrow Airport and drove them to Coventry for a few days' rehearsal. I told the crew we would travel through five cultural regions on this tour. Vance joked that he thought I was talking about the route between London and Coventry. What I actually meant was the UK, Anglo-Saxon Northern Europe, Nordic Scandinavia, Communist Eastern Europe and Latin Southern Europe, five very different cultural areas.

Pat's stage manager asked for a drum riser. Vance asked me if I could build him one, which of course I could and I did. Whilst the band were rehearsing I popped around to the local DIY store, picked up some timber, sheet ply, wood glue and screws, everyone was pleased with the result and it was put on the truck for its first gig in Sweden. On arrival in Sweden the drum roadie decided it was too small and dumped it backstage where it was left and we didn't use it again. He'd made a mistake with the measurements. I still had the drawing that was given to me so I could show him that I had built it to the size they'd requested. So that was a waste of time and money, the timber probably came from Scandinavia originally anyway, so it was now back where it came from.

As well as being production manager and looking after the stage, I also had to look after the dressing rooms, the front of house foyer and manage the security staff. One of the items requested on the rider was a bucket of ice for Pat's Coca-Cola, he wanted this in his dressing room, but in Porsgrunn in Norway no ice showed up. I asked the promoter for the ice and he said he couldn't get any, I said to him, "How can you not have any ice in a country like Norway?" There was a mountain of snow outside, so I said, "If you can't get any ice then shovel some snow into a bucket, Pat will not be happy if his cola is warm."

At one show I held the doors closed until all the security staff were in their allocated positions, much to the annoyance of a noisy crowd trying to force the doors open. The road crew were a bunch of wimps and needed a babysitter rather than a production manager, always whingeing about something. I kept telling them, "This is Europe, get used to it or get over it."

After the show in Stuttgart, West Germany, we headed for the border crossing into Communist East Germany on our way to Poland. The scene was something out of a spy movie, we proceeded through the checkpoint of West Germany and slowly drove up to the East German checkpoint, it was dark, cold and misty, with a damp fog hanging in the air and the orange fluorescent street lights made the fog look murky. The crew bus drove through a gate into an area set aside for coaches which had fifteen-foot-high fences with barbed wire on top. Ahead was a similar sized gate which was closed. As we approached the gate in front of us, the gate behind us closed, locking us in. Normally I would have taken the sixteen passports into the checkpoint to get them stamped, but there was nowhere for me to go. We waited and waited until an East German border guard walked over and came on board, he asked for the passports, took a look around the bus and disappeared with the passports into a dimly lit office behind the fence. I guess they liked to play games with us just because they could, and it amused them to know they could hold up a British bus full of Americans.

After an hour we were eventually allowed to proceed ahead into East Germany en route to Poland. By this time it was starting to get light and Leo looked on in wonder and disgust, mumbling, "So this is where the Communists live." He didn't understand, I tried to explain that not everyone in East Germany was a Communist just as not everyone in America is Republican. The World War II occupying powers of Russia still controlled the eastern side of the country and only allowed the Communist party to take part in elections, all other parties were banned and anyone who protested against Communism was arrested, jailed or sent to a Russian gulag in Siberia.

The country was desolate, grim and grey, it hadn't changed in forty years since the end of the war, looking just like a scene from a World War II movie. No neon signs, no advertising boards, no shopfronts, there was no point in advertising anything as everything was supplied and sold by the government in government-controlled shops, the government set the prices including everyone's wages, there was no free trade so no need for advertising.

We did four shows in Poland to huge venues including the famous Volk Hall in Wroclaw, a monstrously huge building built by a Prussian king and originally part of Greater Germany before the war. It was used by Hitler for some of his Nazi rallies and had some interesting architecture. Then onto Katowice, Warsaw and Krakow. The Polish crowds were very receptive to Pat's music as they didn't get to hear much live music from a Western artiste.

From Poland we went through Czechoslovakia into Hungary. On the checkpoint leaving Poland into Czechoslovakia we were held up at the border. I was asked to come into the office where the border police spent an hour going through each passport and making telephone calls. They were either checking our identity or the men had never seen British and American passports before. Outside sat two Russian soldiers armed with semi-automatic machine guns, they occasionally came in and looked at me like I was a freak. I politely smiled and tried to look calm. When they eventually let us go I was stunned at the beautiful countryside driving through the Slovakian mountains and the Low Tatrus National Park that again had been untouched since the Second World War. I guess it's all changed since these countries have now joined the European Union. We played Budapest Congress Hall in Hungary before crossing into Austria and Western Europe.

I hadn't been feeling too well for a few days, ten days in fact since we'd crossed over into Eastern Europe. I put it down to the water or the food or the unsanitary conditions backstage. At the last gig in Vienna, Austria, I had incredible stomach pains and had to lie down during the show backstage and try to hide my pain during the load-out. We then had an overnight drive 220 miles to Graz in Austria. When we reached the hotel I walked into the room and collapsed onto the bed, I was in so much pain I couldn't move. Pab saw what was happening and called a doctor, the next thing I remember was waking up in hospital with tubes coming out of my arms and a doctor telling me I had nearly died due to my appendix which nearly burst inside me. By this time the band had done the show in Graz.

The next day Vance came by and left me my suitcase and apologised for leaving me, as the tour bus had to move on to the next town, Innsbruck. I was in hospital for a week surviving on nothing but black tea left for me in a flask, and only having solid food on the sixth day, scrambled egg on toast. That was the best egg on toast I ever had. On being discharged I spent another two days in a hotel before I had the strength to walk again and be able to carry my suitcase to the taxi which took me to the airport. I have to say, Barrie Marshall's office were brilliant, they set up everything for me at the hospital, the hotel and arranged my flight home. Vance had to get another production manager out to cover for me as I was in no state to continue working, not for a week or two anyway.

I spent the next couple of weeks at home recovering. When the tour arrived for the London show I went down to Hammersmith Odeon as I needed to collect some belongings I had left on the bus and was disgusted to find that everything, including presents I'd bought for my children, had been taken, moved, lost or stolen, take your pick. Vance didn't know what to say about my missing items, he wasn't on the crew bus so he didn't have any knowledge of what had happened to my items. The tour only had a few dates left and I knew I didn't want to continue on tour with that crew.

Based on what the hospital doctors told me it's fair to say Pab probably saved my life that night.

DR HOOK FAREWELL TOUR

Dr Hook did a 36-date tour around the UK for what was billed as their 'Farewell Tour'. The band had decided to fire their manager Ron Haffkine and go it alone after a number of fall outs, mainly to do with money or rather the lack of it. Haffkine said that if the band wanted to get out of their contract it would cost them a million dollars, an off-the-cuff remark which the band accepted, meaning that they had to work to pay off the money owed to Haffkine. Luckily Haffkine didn't come on tour this time and the Hook road crew made up some amusing T-shirts with a 'Haffkine Prohibited' road sign logo on the front.

I was production manager and mixing FOH again so I used Concert Sound for the PA and Supermick for the lights, Eurotrux for the trucking, Len Wright for the crew bus and Starcruiser for the band bus.

Paul Boothroyd (or Pab as he became known) was fairly new to Concert Sound. After working with him on Pat Metheny I asked him to come on this tour and gave him some more advice on rigging sound. I must have done a good job as he eventually ended up as the soundman for Paul McCartney for a number of years and still is to this present day.

The first three nights were at the Birmingham Night Out nightclub. The unusual thing about this venue is that they have their own Martin PA system but you have to supply your own FOH and monitor mixers. There must be some money in nightclub residencies as we went on to do Lakeside Country Club and four nights at Watford Baileys, unusual venues for a band who had sold out two nights at Wembley Arena in 1982. We also did two nights at Hammersmith Odeon, the rest of the tour was the usual theatres, cinemas and city halls: Ipswich, St Austell, Oxford, Portsmouth, Brighton, Birmingham, Preston, Sheffield, Edinburgh, Aberdeen, Glasgow, Newcastle, Halifax, Harrogate, Liverpool, Hammersmith, Bristol, Manchester, and Leicester.

So for the last of the many Dr Hook tours, I was saying farewell to a band and their crew that I'd worked with since 1974. The band had a few personnel changes along the way: Ray Sawyer, the guy with the eye patch, left in 1983, George Cummings the slide guitarist left in 1975, instead we had new guitarists Rodney Smarr, and guitarist Leonard Wolf, who briefly joined the band before getting sacked for bad-mouthing one of the crew. Some original members were still there, Dennis Locorriere the unmistakable voice of the band's hits, Rik Elswit on guitar, Jance Garfat on bass, Bill Francis on keyboards and John Wolters on drums.

The road crew I was especially going to miss, Nineyear Wooldridge the tour manager from the start went on to tour manage country singer Nancy Griffiths, you could always pick Nineyear out of a crowd as he often wore an American football shirt with a number 9 on it. My old Limey Sound comrade

Gary Doon went on to work on video projection for Madonna and Janet Jackson. Backline crew Rodney Groth I saw again working for saxophonist Kenny G when he did a TV show with me at Tyne Tees Television. Richard Davies became production manager for U2, Mark Smith I didn't hear of again and Steven (Brutus) Schwartz the lighting designer I never heard of again either.

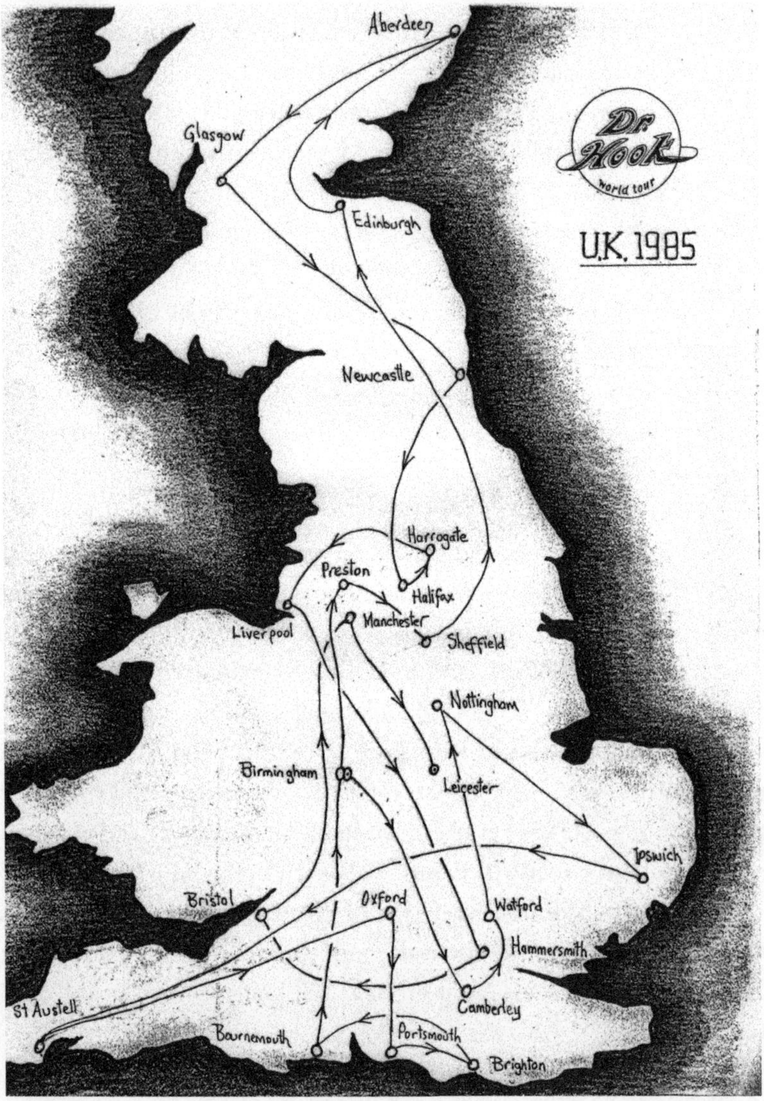

A routing map for the Dr Hook Farewell Tour. 1985

JASON & THE SCORCHERS

As soon as I got back from Dr Hook I was asked to fly straight out to Helsinki in Finland to do FOH sound for an American act from Nashville who could only be described as a cross between country and western and punk. To look at them on stage you would think they were a country hoedown hillbilly dance band, they were wearing typical cowboy outfits, ten gallon hats, big boots and tasselled jackets. But to hear them on stage you might mistake them for the Sex Pistols. They basically took old country standards and 'punked them up'.

When I arrived I went straight to the hotel where the band was staying and was met by their road manager, he explained to me that the band was not happy with the sound they were getting and wanted a replacement soundman. I was then taken down to the gig where they were performing but the soundman who was working for the band hadn't yet been told that he was going home tomorrow. I felt sorry for him as I was standing behind him, he didn't even know that I would be taking over doing the sound tomorrow.

I could understand why the band were not happy, it did sound pretty awful, I also knew I had a job on my hands to make it sound any better. After the gig he was told he would be flying back home to America and the band already had a replacement, I didn't make contact with him, I thought it best not to embarrass him any more than necessary.

Using only the band's backline equipment, the band, crew and equipment all fitted into a tour bus with the backline going in the boot. The sound was supplied by local companies so it was a small, low-budget tour but a lot of fun and I got on really well with the band. They seemed happy with what I was doing and even complimented me on some of the shows I had recorded onto cassette tape.

It was on this tour whilst at an outdoor festival that I detected a loudspeaker out of phase on one of the PA stacks. When I told the local sound tech guy that one of his bass bins was out of phase, he laughed at me and poo-pooed the remark saying, "You can't hear a speaker out of phase." I walked the 50 metres down to the stage, put my head into each cabinet until I found what I thought was the offending speaker. I pulled the plug out and instantly the bass volume increased. This proved I was right; then by using my own reverse phase adaptor which I always carried with me, I re-plugged the speaker and the bass sound increased even more.

What some people don't understand is that loud peaker phasing is so critical to correct alignment of sound, it's not like plugging in an extra light bulb and doubling the amount of light. If you have two speakers, one pushing the sound out forwards and another pushing the sound out backwards, the two will cancel each other out reducing the volume as they are fighting against each other. Having both speakers pushing in the same direction you get double the sound plus more. The local sound tech had to agree I was right and conceded that one can actually 'hear' a loudspeaker that is wired in reverse (out of phase).

The band had already done 14 shows and I picked up the tour in Helsinki, Finland, travelling on to Virrat, Saarijorvi, Valkeakoski in Finland, Stockholm, Uppsala, Malmo in Sweden and the Roskilde Festival in Denmark where we had a 7.30pm slot on the festival list just before The Cure who went on headlining at 10pm. We went on with no soundcheck, but that was no problem for me, I knew the Roskilde stage well. Also on the bill for the other two nights were The Clash and The Ramones. Roskilde Festival I knew well having supplied the sound system for the festival for three years whilst working for Colac. This year the sound was again supplied by Entec, which was great as I knew most of the crew.

Roskilde, which is on a 200-acre site, has grown somewhat. In 1972 when it started out it had 15,000 people, this year it had 70,000. Then we headed onto Osnabruck in Germany, Gent in Belgium, Brighton, Leeds and finally the Electric Ballroom in Camden High Street, London. Luckily I knew the sound company putting the equipment in for that show, I pulled a few favours and got them to add a bit more gear and I also got some extra effects thrown in which they wouldn't normally have done for that venue.

Jason and the Scorchers were a basic four-piece, two guitars, bass and drums. Also on the bus was a tour manager, three backline crew and me. I got on well with Kevin Jennings, one of the backline crew, he invited me to come back to the States and work with him with another band he had connections with, The Georgia Satellites. As much as I liked him I didn't want to go to Georgia to work with a band I hadn't heard of, but the following year I did get to hear about them big time when their single 'Keep Your Hands To Yourself' reached No 2 in the US and No 69 in the UK.

ADAM ANT

Next I did a one-off television special for ITV Southern Television at their studios in Maidstone featuring Adam Ant who performed a couple of songs. As he arrived in normal clothes I didn't recognise him, he looked a lot older than he did on TV. Once on stage with his well-known make-up style he looked quite different and a friendly bloke he turned out to be.

JOHN MCLAUGHLIN

I just happened to walk into Marshall Arts office to sort out some paperwork for the previous Scorchers tour when Barrie Marshall saw me. Straight away he asked, "What are you doing on Friday?" I said, "Nothing so far," "Right can you do a gig with John McLaughlin at the Royal Festival Hall?" So I had the pleasure of working with John McLaughlin again mixing his sound, this time with his friend the bass player Jonas Hellborg from Sweden, a great show.

MAHAVISHNU ORCHESTRA

Through Barrie Marshall's office John McLaughlin asked me to do an American tour with his band The Mahavishnu Orchestra, an electric jazz-fusion rock band, quite different to his acoustic guitar style. The band consisted of John on guitars, Jonas Hellborg on bass, Danny Gottlieb on drums, Mitch Forman on keyboards and Bill Evans on saxophones. I was mixing front of house sound again. As the band was an instrumental outfit it didn't need any vocal mics and mixing sound on this tour I managed to produce the best live sound I ever got from any band at any time.

During a week of rehearsals at The Backline Studios in New York I convinced the bass player Jonas Hellborg to dump the bass stack in favour of a DI Box (Direct Injection box) plugged into the main PA. I fed him a signal back through his monitors, he liked it very much and told me it was the best bass sound he'd ever had and would use this technique again. I'd used this technique before so I knew what the advantages were, for a start I didn't have a bass stack chucking out loads of unwanted bass frequencies from the stage and second it saved transporting extra equipment around.

My old friend from Marshall Arts, David Green, was our tour manager and has the ability to speak several languages. I once called into the office to see David and while I was there sitting at his desk, he was asking me questions in English, whilst at the same time speaking to a promoter in Italian into a phone with his left ear and to a promoter in Spanish with his right ear, we were having a three-way conversation in three languages. The man looking after the backline was PJ from England, he once joked that it was the first time he had worked with a band that didn't wear make-up. I replied that I had never worked with a band that wore make-up. That shut him up.

The first show at The Rainbow Music Hall in Denver actually had a decent PA system surprisingly and happened to be on my birthday. Ot was a totally brilliant show, a 1,300-seater theatre, the acoustics in the room were perfect, the band played well and the sound mix was one of the best on the whole tour. I'm glad I took the trouble to record the show and now have it on CD, easily as good as a live album, one that I'm proud of and still listen to today.

After a few shows I had accepted the fact that the PA specifications I'd asked for I was rarely going to get. Some venues had in-built sound systems and others hired in a system from a local sound rental company, it's a case of turn up and do the best with the equipment that's given to you. Usually in clubs and theatres the venue will have a system already installed, the sound tech guy who works there has lost interest long ago because the venue will not put any money into updating or even repairing broken parts. The usual problems to face would be a microphone channel that doesn't work or a speaker on one side that has blown and they don't have a replacement, the effects units you've asked for aren't available so you have to make do with what they've got. I do pride myself with the ability to get the best sound out of a rubbish sound system by tweaking it here and there, sometimes doing things without the house tech knowing what I've done. The specs I asked for were not a lot, all I wanted apart from a 24-channel mixer was a 27-band stereo graphic equaliser, a Lexicon reverb unit, a Roland digital delay and BSS or dbX stereo compressors. Not a lot to ask for but I very rarely got those. Sound systems from hire companies were generally better than venue-installed systems as they looked after their equipment.

We flew to San Francisco, Palo Alto and San Diego then onto the famous Hollywood Bowl in Los Angeles, a 17,000-seater outdoor amphitheatre. The mixing position seemed like a mile away from the stage and seemed even further when making the hike up and down the concrete steps. The local sound crew were having problems getting the system working, they couldn't get any of the microphone channels to come up on the mixer. I told them it must be a multicore cable problem and it was, after about an hour they finally sorted it. The show started with the sun setting behind the stage, it was an amazing California sunset. It was a warm evening and the audience looked like a crowd from the celebrity world who were more interested in drinking their cocktails and ordering top-ups from the walk-around waitresses than watching the show.

Also on the bill was Lee Ritenour who was a brilliant guitarist and a young guy called Stanley Jordan who came into the dressing room with a guitar case and wanted to show John McLaughlin his guitar style. He took out his guitar and started to play, it was an unusual two-handed tapping technique I'd never seen before, where his left hand was over the neck instead of under it. Back then I thought he was weird to play like that, but he is now a very well-known and successful jazz musician.

We then flew to New York and spent a week in the Bottom Line Club, it was very small but it had a great sound. The promoter hired in a system from a local sound company that delivered what I wanted and what a difference, the sound I got was great and as a result I received a lot of compliments after the shows.

On August 20th I had a night off so I stopped off at The Blue Note Jazz Club on West 3rd Street to see Dizzy Gillespie, one of the greatest jazz trumpet players. It was a privilege to see him in the flesh playing live and in the most famous jazz club in the world, it was one of those nights to remember and one of the last shows he did before he died.

The world famous Newport Jazz Festival was next with Spyro Gyra and Freddie Hubbard on the bill, the following day was BB King, Sarah Vaughn and Stevie Ray Vaughan. This is where experience comes in, no soundcheck just a line check through your headphones to make sure you've got all the microphones working, you're on a sound mixer you've never seen before, in front of thousands of people who expect the band to sound like their album. As soon as the band starts playing it has to be right, or at least within the first 30 seconds, after that you can relax a little and enjoy the show. The festival site is set in an old colonial fort built in the 18th century on the coast with beautiful views out to sea.

In Cleveland we did the Front Row Theatre, a 3,200-seater venue where the union crew played havoc, gigging in America is really frustrating sometimes compared to the UK or Europe due to the fact most large venues are run by unions and they control everything. The job of unions is to make your day as difficult as possible (because they can), they have been around a lot longer than rock and roll groups.

You cannot unload or move any of your own equipment, run your own cables, take amplifiers out of cases or place speaker cabinets on stage where you want them, you have to 'direct' the crew where you want your stage equipment to go. You are not allowed to go onto the stage unsupervised or when there is a union rest break, failure to comply with these rules risks a walk out and having the whole show cancelled. Having said that I found most union crews helpful, but only if they are into the band you're working for. Officially they won't let you mix the sound or control the lights, you have to relay messages to the union sound and lighting guys. By the time you've given them the instructions it's usually too late and you have to move on to the next instruction and hope they react faster next time.

When I reached the Front Row Theatre I reversed the van up to the stage loading door. The stage crew introduced themselves and promptly stopped me from unloading the equipment from my van, telling me, "This is a union building and you can't do unloading, the unloading crew did that." I said, "OK, can you unload it then?" They said, "No, we are the stage crew, we only take it from the stage and set it up." "Where's the loading crew then?" I asked, "They are not here yet, they'll be along shortly." I waited until the unloading crew arrived to unload the equipment from my van and carry it to the stage, where the stage crew took it and placed it where I asked them to, they unpacked the cases and set up the equipment, I waited until they had gone for their break and I went onto the stage and moved it around a bit.

The union soundman in the Front Row admitted that he wasn't up to mixing the band's sound and gracefully stood aside while I did the mix, with him looking over my shoulder in case his boss was watching, I didn't mind that as he was really into the band and was enjoying the music.

Next we travelled to Detroit and Chicago. At the end of the tour John McLaughlin insisted I make myself available for the European leg of the tour which I said I would do.

PACO DELUCIA

September brought me back with Paco DeLucia and his six-piece Spanish flamenco band. Three Spanish guitars, a Spanish acoustic bass guitar, percussion, flute and sax and Juan who was listed as a 'dancer', though he didn't really do much dancing. Dave Catlin from Concert Sound did the monitor mix again. After loading the truck at the warehouse in Watford we flew from Heathrow to Geneva to pick up the band who had just flown from their homes in Spain. On this tour we rented a BMW hire car which we picked up at the airport.

Here we did five shows in Switzerland. The overnight drive from Frankfurt to Berlin was memorable. I felt sorry for the East Germans on the Berlin autobahn linking West Germany with West Berlin, they were trundling along in their little Trabant cars belching out black smoke with West German Mercedes and BMWs flying past doing 100+km/h. I often wondered what they thought. As we approached the West Berlin checkpoint via the East German corridor I saw a Russian tank up on a column as a reminder of the Russian conquest of Eastern Germany in 1945. The track that came on the radio was Elton John's 'Nikita', a song about a girl who longed to be with her lover but was separated by the Berlin Wall which the Russians had erected in 1961. It was an eerie feeling listening to that song just as the border guard was checking our passports, I found the words to that song very moving.

We did five shows in Switzerland, one in Holland, seventeen in Germany, I'd done twenty-three dates into the ten-week tour when I was having problems with one of Paco's brothers Pepe, who didn't seem to like me for some reason. Another problem was that Paco right from the start wanted his favourite tour manager and soundman Vance Anderson, who wasn't available at the time as he was out doing a tour with someone else. I know that he was hassling Barrie Marshall to get Vance off his other tour but Barrie said no and Vance didn't want to do it. The last few days in Germany Paco kept saying that he wasn't happy with the sound, "Not enough treble on the bass," he said in his broken English, whatever that was supposed to mean. I heard from the tour manager he was telephoning Barrie Marshall in England to get Vance, so Barrie Marshall and David Green from the office both flew out to Berlin to see for themselves what the problem was. They both sat behind me at the sound mixer during the show and both said the sound quality was exceptionally good, they told me I had nothing to worry about and Paco was just making mischief, which really pleased me but upset Paco as he now had no excuse to replace me. Dave would take the mick out of Paco by saying, "Wilf, more treble on the bass."

However three days later after a drive from Kiel for a day off in Copenhagen I had a telephone call at the hotel to say I was coming home and was being replaced by Jeff Hooper, another one of Concert Sound's engineers. He wasn't Vance but Paco was having a strop because he couldn't get Vance. Paco tried to apologise to me saying it wasn't personal, but I felt it was personal because I wasn't doing anything wrong nor was I doing a bad sound. That ended my relationship with Paco. I never saw him again.

As I headed home I was looking forward to doing the next Mahavishnu tour in Europe, so I was disappointed to find that after a series of phone calls to Barrie Marshall's office, Barrie didn't return my calls.

Barrie Marshall in typical Barrie style just took off without me, he didn't even have the decency to say he was using someone else. That someone else was my old mate Pab. Despite repeated calls to Barrie's office I was told he would call me back but he never did, I even spoke to his lovely wife Jenny who couldn't apologise enough for her husband's behaviour and said she would definitely get him to call me. He didn't. I guess he was too embarrassed or didn't have the nerve to speak to me. I wouldn't have minded if I'd done a bad job last time, but I didn't. John McLaughlin said he wanted me to do the next European tour so it had nothing to do with my ability to get a good sound. It might have had something to do with Paco DeLucia. But no hard feelings towards Pab. I didn't have a problem with Pab doing it, he was a friend of mine and a good engineer, the guy I once took on tour as a new boy now took over from me and went on to become Paul McCartney's sound engineer for many years, so I must have done something right. Of course I won't forget the day he saved my life in Austria on the Pat Metheny tour.

It's a real shame that I lost all respect for the man I had once admired and I never worked for Barrie Marshall again (at least not directly). I didn't see the tour manager David Green again either, the last I heard of David he'd been arrested and extradited to Italy to face charges relating to his family who were allegedly involved in Mafia activities. Never mind, I had other things to do.

LINDISFARNE

December came around and it was time to start another Lindisfarne Christmas tour, a modest 24 shows starting off in Leeds University where The Who recorded their *Live at Leeds* album, and the usual big cities Sheffield, Nottingham, Manchester, Leicester, Bradford, Birmingham and another sell-out show at Hammersmith Odeon plus eight shows at Newcastle City Hall. I was using Dickson Kirkwood from Limit Audio for the monitor mix this year and we had along my friend Micky McGuire, a lighting tech who also had a pyro licence and was a wizard at explosives on stage. Jim Moore was the backline roadie.

An addition to the band was Steve Daggart who came along as part of the road crew, he also played keyboards on stage during the show to add some extra sound; later on he became a permanent member of the new Lindisfarne band. Sue and Kim Brown came along on tour to fill the stage with decorations which they did brilliantly, decorating the stage with a Christmas tree, tinsel, chains, balloons, and general Christmas decorations, sometimes it was a bit over the top but that made it look even better. Everyone who entered the venues were given a party hat before taking their seat and the whole venue was in party mood.

During this tour a change in my personal life took place, my wife Estelle and I were going through a difficult time in our marriage and we talked about divorce. Jim Moore the backline roadie for Lindisfarne and Gordon Rae the band's lighting engineer had set up a lighting company called Nitelites, a lighting company who supplied the lights for Lindisfarne. Jim offered me a one-third partnership in the company, with the intention of me expanding the business into a sound and lighting rental company.

They did have a very small PA system for doing pubs but they were not in the concert league. I gave it some thought and after a discussion with Estelle we decided that our marriage was over. It was the hardest decision I had ever made and I did not take that decision lightly, it was not what I wanted but I can only blame myself for being away so much. No one can ever say we did not try to make the marriage work, a few weeks earlier we left our children with my mother and headed off to Northern France for a 'make or break' weekend to try and sort things out; although we got on most of the time we just couldn't seem to live together when I came back off tour. The hardest part of the break-up was not seeing my children.

Estelle said I was gone too much when the children were growing up and I missed so much of their childhood, which was true, she was right, but that was the price I paid for the career I had chosen. I felt guilty about that and so bad that I wasn't there for them. The two days at home over Christmas sealed the fate, so in January I left home with a few things and went to stay with Jim and his wife Lynne at their home in North Shields, to see if we could work something out with this new partnership idea and whether I wanted to move north. After a few days I made the decision to stay.

Photo: Lindisfarne Musical Productions
Lindisfarne band and crew. Newcastle City Hall.
Top row. Sven, Jim, Rod, Jacka, Simon, Ian, Sue.
Bottom row. Me, Alan, Ray, Marty, Kim.

24

TYNE TEES TELEVISION & NITELITES

Nitelites went from a two-man lighting company to a three-man sound and lighting company; on arrival in North Shields it wasn't long before I started work with the small sound system. They had an old 16-channel Midas mixer, coincidentally one that I had built when I worked at Midas, two copy Martin bass bins which had been confiscated by Dave Martin and sold off as counterfeit. The PA had no effects except for a really old Roland space echo and an assortment of cheap microphones. I was starting to wonder what I had let myself in for. Jim was a former shipyard worker and Gordon a former department store salesman, they could set up a lighting rig OK but had virtually no experience with sound.

I never liked the name Nitelites especially the American spelling. A Nitelite sounded like something you put in a child's bedroom. We changed the name to Nitelites Sound and Light to reflect the company now supplying sound equipment as well as lights, and over the next five years I built it into the largest sound company in the North of England.

Shortly after I left Concert Sound, the MD Mick Anderson had also left and joined rival sound company Entec who I had worked for on the UFO tour in 1977. I stayed in contact with him and discovered that he was selling off some old stock which would do very nicely for my system. Over the next few months I purchased some second-hand speakers and amplifiers from Entec and two Vitavox sub-bass speaker cabinets from Concert Sound. I also purchased some mid-range speaker cabinets from Turbo Sound; they didn't throw the sound as well as a Martin mid-range speaker, but I thought they had a much warmer and more natural sound. As we were not doing arenas (yet), it didn't really matter about throwing the sound long distance.

After three years I ended up with a 10,000-watt system capable of delivering a good sound in a Wembley Arena-sized venue, two sound mixers, a TAC 48-channel front of house desk, a TAC 18-channel front of house desk, and a TAC 24-channel monitor mixer, an effects rack with all the effects and audio processors I wanted.

TAC mixers were not as good as Midas mixers but they were a lot cheaper. An equivalent comparison between TAC and Midas would be between Jaguar and Rolls Royce. For the work we were doing a TAC (or Jaguar) is more than good enough and it had all the facilities I needed, spending out on a new Midas (or Rolls Royce) would have been over the top and unnecessarily expensive.

One of the first gigs I did was a show at Queen's Hall, Hexham, with Alan Price, someone I knew well and had worked with back in the Colac days. An arrogant little man and one of the most miserable artistes I've worked with. Then a white glove job with Lindisfarne at the Royal Albert Hall for a charity event, so-called white glove job because you don't get your hands dirty, I just turned up and mixed the show, someone else was suppling the PA system.

Then I was about to experience a different type of sound job, something that I hadn't done before: a theatrical stage show of *The Little Shop of Horrors* at the Newcastle Playhouse with Richard O'Brien playing the lead role, he wrote and created *The Rocky Horror Show* which went on for years in London.

The Little Shop of Horrors, written by American Howard Ashman, is a rock-horror comedy musical set in New York. It involved a small plant that grew into a massive monster, at the end it took up the entire stage and eventually ate the theatre, including a stunt actress sitting in the audience that got plucked out of her seat in row C by one of its branches and hoisted up into the roof screaming. Some stunning special effects were performed for such a small theatre.

Although I hadn't done theatre before I approached the job as if I had, and as there was a live band playing in the orchestra pit I treated it like a rock concert, although using hidden radio mics on the actors was a challenging experience I soon got used to.

Throughout the two-day rehearsals the director was more interested in the cast's performance and the stage lighting than he was with the sound, it wasn't until all the rehearsals were over that he came up to me at the mixer and apologised for not spending any time with me. He said I was doing a good job with the sound and was happy with what he heard.

I really enjoyed the week long experience, I got on well with the cast and the stage crew, The Playhouse front of house bar became a regular watering hole and I met up with the stage crew quite regularly after that.

Immediately after the *Little Shop of Horrors* shows Lindisfarne undertook a national club tour in smaller venues, sixteen gigs in sixteen days, that's not unusual, it costs money to keep a band and its crew on the road, better to slip in a low-paying gig, at least it pays the hotel bills. We were doing small venues like pubs, clubs, universities and theatres. London's Mean Fiddler pub is a well-known music venue having featured some well-known acts over the years. I was carrying a 6kWatt sound system in a 3-ton truck, Jim was driving another 3-ton truck with the backline and a small lighting rig, a four-man crew in all.

In August Lindisfarne did the famous Cambridge Folk Festival with its awful Bose sound system, I'd done that festival before and the sound equipment hadn't improved any since the last time. The mixing equipment was OK but the speakers just couldn't deliver the sound that was required, the speakers distorted and couldn't cope with the wide range of dynamics that came with Lindisfarne, it might have been a folk festival but the acts were by no means all folk, there were also rock, blues and jazz artistes. The following week it was the Edinburgh Festival and this time I was very impressed with the sound system that was supplied by a local sound company and the band sounded good, sometimes you win.

Life didn't just involve doing local gigs, the band were asked to do a TV show in Geneva, Switzerland, which meant flying from Newcastle to Geneva and mixing on a local sound system again. It was live and the TV company took an audio feed from the stage microphones.

I didn't expect to be getting about so much when I moved north, a trip up to Lerwick in the Shetland Isles was an eye opener, I'd never been there before, I'm told there are more sheep than people, but the rumour that the natives only had one eye in the middle of their forehead and were all related to each other was not true. A few shows were slotted in at Inverness, Ulster Hall in Belfast and the Opera House in Cork, Ireland, venues I knew well.

It's good to catch up with old friends, Gary Doon, ex-Dr Hook crew and ex-Limey Sound partner, got himself a job working for Madonna operating her video screens. He said the production was a nightmare with so many crew working on the mammoth festival stage, enormous amounts of sound, lighting and video equipment had to be installed with miles of mains and signal control cabling, it took the crew two days just to erect the stage. Madonna was doing some shows in Europe and I made contact with him while he was in England and I got to see him at Leeds. He left a backstage pass at his hotel which I picked up on my way through. I was not especially a Madonna fan but it certainly was a great show to watch and she really worked hard on stage.

BUTLINS

When I got home I had a call from an old friend from the Steve Hackett tours, Kevin, who was running his own sound company Stage Audio Services (SAS). He asked if I wanted to look after a stage at a 60s festival at one of Butlin's holiday camps at Barry Island in Wales, it meant leaving Nitelites for a week, but as there were no other jobs on I said I would do it.

I was in for a shock when I got there as there were three rooms with sound systems already set up, I had one room and the other two rooms were run by SAS crew. It was a one-man job running the stage, moving microphones during changeovers and dashing back to the mixer to mix the show, it was a very low-key event but it had some interesting artistes on the bill. The Searchers, The Troggs, Del Shannon, Swinging Blue Jeans, Merseybeats, The Foremost and lots of other 60s acts not so well known.

The accommodation was a chalet made for Hi-de-Hi holiday makers, felt like it was made of cardboard and it didn't even have a 13 amp socket in the room, just a bed, a chair and a bathroom if you could call it that. The food they supplied us was served up in the staff canteen, with employees on one side of the room having to eat off plastic tables and on the other side were the managers' tables with white cotton tablecloths. I felt like sitting on a managers' table just to make a point but thought better of it, I didn't want to embarrass my mate Kevin who was paying me. The weekend went off OK and I went home having had a good time despite the conditions.

In August 1986 my old mate from The Scorchers tour, also called Kevin, sent me a postcard from Atlanta, Georgia, with the message, 'Get over here end of September and I'll put you to work'. He was about to go out on tour with The Georgia Satellites that I mentioned earlier, and he wanted me to do their sound. I wrote back 'Sorry can't do it due to other commitments.' He then sent me a tape of The Georgia Satellites' new album in a way to tempt me over, but I had just moved to Newcastle and wasn't interested in moving to Georgia, it was nice to have received the invitation and nice to know you're wanted and not forgotten.

On 24th October 1986 I heard from Concert Sound that my dear friend Peter Grainger had been killed, run down whilst walking his son to school. A drunk driver mounted the kerb killing him outright. It was a shock throughout the entire Concert Sound camp. Peter had been the main sound engineer for Dire Straits and was on their ground-breaking *Brothers in Arms* tour which launched the CD and the new Philips CD player. Dire Straits went on and dedicated their next album to Peter who had worked for the band from the very beginning.

It was only three years before that Peter had come with me as my sound crew assistant. I wasn't sure why Peter was assisting me as it should have been the other way around, but Concert Sound put me out as the main man looking after front of house for the band's engineer. Peter wanted to come along as a sound crew member, he told me he just wanted a low-key gig for a change without the pressure and was happy to be number two on the crew. Such a nice guy.

The end of the year ended like most of the other years doing another Lindisfarne Christmas tour, apparently this tour was the biggest tour undertaken by anyone so far with 47 shows in 51 days with just two days off for Christmas, and two days for New Year. For some strange reason there was no show on 2nd December, it must have been impossible to find an empty venue anywhere in the country otherwise the date would have been filled. The tour included of course eight shows at Newcastle City Hall, the last show on the tour was a brilliant and massive sell-out concert at Hammersmith Odeon on 3rd January. The shows were being co-promoted by some local radio stations and most were recording them live for broadcast or future transmission, including BBC Radio Merseyside, Leicester Sound, Radio Trent, Radio 210, Radio Invicta, Beacon Radio, Plymouth Sound, Radio Wyvern, Hereward Radio, County Sound Radio, Signal Radio, Marcher Sound, Viking Radio, Red Dragon Radio, Southern Sound, GWR Radio, Piccadilly Radio, Pennine Radio, BRMB Radio, I didn't know there were so many local radio stations out there.

The band had a Yamaha CP70 electric piano but unlike pure electronic pianos this had strings and had to be tuned every day, so at 3pm during set-up we had to keep quiet so the tuner could tune the piano on stage.

The new album *Dance Your Life Away* was released this year and produced by Steve Daggart who played keyboards on stage during some of the songs. Mick Elliot a local comedian and compare came on as Santa, told a few jokes and introduced the band, very festive. HoHoHo.

Lindisfarne Christmas Party. Newcastle City Hall. 1986

Whilst I was living in Newcastle I had the opportunity to work for Tyne Tees Television, part of the ITV network, as a sound engineer for a live show *The Tube*, thanks to Mick Anderson who was now the MD at Entec. Entec had a permanent PA system installed in the studios of Tyne Tees Television for the rock music programme. Mick Anderson called me as he knew I was living in Newcastle, he asked if I would cover for one of his engineers. I ended up doing all the remaining shows. The first show had The Christians, The Mission and Timbuck 3.

Unlike other TV music shows I'd done, *The Tube* was actually broadcast live, not just recorded live but actually transmitted live, as the bands were playing on stage you were watching them at home on your TV, no time to correct mistakes, no time to edit out errors, it was really live.

My job was to set the mics, soundcheck the band, set the monitors and mix the sound for the studio audience. The TV sound was mixed upstairs in the main control room alongside the lighting mixers and the director who controlled the cameras. As well as the TV sound mix and the studio audience sound mix there was a mobile recording studio parked outside in the car park for an American TV station. Their instructions were to record every channel at 0db with no EQ, no effects and no mixing, just record the bands straight, easy work for those guys.

The show, which went out weekly on Channel 4, featured three or four artistes, it was broadcast on a Friday evening and involved a set-up, soundcheck, camera check, and rehearsal on the Thursday before, so it was a two-day job and Tyne Tees paid very nicely thank you.

A pub next door called The Egypt Cottage was a regular hangout for the crew and for most of the artistes after rehearsals and after the show. Before going home I'd call into the staff canteen and have a subsidised dinner with their excellent apple pie and custard.

Whilst working at the Tyne Tees studios, one of the band members asked the floor manager for a fan to keep the stage cool, it was always hot under those studio lights. The floor manager asked a stage technician to bring a fan, he said "No it's a prop, I can't touch a prop, it's not my job," so he asked the props department to bring a fan, props brought it to the stage and put the fan down on the stage and left. The floor manager went to the props man and asked if he could plug the fan in and switch it on. The props man said, "No, I can't do that, that's an electrician's job." The floor manager unable to plug it in himself for fear of a walk out had to call the electrician who came and plugged it in and switched it on. That's how stupid union power became in the 1970s and 1980s. Thankfully those days are gone.

The BBC were no better, they were held hostage to the unions who took great delight in making life as difficult as possible just because they could, with a threat of a walk out you had to work by union rules even if you were not in a union. Whenever I worked at *Top of the Pops* or the *Old Grey Whistle Test*, the floor staff would hang around the studio watching and would go ape if you ever tried to move anything on the set. That was their job, they probably felt that if I could do it then they wouldn't be needed, which to some extent was true.

One of the presenters on The Tube was ex-Squeeze keyboard player Jools Holland, the other was Paula Yates, daughter of the talent show host Hughie Green. She was married to Boomtown Rats front man Bob Geldof. Paula was a different type of presenter to Jools Holland and she would always be messing about and constantly flirting with anyone and everyone. At one point whilst Jools was doing camera checks Paula walked up behind him, put her hand between his legs and squeezed his private bits in full view of everybody, she was the only one who thought it was funny. I will always remember the embarrassing interview she held with INXS front man Michael Hutchence on a bed.

Rumours in the studio were that the management were looking for an excuse to drop the show and it was Jools Holland and Paula Yates that killed it off, they gave them their excuse. The Tube lasted until April 1987 when it was felt it had run out of ideas and audience numbers were dropping.

But this wasn't the end of my work at Tyne Tees Television, they were already working on a replacement show and they called it *The Roxy*. *The Roxy* was a television music programme that was broadcast on ITV from 1987 to 1988 and featured a vast range of well-known artistes.

Unlike its predecessor *The Tube*, which concentrated on rock bands and up-and-coming artistes, *The Roxy* showcased mainstream artistes that dominated the British pop charts, more like *Top Of The Pops*. This was actually a more enjoyable show to work on and was recorded on a Thursday for transmission on the Friday.

The Roxy was not live but instead used backing tracks. Tyne Tees picked up a trick I'd seen at the BBC on *Top of the Pops* where the drummer's cymbals were replaced with cardboard ones which didn't make so much noise when the drummer hit them, and the drum skins were covered with rubber pads which didn't make any noise at all. The guitars and keyboards were not plugged in but unknown to TTTV I'd made up a few dummy jack cables to plug into the instruments. One thing that really annoyed me on *Top of the Pops* was that no attempt was made to disguise the fact that the band were not playing live. Seeing someone playing an electric guitar without it being plugged in just looked plain stupid in my opinion. I tried to make the stage look live even though it wasn't, I even put some dummy mics on the instruments and drums.

During my time at the Tyne Tees Television I worked on some great shows with ABC, Bananarama, Billy Ocean, Black, Boy George, Bryan Adams, Brian Ferry, Broken English, Bros, Chris Rea, Christians, Cliff Richard, Communards, The Cure, Curiosity Killed the Cat, Cyndi Lauper, David Sanborne, Def Leppard, Depeche Mode, Echo & The Bunnymen, Eddy Grant, Erasure, Errol Brown, Freddie McGregor, Gary Numan, Housemartins, Hue & Cry, Joe Cocker, Johnny Hates Jazz, The Kane Gang, Kenny G, Kim Wilde, Level 42, Living In A Box, Lloyd Cole, Los Lobos, Marillion, Marrs, The Mission, New Order, Patsy Kensit, Pet Shop Boys, Proclaimers, Pseudo Echo, The Rainmakers, Ray Parker Jr, Rick Astley, Robert Plant, Samantha Fox, Shakin' Stevens, Shirley Bassey, The Silencers, Simply Red, Sinitta, Siouxsie & The Banshees, Sisters of Mercy, Squeeze, Status Quo, Steve Winwood, Swing Out Sister, Taylor Dane, Terence Trent D'Arby, Then Jericho, Timbuck 3, Tom Robinson, T'Pau, UB40, Vow Wow, Was Not Was, Westworld, Wet Wet Wet and a few others.

One memorable occasion when The Jesus and Mary Chain were going through a camera check in the afternoon for one of the shows, the director was so fed up with the attitude of the band that he told them to pack up and go home, later telling us it was because they looked too miserable on camera, he didn't want them on the show. That was a quick decision, they were gone.

I got to meet up with some old friends whilst I was there, Def Leppard who I'd toured with in 1980 when they were first starting out turned up and remembered me. The drummer Rick Allen who'd lost his arm in a car crash brought in his new electronic drum kit which he played with one arm and two feet. To listen to him, you would never know he only had one arm. His impressive array of pedals was a practical substitute to him losing an arm and I have to admire his determination to carry on drumming after that accident. Many drummers would have given up and I suspect many bands would have replaced their drummer. Whilst his drum tech was setting up the kit, Rick showed me how his kit worked. He had four foot pedals for his left foot which triggered a hi-hat, a snare, one rack tom and a kick drum, his right foot played another kick drum, his right arm played the remaining rack toms and floor toms. The kit was all electronic pads with his original Ludwig acoustic drum kit sampled into an electronic drum machine, so whenever he hit one of his pedals or drum pads it activated the original sound of his Ludwig kit. Listening to the PA system you wouldn't know it was an electronic drum kit it sounded so real.

My old friend Rodney Groth, the stage crew boss for Dr Hook, came in with American sax player Kenny G, he was pleased to see me and we managed to catch up with some old news. He told me one of Dr Hook's crew Marc was now production manager for U2, Dr Hook's road manager Nineyear was working as tour manager for country artiste Nanci Griffith and Gary Doon was working as a sound tech in a Nashville country music venue.

Unfortunately that was the last time I ever saw Rodney, about a year later I heard some bad news that Rodney had developed a brain tumour that wasn't diagnosed early enough and he'd passed away. Not long after that Gary Doon passed away after a long illness. I was saddened to hear the news about my friends.

Chris Rea came in and did his latest single and we chatted about the old times on the Lindisfarne tour we did together in 1978. I did a show with Joe Cocker on *The Roxy* and afterwards the Tyne Tees production team had arranged for Joe to do a private performance at an after-show party, (one of a few). I got Nitelites to put a small PA together for the event which was held in a nearby nightclub. It goes without saying I did the sound for that as well.

In between doing *The Tube* and *The Roxy* for Tyne Tees I managed to fit in a short tour of Norway with Lindisfarne, flying to Bergen we did the whole tour by train. Quite a memorable experience and an enjoyable change, taking the train from Bergen to Trondheim, one of my favourite Norwegian cities, we went through mountains, tunnels, bypassed fjords and gushing rivers. As it was only March there was still a lot of snow was on the ground. From Trondheim to the capital Oslo we took an overnight express so we didn't see a lot as we slept in our bunks, then on to Kristiansand, Stavanger and back to Bergen for another night at the Exodus club. In all a very enjoyable trip, the equipment was supplied to us locally and the gear was pretty good, the club PA systems were what you would expect from a club but we got by OK.

In between the television jobs Nitelites got some small club gigs, what I called 'bread and butter jobs' to pay the bills and rental on the warehouse. They were at the local Newcastle University, Polytechnic, Mayfair Ballroom or the Riverside Nightclub, they were just local bands or visiting artistes on tour who required a PA system. That is where we cleaned up as there were no other sound companies in the area who could match the size and power of the system I had built.

One of these jobs was a talent competition called 'Battle Of The Bands' sponsored by Wella hair products, there were seven local heats around the country, Newcastle, Birmingham, Manchester, Liverpool, Glasgow, London, Chippenham and a final at the Hammersmith Hippodrome night club. I had to be totally impartial and mix each act exactly the same, of course it didn't matter to me who won as I didn't have a preference or any conflict of interest. The winning act in London turned out to be Really for Real, a band playing electronic dance music, they even gave me a copy of their album after the final. I'd never heard of them before and never heard of them since but they were very good at what they did.

The last show of *The Roxy* at Tyne Tees Television was in 1988 but was not the end of my career at the studio, TTTV had organised a 24-hour telethon for a number of charities in direct competition to the BBC's *Children in Need.* It went on all night starting at 12 noon and ending at 6am in time for breakfast TV. Needless to say I was completely exhausted after that long stint behind a sound mixer. Most of the time it was just controlling presenter's microphones with the occasional guitar mic or a full band mix, this was mixing for the in-house audience in the studio, rather boring some of the time but TTTV paid me well.

The following month I rigged a PA system for an outdoor television show with Bros, lots of girls screaming their heads off at the sight of this new teen throb boy band. Then a Raymond Frogget Country music special in TTTV studios and then Mica Paris and Courtney Pine for a Jazz Special TV show. The studio kept me busy.

The Lindisfarne Christmas tour this year was 46 shows in 48 days with eight shows at Newcastle City Hall. Lindisfarne had just released a strange and very unconventional record for them called *C'mon Everybody*, an album consisting of 50s and 60s Rock'n'Roll cover tracks. The album itself was actually very good musically and the band reproduced the originals very well. The album wouldn't have been so bad if it wasn't for that awful album sleeve which featured disco dancers in a discotheque. Not what you would expect from Lindisfarne and definitely not the right album sleeve for a Rock'n'Roll album. Whoever designed that sleeve should have been shot.

Some of the audience were a bit perplexed when they heard the first half of the show hearing all these 50s and 60s cover songs; as great as they were, it wasn't Lindisfarne and the audience wondered if they were listening to a tribute band, some even looked over my shoulder to read the set list and asked why they were doing those songs. The second half of the show was the typical and well-known Lindisfarne set list. 'Run for Home', 'Meet Me on the Corner', 'Lady Eleanor', 'Fog on the Tyne', 'We Can Swing Together' and others.

The following year was spent building up more sound equipment. I was doing larger jobs but still having to do the smaller clubs and pubs. By now we had so much equipment the warehouse was getting too small, as well as sound equipment, Gordon was buying more lights to do bigger lighting jobs, aluminium 40-foot trusses, Genie Superlift and motor hoists, follow spots and smoke machines. It all helped generate income but the sound rental was the biggest earner.

Other jobs included Tom Robinson at a miners' gala in Beamish Museum, Alan Price at Newcastle Playhouse, London Beat at the Polytechnic and a regular venue The Riverside, a nightclub which featured mostly rock bands and up-and-coming acts, I had some really memorable nights there.

In June when most of the world was watching the Mandela concert at Wembley Stadium I was in Durham doing a kind of mini-Mandela concert. I was there while my partners were sat watching the real thing at home on TV with their families. I started to think something wasn't right here, sound brought in 80% of the income and I was doing 80% of the work but wasn't receiving 80% of the benefits. I was becoming restless, something had to change and I was thinking of getting out from the business. I said to myself, *I will give it 12 months and if things don't change then I'll decide whether to stay or go.*

Meanwhile life had to go on, I did a few firework shows where the firework display was set to music. On the quayside at North Shields I put in a 10,000 watt system and several delay towers running down the quayside, I was told they could hear the music in Tynemouth down the River Tyne. A Revox tape machine was set up inside the mixing tower and the firework controller was stood next to me while he co-ordinated the firing of the fireworks by walkie-talkie exactly to a pre-set order. It sounded great especially the sub bass W bins that complemented the bangs in the air with an earthquake rumble through the ground, I made sure that my in-rack cassette player was set to record, so I had a copy of the music for future use, the tracks were a mix of Vangelis and classical orchestra music.

A typical Nitelites PA stack at the Fish Quay Festival

A week later I did another firework display for the opening ceremony of a new AMC multiscreen cinema complex, this time I rented a delay system from Asktam in London and together we had 20,000 watts of power. You could feel the ground shake and that wasn't just the fireworks.

The year ended as usual with another Lindisfarne tour but much smaller than earlier ones, could the great Lindisfarne be losing their appeal? This time only fifteen shows in December with six shows at the Newcastle City Hall. This tour must have been a 'make the most of it' tour as the band forwent their hotels and decided to use a sleeper bus to save money, the crew had a sleeper bus as well. I was used to it but some of the crew had never slept on a tour bus, the only saving grace was Rachel from the catering company cooking us all a good English breakfast before we started work.

We had a bit of a problem at Hull City Hall, one of the regular gigs on the tour circuit; normally the local stage crew were a gang of Hell's Angels who would unload and reload the trucks and were a good bunch of lads who always worked hard and did a good job. This year the Newcastle crew did a deal with the band in which they would cover all the venues in the North East of England. The problem was when we turned up in Hull the local crew were waiting for us and they were not happy, it looked like a confrontation was about to happen. Hull was their territory and they didn't like an outside crew coming in and taking their work. Jim tried to calm them down but they spent the whole time harassing the Newcastle crew as they unloaded the truck, making comments as they passed by and deliberately standing in their way. It looked like it might get out of hand but there wasn't anything I could do, I continued to set up the equipment as the flight cases arrived on stage.

VENUES

When you walk into a venue for the first time you sometimes dread what you are going to be presented with. It's not always a modern music venue with state-of-the-art equipment. It could be a sports arena or a seedy nightclub. It may be a town hall with gold-plated ornaments, a warehouse with a tin roof or a converted rock club that smells of beer and stale cigarettes. It may have modern theatre dressing rooms or it may have filthy dirty ones where the walls are covered with graffiti and the toilets haven't been cleaned in four years. The house PA system has a blown speaker and the amplifiers you want to get to are somewhere up in the roof or in a basement. On the mixer the lights don't light up, the switches don't switch, the faders feel like they are sliding on sand, the mixer is covered in beer or Coke and then channels 2, 11 and 16 are not working.

The stage crew arrive late and stoned and don't really want to be there. On a bad day it could be even worse.

25

FOG ON THE TYNE

The New Year started with Lindisfarne doing a tour of Italy starting at The City Square nightclub in Milano. The band released *Amigos* their new album, but Steve Daggett left the band and was replaced by Steve Cunningham on bass which allowed Rod Clements to move onto guitar.

Next I did three shows with The Flying Pickets, a five-piece a capella group who in addition to singing also played the musical instruments with their mouths. Brilliantly done and professionally presented. All I needed was five vocal mics and I inserted five compressors into their channels to give me greater control over their dynamics to mix their harmonies, added some reverb and it sounded good.

LABI SIFFRE

I received a call from Mick Anderson who got me the job at TTTV whilst he was working for Entec. He had returned to Concert Sound and asked if I wanted to do a European tour with Labi Siffre who'd had a big hit with his single 'Something Inside So Strong', a song about apartheid in South Africa. Mick knew I was involved with Nitelites but he asked me anyway. I was getting increasingly unhappy with what was happening at Nitelites and told my partners I would be away for four weeks, they were not too pleased but I needed to get away from Newcastle for a while, or Nitelites at least.

I drove down to Luton to their new warehouse having just moved out of their cramped railway arch in Watford for a brand new supersized warehouse on an industrial estate. Before the tour started I was in the warehouse preparing the sound equipment I was to use, when Mick needed some extra sound equipment delivering to the guys on a Tom Jones tour at the NEC in Birmingham. I knew my mate Paul Boothroyd (Pab) who'd worked with me on Pat Metheny and Dr Hook tours was on the crew so I volunteered to take the equipment there, it was just a few microphones and replacement loudspeakers. When I got there I was talking to Pab and he was trying to get me to come along on the Tom Jones tour but I knew Mick wanted me for the Labi Siffre tour.

There were six on the road crew, two on lights including my old mate Finbarr Quinn, two on backline, me on front of house sound and Dave Catlin on monitors, as well as a tour manager and a stage manager. We flew to Amsterdam and picked up two minibuses, one for the band and one for the crew, the truck driven by Mike from Trans Euro went by ferry. We did four shows in Holland, one in Austria, three in Germany and three in the UK. A really enjoyable tour, Labi was a pleasure to work with and his music was easy on the ear and easy to mix.

The Amsterdam show had a film crew present with us all day, filming us setting up and filming the live show for a documentary. In Cologne the band did a TV show lip-syncing to a playback track so it was an easy day for the sound crew, no lights were involved as it was done in the TV studio. After the show the record company Polydor took everyone out for a meal.

In Vienna we did the Amhof Festival which meant it was a set up and play situation, no soundcheck. In Munich we played the Schlachthof which translates to Slaughterhouse. I hoped they were referring to the venue's previous use not its present use for visiting artistes. Back in the UK the Reading gig at the Hexagon was a live recording for the BBC, a live 'In Concert' program where the BBC took all the microphone splits off my stage microphones, nice venue and a good sound.

Meanwhile back in Northumberland Gordon Rea had gone off on a lighting tour for Yamaha to sponsor Yamaha musical products and managed to get one of their Japanese staff pregnant, or to be more accurate, she got pregnant by an English bloke so she could give birth and stay in England. Gordon fell for it, which put pressure on him to support his girlfriend.

A mixture of gigs followed including Katrina and the Waves who'd won the European Song Contest with 'Walking on Sunshine'. I was reunited with an old friend, Keith Davies, a crew member I worked with on the Ralph McTell and John McLaughlin tours, he was working for Katrina as lighting engineer. He said he couldn't help but notice that most of the investment in Nitelites had gone into sound equipment rather than lighting equipment, I told him that's the way it should be as most of the money is earnt by the sound equipment, I was hoping he'd report back to his brother Clive who by now had retired from sound and lighting after selling Colac and bought a hotel in Sri Lanka.

An outdoor music festival the River Wear Festival in Sunderland was almost a complete washout, the organisation was pathetically amateurish. Martin Stephenson and the Daintees were headlining with an assortment of B-list bands and artistes. The day started off well enough, I rigged the sound system and set up the mixing console in what was supposed to be a mixing tower, turned out to be a scaffold frame with tarpaulin covers. This was OK until it started to rain, the rain just poured into the tower and soaked the sound mixer, I managed to throw some covers over the top to limit the damage. On stage it got worse, the rain started collecting in the roof and with the weight of water it was creating a small lake above everybody's heads. No one on the stage could see it so I contacted the stage via my intercom as they were totally unaware of the increasing ocean of water accumulating above their heads. When they tried to relieve the pressure on the canvas roof it only made things worse resulting in them diverting the water over the edge, down the back of the stage to where all the power cables were run.

My sound system at the River Wear festival in Sunderland

By this time I'd had enough of the fiasco and made a management decision on grounds of safety and pulled the plug. I told the stage manager I was turning off the mixer and told them to shut down the power and leave the stage. I turned off the mixer to prevent any further damage to the equipment and waited until the rain stopped and it was safe to continue. About an hour later the rain had stopped and we resumed the show having dried out the equipment.

Another meet-up with an old friend, Pete Eustace, the front of house engineer from Thin Lizzy who was now working for The Soup Dragons and was doing a show at Newcastle Poly, it's always great to see old friends from way back that you've worked with on different tours.

Another reunion, this time with fellow Balls musician Steve Gibbons who played guitar with Denny Laine and Trevor Burton back in 1970 and 71, he was the support band for ex-Small Faces singer Steve Marriott at the Newcastle Mayfair Ballroom. A terrible place to load in and load out, nice inside but the only way to get the equipment down to the stage is down a long narrow staircase or via a catering lift which was only big enough for a tray of chicken and chips. It took forever to get all the speaker cabinets and amps inside.

The year ended with a Lindisfarne Christmas tour, 33 shows this time with six at Newcastle City Hall.

As well as supplying sound for music events, I was also asked to supply sound for what you would call corporate and sporting events. I had already opened a multiscreen cinema and now Nissan were opening their brand new factory in Sunderland to build cars, initially with Japanese parts but eventually using UK-manufactured parts. The opening ceremony was performed by the Prime Minister Margaret Thatcher and security was tight. The day before, I went along and set up a PA system either side of a makeshift stage and placed two microphones on a lectern, at the entrance gate were police and security staff. Army bomb disposal teams and sniffer dogs patrolled the site all day checking under and around anything that could hide an explosive device. The second day security was tight again, our special passes were checked and we were allowed to enter. Margaret Thatcher did her speech to a throng of television cameras, press reporters and officially opened the site.

Sporting events were easier to deal with. Supplying sound for events such as darts on live television, boxing matches, synchronised aerobics and children's television show *Get Fresh*. On the darts television show I was asked to place a microphone behind the dart board so the TV viewers could hear the 'thud' of the dart as it hit the board. The first dart was thrown and as I had the microphone level cranked up higher than I thought, half the audience fell off their seats in shock as the loud thud echoed into the hall, I quickly pulled the volume down as the producer came running over to me waving his arms in a panic, it made a few people laugh though including me.

Unloading and loading 20 tons of equipment everyday can be exhausting work even with the help of stage crew. I like to be in the back of the truck stacking those flight cases and speaker cabinets, it keeps me fit and I enjoy the adrenaline rush after a show. Stacking equipment on stage is an art and strength is not always essential. Take for example one venue we did which was in a sports arena where the stage crew were actually the weightlifting team. There's no doubt they were strong and pumped a lot of iron but they didn't have a clue how to get a bass bin weighing 150lbs on top of a seven-foot tower. Three men huffed and puffed and tried lifting it in all sorts of angles and couldn't get the bin up to the height. I politely said, "This is how you do it," I called my crew member over and the two of us swung it up in what must have looked like an effortless lift straight on top of the seven-foot tower. When you do it every day you get used to it and can make throwing around a 150lb bass bin look easy. It's not the strength you need, it's the technique and I've said that about a lot of things throughout my life.

I did 32 shows through November and December including five at Newcastle City Hall with Lindisfarne and this was the last tour I did with the band but not the last show. My son Alex came along on part of this tour and helped me set up the sound equipment. After the soundcheck I let him play around on the mixer and the outboard effects, he was familiarising himself with the echo machine, reverb and delay unit and recording some music on the cassette player. This got him interested in a career as a sound designer a few years later which saw him make his own records, design sound effects and background music for corporate events, commercials and videos. Jim's two children came along sometimes although they were much younger and some of the crew thought they were too young and just got in the way.

In 1990 I did a television show for ITV in the Central TV studios in Nottingham with an enthusiastic audience which ironically was one of the best shows I've ever seen them do. The show was later released as a video and I finally got my name mentioned for sound at the end of the credits, together with Ian Byron who did the monitor mix. You can still catch it on YouTube.

The popularity of the band was waning a bit although all the shows we did were sold out, the venues were getting smaller and I could see things were starting to slip, although it wasn't Lindisfarne I needed to get away from, it was the working environment at Nitelites.

I wasn't the only one thinking of leaving the band. A shock announcement after that TV show was that Ray Jackson (Jacka) was leaving Lindisfarne, I was told it was due to Lindisfarne not having enough work to keep the band going financially, but there may have been other reasons. There was a collaboration with Newcastle footballer Paul Gascoigne on a reworked version of the Lindisfarne hit single 'Fog on the Tyne' which didn't go down well with Jacka and may have been the last straw for him, it didn't go down well with many of the fans either but they did get to perform it on *Top of the Pops*.

After five years of doing small gigs around England I'd become homesick for the south, for my family and the southern weather. A visit south one Easter was when I realised that spring arrived a month earlier in the south than it did in the north, there was a definite three degree difference in the weather between north and south. I also missed my children who I didn't get to see very much because I lived so far away.

I was also not happy the way the business was being run. Things were coming to a head with my partners. I didn't feel the assets and benefits were being evenly distributed between the three of us, to me some appeared to benefit more than others. I also felt that not all were pulling their weight as much as they should which made me resentful and unsettled. Whenever I attempted to raise the subject it caused some friction between the three of us and the issues were never resolved.

Whilst I was generating the majority of the income with my sound system with the help of a hired employee, I was receiving a less than one-third share of the benefits, time was getting close for a showdown and it couldn't come soon enough as the lid on my pressure cooker was about to blow. I was thinking it was time for me to get out of the partnership.

Another Tyne Tees Television all night Telethon program was organised and I drew the short straw again as it only involved sound and no lights, I didn't mind being there as I enjoyed doing it but I was really exhausted again after being up all night working. I left the studios at 7am when the show finished and went home for breakfast before heading down to the Fish Quay Festival at North Shields for another all-day event which included Lindisfarne headlining at midday. Unfortunately I sat down at home, fell asleep and didn't wake up until the band was on stage. Ian who usually did monitors did the front of house mix and Jim did the monitors.

My view from the front of house mixer at an outdoor festival

When I woke up and realised I'd overslept after the all-nighter I made my way down to the quayside to finish off the rest of day, to be met with some hostile looks, never mind the fact I'd been up all night earning money for Nitelites and hadn't slept, I got no thanks for it either.

I took over doing the front of house mix for the rest of the day with Desmond Dekker and the Aces who ran through his hits from the 60s, 'The Israelites', '007 Shanty Town', 'You Can Get It If You Really Want' and other reggae songs.

Even though Jim was a friend of mine I was getting comments which I thought were out of character for him, Gordon was close to getting his face punched in. Jim was easily influenced by Gordon and didn't see that he was being ripped off and taken for a ride by his partner. I liked Jim and he was an easy-going sort of guy and usually went along with what Gordon said. The next day back in the office I decided I'd had enough and it came to a head when I said I was not happy with the way the company was being run, it was more like a dictatorship than a partnership and I resigned from the company. I collected my toolbox and personal items from the warehouse and went home.

I could have threatened the nuclear option by taking my sound system with me, but I didn't want to destroy a company that I had built up and put people out of work, so I decided to come to a financial agreement and sold my share of the partnership. Although I was fairly happy with the deal at the time, looking back my ex-partners got the better end of the deal.

Although the people at Nitelites may have changed since I left and the equipment may have changed, it was what I did in the early days when I built up the sound system from nothing to being the largest sound company in the North of England that is the legacy that I'm proud of today.

Although I enjoyed living in the north-east and the people were very friendly and welcoming, especially the ladies, I didn't want to spend the rest of my life there. I felt cut off from the rest of the country and my family. I put my house up for sale, made a good profit on that and moved down south to Northamptonshire, I asked my girlfriend at the time Judith if she wanted to come with me and to my surprise she said she would.

We found a house in Irthlingborough, Northamptonshire, and moved there as soon as things were settled with Nitelites. The rest of the year I took off and spent it doing up my new house, decorating, redesigning the garden and taking some time out to consider what I would do next. I didn't have to wait long.

26

ROCKY MOUNTAIN WAY

After a while, I realised that although I was enjoying the time off, I needed to get back into work, quite what to do I hadn't decided. Either to start another sound company, retire from music and do something totally different or try and get some work with one of the old sound companies I'd worked with before.

Once I decided what to do I wasted no time in picking up where I left off and the first thing I did was to contact Mick Anderson at Concert Sound who'd got me the job at Tyne Tees Television Studios. I told him I had moved back south, well at least to Northamptonshire, that's a start. He told me there was plenty of work for me if I wanted it and he was pleased to have me back on board again. Apparently they had been trying out some new sound engineers or rather wannabe engineers with disastrous results and they didn't measure up to Concert Sound standards.

JOE COCKER

I drove down to what was now their new warehouse in Luton, not far from where I lived and closer than the old warehouse that used to be in Watford. Mick Anderson asked if I wanted to go out with Joe Cocker running the front of house for Joe Cocker's FOH engineer on a tour supporting Rod Stewart and Status Quo. I thought that would get me back into the big league again after messing around with (with the exception of Lindisfarne) second-rate bands and small venues. So on the 1st June we headed out on tour and opened up the show at the massive 60,000-seater Celtic Park Football Stadium in Glasgow.

Joe Cocker had been using his own FOH engineer for some time so I was back in babysitting land again. We supplied the mixers, the mics and monitors. The main PA system was supplied by Rod Stewart and all I did was to patch my mixer into their main mixer. Status Quo did the same thing. On the sound mixing tower there were three mixers, Rod's was at the front, behind that was Quo's mixer and mine at the back with my outboard effects racks. The changeovers went quite smoothly, when working on large festival stages, all the equipment was lined up backstage and wheeled on, plugged in and checked within a matter of minutes. Meanwhile Joe Cocker's equipment had been unplugged, wheeled off and was being broken down backstage around the back out of sight, a slick, professional operation.

Whenever I heard Rod Stewart perform 'Maggie May' on stage it always reminded me of when Jacka (Ray Jackson of Lindisfarne) used to tell us about the recording session when he was asked to perform the mandolin part on 'Maggie May'. Disappointingly when the album came out Jacka didn't even get a credit on the song, all he got was 'The mandolin player from Lindisfarne I can't remember his name', which really annoyed him and then to add insult to injury on *Top of the Pops* DJ John Peel stood in and 'pretended' to play a mandolin, and very badly at that. Despite the song being an international smash hit all Jacka got was the musician's union fee of £15. When Alan Hull of Lindisfarne came in to sit in the control room and said hello to Rod, Rod totally blanked him and didn't even acknowledge him. Funny how fame goes to some people's heads or was Rod having a bad day?

Rod's girlfriend Rachel Hunter was backstage most days tottering around in her ridiculously high heels, short mini skirt, and her long flowing blond hair, fake tan and manicured nails. Escorted at all times by a six-foot-six bodyguard built like a refrigerator wearing that essential piece of security equipment, the earpiece, with a wire disappearing down inside his shirt collar and dark glasses as if he was protecting the US president, looked like overkill.

After Glasgow we headed off in convoy like a travelling circus with eight 40ft articulated trucks and five tour buses down to the International Stadium at Gateshead where I ran into some old friends and local stage crews, Old Trafford Stadium in Manchester, back for another show in Gateshead and on to Ipswich Football Stadium and finally Wembley Stadium.

Back in the warehouse after unloading the truck, a call came in: Debbie Harry was rehearsing in London and needed some monitor speakers, so I volunteered to take them down. I stayed around awhile for a listen as she went through her songs for the next Blondie tour. That was an unexpected pleasure meeting the bedroom poster girl of the 1970s, (though I must add, not my bedroom).

After the Rod Stewart tour in the UK, I continued to tour with Joe Cocker but this time he was headlining his own shows for the 'Ova Deya Tour', starting in Switzerland at the Paleo Arts Festival in Nyon. We then travelled to Austria, France, Spain, Portugal, Israel and Malta, going back and forth for a total of 13 concerts. Joe's eight-piece backing band was actually The John Miles band who had a hits with 'Music (is my first love)' which got to No 3 in the charts, 'Slow Down' which got to No 10 and 'Highfly' No 17. A great sounding band with some really good musicians, The John Miles band also worked as the backing band for Tina Turner.

The Joe Cocker venues were mostly outdoor arenas and football stadiums. The first show was the Paleo Arts Festival in Nyon, Switzerland, also on the bill supporting us was Suzanne Vega. I set up the mixer in the control tower and just patched into the house speakers that everybody used, it's so much easier now.

We went through Zell-Am-See and Antibes, Gijon in Spain where Elvis Costello supported us, Lisbon in Portugal where we were supporting Simple Minds and U2 at the 52,000-capacity Jose Alvalade Stadium, where I ran into my old friend Richard Davis from the Dr Hook road crew who was now working as production manager for U2.

The front of house mixing tower was a bit cramped, even more so than the Rod Stewart / Status Quo shows. Simple Minds had their mixer at the front of the tower with U2's mixer behind and my mixer behind them both at the back, that's the hierarchy and that's the way it works. I remember the old days when all bands used their own PA, then the speaker stacks got so big everybody had to the use the main act's PA and the same mixer, that's where the support acts got a raw deal as they wouldn't have been allowed to change any of the settings. Thankfully we've moved on from that situation and we all now use our own mixers, effects and control gear and just plug into the main act's speakers, so much more civilised.

Then on to Tarragona and Alicante where we played the Plaza de Toros which was a bullring and the dressing rooms were the slaughterhouse where the bulls were slaughtered. It wouldn't have been so bad except there was still blood on the floor from a previous bullfight. Then the Les Arena D'Arles in Arles, after that show we were due to fly from Marseille Airport to Israel for two shows. As we were flying on El Al, the Israeli state airline, security checks were extra tight, we were not allowed to transport the equipment ourselves to the airport which consisted of a complete 40-foot trailer full to the roof. Instead a truck owned by the Israeli airline security turned up backstage with four armed security officers and sniffer dogs. Every box, case and piece of hardware was meticulously checked over by the Israeli security force and packed onto their own truck by their own people. We were not allowed to touch it, once the equipment had been loaded and locked it disappeared and we didn't see it again until it was delivered to the Galilee Park amphitheatre venue at Karmiel, Israel.

It's interesting to know that as one of the most targeted nations in the Middle East at that time, no one had ever blown up an El Al flight and they were the first airline to install bomb-proof cockpit doors. On my previous flight to Israel our bags were checked by Israeli security before we even got to the check-in desk, only after being cleared there were we allowed to proceed through to the normal check-in desks. During the 1960s El Al the official flag carrier of Israel suffered several terrorist attacks on its planes and offices but has only been hijacked once: in 1968 two Palestinian terrorists attacked a Boeing 707 from Rome to Tel Aviv, all hostages were freed in Algeria.

The venue was scorching hot and we struggled to set up the equipment in the burning sun, when I looked around it seemed we were the only ones working. Mad dogs and Englishmen came to mind although it was a beautiful setting once the sun went down and Joe did a cracking show with the sun setting behind the mountains. The next day we were at Park Hayarkon in Tel Aviv, a city I've always loved. Although Israel is a Jewish state there are many secular Jews who are not Orthodox and don't go to synagogue just as there are many secular Christians living in England who don't go to church but claim to be Christian. Many Israeli Jews don't actually like the Orthodox Jews claiming they are more fascist than the Germans were, that surprised me.

On the flight from Ben Gurion Airport at Tel Aviv I sat in my requested aisle seat 18D as I like to have that extra space on the aisle, there was a young lady already in seat 18F by the window leaving an empty seat in the middle. After a while an Orthodox Jew boarded the flight and asked if I would move to the middle seat, I politely explained that I had requested an aisle seat and I wanted to keep it thank you. He then spoke to one of the flight attendants and she came back and said for religious reasons he cannot sit next to unaccompanied females. I politely told her that was his problem not mine and he should have got up earlier if he wanted an aisle seat. He was eventually found another seat elsewhere. I can't imagine why he objected to sitting next to this young lady. I later learned that there have been a number of these requests from Orthodox Jews with this problem, but El Al have refused to make a ruling on it even though they are the official state airline for Israel.

After two shows in Austria in Wiesen and Wels we flew to Malta, to the Marsa sportsground which was a football stadium, no grass, just sand, as usual we used a local sound company to supply the amps and speakers. Carrying just the sound mixers and stage gear had the advantage of reducing the freight costs.

Whenever there was a day off, the band and crew would eat out together with Joe Cocker, there was always a fight with some of the entourage to see who would be sitting around the master at his table, sad really, I just sat back and watched the circus with amusement.

I saw the same thing with David Bowie. We were staying at the same hotel somewhere in Europe, Bowie was sitting at a nearby table accompanied by two of his colleagues having breakfast, and I was at a table nearby. David Bowie's table was only laid for 4 people but as more of the Bowie party came in they all wanted to sit at the same table as their master. Embarrassingly instead of sitting on one of the many empty tables nearby they all attempted to push their way onto his table with their breakfast with the result that 6 or 7 were crowded onto the same table making themselves look like frustrated groupies desperate to be near their boss. I just sat back with my scrambled egg and toast watching the circus get bigger and bigger.

Joe Cocker was a real gentleman and a pleasure to work with, no big egos, no tantrums just a guy with a great voice who got up on stage every night and gave us a great show. Brilliant.

When a one-off concert in Athens was being planned for Joe Cocker, Concert Sound asked me to fly out from Heathrow to Greece to check out the local sound company to see if their speakers were up to the job. I spent the day with the sound company discussing the PA system they would supply and looking at their equipment, specifying what we needed and they were very helpful. However as I got back to the hotel I received a call from Concert Sound to say that the concert had been cancelled and I flew back home to England the next day, a totally wasted trip but I had an enjoyable visit to Athens.

Back in England I did three days at Hammersmith Odeon with a band called Guy, (no, me neither), but apparently they were an R&B hip hop soul band from America featuring Teddy Riley on vocals, never heard of them but they sold three nights at Hammersmith so they must have been fairly well known. Then a couple of one-off shows with an English band The Blessing, a blues and soul band who's single 'Highway 5' reached No 40 in the charts whilst I was doing these gigs, but then it was remixed in 1992 and reached No 30. Their album 'Prince of the Deep Water' featured guest musicians Bruce Hornsby, Rickie Lee Jones and Nicky Hopkins, quite impressive.

By this time, the Martin speakers that most people had been using for the past few years were being phased out in favour of the new EAW speakers (Eastern Acoustic Works), they had flying hooks on the top and bottom which started the line array fashion of hanging one speaker under the other. The new EAW speakers were a one-box cabinet which housed a 15" bass speaker, a 12" midrange speaker and a high frequency horn. On the top and bottom were hanging bars which could be used to hang the speakers in the air with other speakers underneath in a line, what we now call line array. These speakers could hang themselves with a specially designed frame above set at just the right angle. For the sub bass, a block of EAW sub bass speaker boxes were placed on the floor either next to or under the stage. For small in-fills for the front of the stage small 10" speakers could be placed in strategic positions to fill in blank spots. The old PA speaker systems were now old technology.

JOHN DENVER

Jeff Hooper, one of Concert Sound's engineers, was doing FOH for John Denver, I was asked to rig the system and help Jeff. Ten shows around the UK, doing all the usual venues, Manchester Apollo, Newcastle City Hall, Edinburgh Playhouse, Birmingham NEC, Bournemouth BIC, St Austell Coliseum, London Royal Albert Hall, Brighton Dome, Bristol Colston Hall, and a trip over to Ireland for a show at The Point in Dublin. I used a much smaller sound system as John Denver was only performing with his acoustic guitar and a small band with a string quartet. John Denver was another gentleman of the music business, a rare quality indeed and a pleasure to work with.

DOVES & ENERGY ORCHARD

A couple of one-off shows with English rock band The Doves at the University of London Union (ULU). The Doves made four studio albums, two of which got to No 1 in the UK charts. Then a show with Energy Orchard at a college in Canterbury, a band from Northern Ireland whose sound is a mix of Irish folk and Rhythm and Blues, those two shows took me back to my old college gig days driving my old transit van.

LEVEL 42 / THE BLESSING

A couple of days later I was relaxing at home looking forward to some time off when I received a telephone call from Concert Sound, "Can you fly to Hamburg tomorrow?" They wanted me to take over mixing FOH for The Blessing, a band supporting Level 42. They were halfway through a European tour and had just sacked their soundman who wasn't getting the sound the band wanted. That was my time off out the window, I packed my suitcase for another four weeks on the road. I arrived at Hamburg airport and made my way by taxi to the CCH venue, a huge warehouse exhibition type building with horrendous acoustics.

Level 42 were just finishing a soundcheck and I arrived in time to see the stage set being changed for The Blessing, at least I had the advantage of already having mixed two shows with them a few weeks earlier, so I knew the music and I had met the band, they were easy guys to get along with. The set-up time was running late and doors were about to be opened. Without any delay I went straight through a soundcheck in record time much to the amazement of the rest of the crew who were not used to soundchecking the band so fast. I reset the mixer from how the last guy had left it and I was ready for the show. Nine shows in Germany, two in Sweden, one in Finland, one in Holland, three in France ending up at LaCigale in Paris. The tour was a mixture of town halls, theatres and nightclubs using a Concert Sound Midas mixer and EAW speakers.

After The Blessing had done their set I would help on the Level 42 show helping Dave Dickson set up. That was a really enjoyable tour and good fun working with Dave.

When I got home I heard that Jake LeMesurier, the younger brother of my friend Robin LeMesurier, had died of a heroin overdose, he had been suffering from depression and a heroin addiction. It must have been difficult having very successful parents John LeMesurier and Hattie Jacques, both successful actors in their own right and a successful brother who played guitar with Rod Stewart. Although Jake worked as a roadie for a while he also played drums, but struggled to find a band. He was a nice guy and yet another wasted life lost to heroin.

MERCHANDISE

It started a long time ago with just a souvenir program, then came the T-shirts, followed by sweatshirts, hats and eventually jackets and much more. Anything sellable was put on sale in the hope that fans would buy it, just because it had their favourite artiste printed on it. Motorhead had the best idea, it gave out free T-shirts to everyone who attended their concert, it was not a huge expense for the band but it resulted in every young kid walking the streets wearing Motorhead T-shirts, a great marketing idea.

Then came tour merchandise given exclusively to the crew. Crew T-shirts and sweatshirts and exclusive tour jackets for those on the tour. On the Van Halen tour everyone had a brown leather jacket, a cross between a flying jacket and a motorcycle jacket, they felt comfortable to wear and looked good. It also caused a few heads to turn when thirty plus people checked into a hotel wearing what looked like a military uniform.

The Thin Lizzy white silk jacket was a bit over the top but seemed to attract the girls when you wore it. I gave mine away to a friend after I got tired of wearing it, white wasn't my colour anyway especially in silk. The Thin Lizzy mirror badges were popular as well. The fashion for silk tour jackets lasted about ten years before promoters and managers decided it wasn't fashionable anymore and was costing too much money to produce, just as well as I didn't really like wearing them. Some crew members wore their tour T-shirts as a kind of campaign medal to show off what bands they had worked with.

There is of course a lot of money involved in tour merchandise. Many bands sold the rights to a merchandise company for a set fee, it's then up to them to sell as much as they can to get their investment back and make a profit. If they back the wrong horse they could lose a fortune without any risk to the band. In 1980 on the Van Halen 'Invasion Tour', the band sold the merchandising rights for $4 million dollars, that's $1 million for each member of the band.

Programmes are generally a rip-off as they usually contain regurgitated photos from old programmes, plus a few notes about the artiste and a list of where the tour is going or has just been, you don't get much for your money. On one tour a 3-ton truck which followed the tour had to get re-stocked on a daily basis as they were selling so much. Then there are the badges, keyrings, posters and signed photographs. Tina Turner even had sweat bands for the wrist although I can't imagine her wearing one. Always on sale are the band's CD catalogue, even small unknown bands try to sell their CDs to fans as they walk out, especially live shows recorded on CD or DVD videos which are relatively cheap to produce.

Nowadays if you can't get what you want at the venue you could always go online to the artiste's website and get a back catalogue of old tour merchandise, that's the stuff they couldn't sell during the tour but is still available while stocks last.

On the Shirley Bassey tour the logo was a red rose on our tour jackets, but everyone called it the red cabbage tour because the rose looked like a cabbage due to its inferior printing.

Status Quo gave out free plastic guitars to the fans as they arrived so they could play along with the guitar solos, I suspect the band was tired of seeing the fans playing air-guitar every night and thought it a good idea to hand out plastic ones instead.

Dr Hook were always good with their tour merchandise, except that the tour jackets always had the year on the back which was a bit off-putting, their T-shirts kept me going for years. Lindisfarne T-shirts were generously handed out, except for one year when someone decided to choose purple as the colour scheme, nobody wanted to be seen dead in it and they ended up being used to wash the car. Michael Ball gave the crew a bottle of Michael Ball champagne after the tour, but I discovered it had another label stuck underneath, nice thought though. The Eric Clapton, ZZ Top, Joe Cocker tour had special chromium keyrings made with the bands' names engraved on it, very good quality and I still have one.

Bootleg merchandise is always a problem outside venues. Only the merchandise stalls inside the venue are genuine and sell authorised products. The merchandise that's offered to you outside the venues are generally cheaply made products of poor quality, with pathetic designs printed on them that look tacky. Dr Hook tour manager John Draper discovered a bootleg stall inside the venue trying to compete with the band's own official merchandise stall, so he poured a can of Coke over the products along the entire length of the table and told him to take his tacky trash away. It may be someone trying to earn a few quid on the side, but as with all bootleg products it's copyright theft and only ends up ripping off the audience by thinking they are getting genuine products from the artiste they've paid to see.

It doesn't end there, venues soon picked up on the amount of money they could make and started charging merchandisers and the band's own sellers a fee to operate inside their venue, in other words they wanted a slice of the profits. Some venues went so far as insisting that only their own staff could sell at their own merchandise stand, some insisting that programmes were only sold by their staff at a marked-up price which is why you often see programme sellers at the entrance doors before taking your seats.

27

EVERYTHING LOUDER – MEAT LOAF

LEVEL 42

1992 started off with another tour this time rigging the sound for Level 42. No support band on this leg of the tour, it was a club tour doing every grotty sleaze pit hole in Europe. Seven days in Spain whose venues are not known for having good facilities, a bullring where the dressing room was a slaughter room and there was still blood on the floor from last week's bullfight, stages too small to fit everything on, mixing positions which were impossible to access and of course the load-ins which took forever due to the fact that these venues were never designed for British rock bands carrying 20 tons of equipment in a 40-foot trailer. Nightclubs still had the smell of last night's beer, smoke and vomit, but we made our way around Spain, France, Italy, Austria to very supportive fans before returning to England to everyone's relief for nine shows in much cleaner and civilised venues ending up at the Cambridge Corn Exchange.

TONY JOE WHITE

On my return I was asked to mix the sound for legendary American singer Tony Joe White at the Grand Theatre in Clapham, a converted cinema and Victorian music hall. A colleague who was there mentioned that TJW sounded a lot better than the support act who'd used the same mixer before me, I was pleased to hear that. Tony went down a storm with his southern drawl accent and swamp rock music. The man from Louisiana played favourite songs he'd written like 'Steamy Windows' and 'Undercover Agent for the Blues' both covered by Tina Turner, 'Poke Salad Annie' covered by Elvis Presley and Tom Jones and 'Rainy Night in Georgia' covered by practically everyone. A very talented artiste and song writer.

GEORGE HARRISON

The next day I had the pleasure of doing a show with George Harrison at the Royal Albert Hall. This was a charity event for the Natural Law Party, one of George's pet charities he was involved in. It has something to do with 'Conflict free politics through holistic health programs and the practice of Transcendental meditation'. Yes, you've lost me there as well, but I'm sure he meant well.

It's always a long day rigging at the Royal Albert, not the easiest venue to get into. The stage is 30 feet below street level and access is via a long aluminium ramp, which on this occasion went missing, presumed stolen due to its high value in scrap metal I'm guessing.

Because there was no ramp this time, the local stage crew had to carry the entire production down a set of stairs from the top of the stalls down to the stage level and some of it down to the arena floor. Rigging is a nightmare at the RAH and seems to take all day waiting for the riggers to drop the ropes from the roof so you can attach the motor chains which will haul the speakers into the air, but first you have to wait until the lighting truss is up in the air and out of the way. The multicore cable runs from the stage to the mixing position. It isn't as bad as some venues, there's a tunnel which runs under the floor and pops up right at the back of the stalls just where the mixer is. Very handy.

During the equipment set-up George was in a good mood and came up to the sound mixer and chatted about the stage set and he seemed like a decent bloke. It was the first time I had met George and he was just as I imagined, dark, sleek and tanned with that unmistakable Liverpool accent. George Harrison was joined on stage by guitarists Joe Walsh from the Eagles, Gary Moore from Thin Lizzy and Colosseum and Mike Campbell from Tom Petty and the Heartbreakers, Joe and Gary each doing their own songs in the first half of the show.

After the interval, George walked on to enormous applause and went through some of his best-known songs including many Beatles tracks. 'Taxman', 'Give Me Love', 'Peace On Earth', 'Something', 'Got My Mind Set On You', 'My Sweet Lord', 'All Those Years Ago', ending up with 'While My Guitar Gently Weeps'.

The guitar solo on 'While My Guitar Gently Weeps' was played by Eric Clapton on the Beatles album, but the guitar solo this night was taken by Gary Moore in what I consider one of the best guitar solos I have ever witnessed from anybody ever. Hearing Gary's guitar solo that night made my bones turn to jelly, it was one of those moments that I will never forget and quite an emotional experience.

This also happened to be the last time that George performed live in Britain before he died and before the very last concert a few weeks later in New York.

Another bonus that night was seeing Ringo on stage playing drums, one of Ringo's rare appearances, and Ray Cooper on percussion which is a show all in itself if you've ever seen him, Ray has worked with practically everyone from the Rolling Stones down. For the encore all the musicians came on stage for a grand finale and did Chuck Berry's 'Roll over Beethoven' with George's son Dhani Harrison also playing guitar. What a night, it was one of those once in a lifetime events that will stay with me forever.

THE HIGHWAYMEN

I then had the pleasure to go out with an unusual mixture of artistes called The Highwaymen. The band consisted of Johnny Cash, Willy Nelson, Kris Kristofferson and Waylon Jennings, these were all very well-known country artistes in their own right. Even though I'm not especially a country music fan I'm well aware of the four names and how big they were. The four took up the front of stage position in a line, each with a mic stand and guitar in hand. There was a house band at the back of the stage who were all top session musicians from Nashville, and some of the best in the business. Each one of the Highwaymen would take it in turn to do one of their own songs whilst the other three sang backing vocals and played guitar.

It was like a family holiday for them, each one of them hired a luxury sleeper coach fitted out like a mobile home and they brought their families over to Europe to do this tour, and do some sightseeing at the same time. Johnny Cash bought his wife June Carter-Cash and their children. Kris Kristofferson's son Clint was part of the road crew as a stage tech and travelled with us on our crew bus except when there were some days off, then he went back on to the family bus. The car park got very crowded some days, with four buses for The Highwaymen plus a band bus, a crew bus and two 40-foot tractor trailers.

I spoke to Waylon Jennings a few times in the catering room when he joined us for our evening meal and I talked to him about Dr Hook, as I knew they knew each other. The Dr Hook band and their crew used to talk to me about Waylon Jennings during Dr Hook tours and the gigs they did together in the States, so I had a few stories to tell Waylon and Waylon told me a few things about Dr Hook and the singer Ray Sawyer before he left the band.

The band first did a few shows around Scandinavia, then we picked up the tour at Wembley Arena, and did four more in the UK before going to Ireland, Holland, Germany and Switzerland. Whilst we were playing the Deutschland Halle in Berlin some of the American road crew asked if I would take them to see the Berlin Wall, the Brandenburg Gate, the Reichstag and Checkpoint Charlie, all well-known landmarks they had heard so much about from Hollywood films. It was their first time to Europe so I did the tourist guide bit with them before heading back to do the soundcheck. We played London, Birmingham, Sheffield, Aberdeen, Dublin, Belfast, Brussels, Rotterdam, Hamburg, Berlin, Frankfurt, Munich and Zurich before heading home. I didn't realise country music was so popular, but with four big names like this on one bill I'm not surprised the shows sold well.

JOHN DENVER

Another tour with John Denver, this time around Europe doing Ghent in Belgium, Ludwigshafen, Bonn, Hamburg, Berlin, Essen, Frankfurt, Stuttgart and Munich in Germany, Bolzano in Italy and the 10,0000-seater Ahoy Arena in Holland. Whilst we were in Bonn, the capital of West Germany at the time, the American Ambassador's wife was a big fan of John Denver and managed to get herself and her husband front row seats as guests. It was a pleasure working with John Denver, such a nice guy and his music wasn't at all painful on the ear, although it did get a bit boring hearing the same songs every night and sometimes I found myself struggling to stay awake. I was pleased when he got to the high tempo songs, I woke up a bit then.

It was a pity to hear of his untimely death a few years later in 1997. John was an experienced pilot and had his own plane, somehow he flew his plane into the ocean whether on purpose or by accident we will never know, although the cause of the crash was an empty fuel tank, there was a rumour at the time he was depressed. I remember him telling us backstage one time that a few years before, when there was an oil embargo by Saudi Arabia and the Gulf States, he had hollowed out the inside of a mountain which backed onto his house, he filled the mountain cavern with aviation fuel for his plane before being caught out and had to pay a fine for illegally storing fuel. John played all his hits including 'Rocky Mountain High' and 'Take Me Home, Country Roads'. As well as playing solo with his acoustic guitar he also had a four-piece string section, bass, percussion and saxophone/flute players.

Staying awake was not a problem with my next tour.

GARY MOORE

Gary Moore, the brilliant ex-Thin Lizzy guitarist, I worked with him when he was in Colosseum II. I knew him quite well by now although he was not a man of many words, a quiet sort of guy. During soundcheck his guitar tech would put X chalk marks on the stage where Gary found good spots for guitar feedback, by standing on the X mark he could hold a guitar note for minutes at a time if he wanted. I rate Gary Moore as one of the best guitar players of all time alongside Eric Clapton, Jeff Beck and Eddy Van Halen, seeing him play with George Harrison on stage just two months before cemented my opinion.

MICHAEL CRAWFORD

Going from one extreme to another and back again is all part of working for a sound company as opposed to working for just one artiste. My next job was a tour with Michael Crawford, he was singing hit songs from the west end shows of Andrew Lloyd Webber. These included *Cats*, *Les Miserables*, *Evita*, *Joseph's Technicolour Dreamcoat*, *Jesus Christ Superstar*, *Starlight Express*, *Phantom of the Opera* and some other hits from West End and Broadway shows.

I remember Michael Crawford as the hapless Frank Spencer in *Some Mothers Do 'Ave 'Em* which ran from 1973 to 1978 on television. I didn't realise he had such a tremendous operatic voice as I found out when he performed some of the hits that he'd actually sung in the West End shows and on Broadway. We had a 37 -piece orchestra and a conductor, another challenge similar to the Shirley Bassey shows having to mic up all the different instruments. Only ten venues on this tour but multiple nights in each place, so the tour went on for three weeks around the UK.

One night as we were having our evening meal in the green room backstage, the television was on and it was showing an old episode of *Some Mothers Do 'Ave 'Em*, I was with the crew watching it as we ate our meal. Michael Crawford just happened to pass through on his way to his dressing room, he paused for a while, looked at the TV and started to smile in amusement whilst looking at himself on television as he was so many years younger, he thought it amusing, everyone was looking at him for his reaction.

I was using the now familiar EAW speaker system that was working out well as a flying system, most of the speakers now went in the air with a small in-fill on stage for the front rows. Surprisingly I was using as many as 44 EAW speaker cabinets and 8 sub bass cabinets. Long gone were the mountains of speaker boxes piled up high on each side of the stage and it did look a lot cleaner. For a mixer I had a Yamaha PM3000 which was now part of the Concert Sound stock, a versatile mixer and very easy to use.

MICHAEL BALL

As if one West End musical artiste was not enough I got called in to do front of house sound for Michael Ball at the Dorchester Hotel in London for an audience of super rich celebrities and invited guests. That was quite an experience. A lot of evening dresses, tuxedo suits, jewellery, perfume and champagne.

The show at the Dorchester Hotel with Michael Ball must have gone down well as I was asked to do the sound at the hotel again for an Egyptian wedding reception, the bride and groom were very rich Egyptian citizens and were living in London. As part of the reception, which was totally over the top as far as presentation goes, they flew in direct from Egypt one of Egypt's top dance bands who arrived from the airport late. I had already set up the sound system and their mics but was unsure what to expect. The only instruction I was given by the band's manager was to put loads of echo on the voice. I did that but apparently that wasn't enough, I was told to put even more echo on, it must be a cultural thing as it sounded like far too much echo to my Anglo-Saxon ears, but if that's what they want. The band were quite good actually in an Arabic kind of way, I was sure that I heard a snake being charmed out of its basket, it was quite hypnotic.

CHRIS DeBURGH

The next week I was out rigging sound for a Chris de Burgh tour, seven shows around the UK. My old friend Jeff Hooper from Concert Sound was mixing FOH and I was helping him rig the system and set the stage mics. I didn't realise that although he was fairly well known in the UK, Chris de Burgh made huge record sales in European and South American countries. He is best known for his hits 'Lady in Red', 'Don't Pay the Ferryman', 'Missing You' and 'A Spaceman Came Travelling'. Although we only did seven shows around the UK he did have a massive European tour scheduled for later in the year. Chris had a five-piece band plus himself on guitars and keyboards, quite an easy show to work on.

On the 4th and 5th October I worked with Gary Moore again headlining his own shows at the Royal Albert Hall for a special one-off, great shows again.

TOM JONES

Next was another one of Concert Sound's regular artistes, Tom Jones. I was not a fan of his but he did put on a good show for the many fans who came to see him, unlike the early days in the 1960s when ladies would throw their knickers on stage, the tradition seemed to have continued except the ladies were older, the knickers were new and they still had the price tags attached. I don't know what happened to them but I know there was a huge flight case backstage where all items thrown on stage were put every night. 22 venues and 31 shows in six weeks. Tom didn't do soundchecks except for the first show which was really a production rehearsal, everything after that had to be right when he walked out on stage. On stage he had a five-piece band plus a four-piece brass section and three backing singers.

DAVID SANBORN

December ended the year with one of my favourite jazz artistes, David Sanborn, a jazz saxophonist. I already had four of his albums, and after seeing him perform live on one of the TV shows I did at Tyne Tees Television I was totally blown away, David Sanborn is someone who is highly regarded as a session player and has played with practically everyone. Best known for his R&B smooth style jazz, but I also see him as the heavy rock sax player of the jazz world. He is without doubt one of the world's best sax players having played with everyone from Eric Clapton, Bob Dylan, Bruce Springsteen, Elton John and The Eagles to Stevie Wonder, and James Brown plus a list too long to include here. A pleasure and a memory not to forget. It was just a short tour really, London, Rotterdam, Brussels, Berlin, Hamburg and Cologne. In the Town and Country Club in London I was able to use the house PA system which was pretty good. This was a low stress tour and quite enjoyable mixing his FOH sound.

The next tour couldn't have been more different but that is what I enjoyed about working for a sound company, you never got bored with the same genre of music. I like all types of music within reason and up to a limit but listening to the same artiste or the same type of music month in, month out, or year in, year out, would drive me mad.

THE RAMONES

So now, The Ramones, a legendary American punk-rock band who had a very strong following. Even today after 20 years you still see young kids wearing Ramones T-shirts who have probably never even seen the band live. They still have a cult following even years after the band split, by 2014 all four original members had died. Last week I even saw a 3-year-old child in a pushchair wearing a Ramones T-shirt.

Joey, Johnny, C.J. and Marky were not brothers even though they all had a Ramone surname as their stage name, as did the other three ex-members of the band. Eight shows in nine days across the UK in some of the best known rock clubs, from Barrowlands in Glasgow to Nottingham Rock City ending up at the legendary Brixton Academy. Johnny Ramone carried his own microphone stand which he had made especially for him as he was almost seven feet tall, I couldn't reach the mic to check it without pulling it over at an angle.

Ramones at Brixton Academy. 1992
Featuring Johnny, Joey, C.J. and Marky

After the Manchester Academy show we had a day off, I was stopped in the street by a young girl who said she recognised me from last night's show and asked if I knew where the band were staying, of course I did know but wasn't going to tell her.

ERIC CLAPTON

I had Christmas off at home and spent some time with my girlfriend. I was asked if I would to do the front of house sound for Eric Clapton at one of his New Year's Eve parties in aid of Alcoholics Anonymous, a charity for which Eric is a councillor. The idea of these parties which Eric organised is for former alcoholics to attend a party in a non-alcoholic environment with fellow members, and not be surrounded by other drinkers which may put temptation in their way. I had a hotel room booked after the show and I made sure my girlfriend came along to celebrate the New Year with me, I wasn't going to leave her at home on this night of the year.

Before the show we had two days of rehearsals and we were booked into a room at the back of a pub near Eric's house. I set up a small PA in what looked like a function room which was probably hired out for weddings, parties and discos. The pub was crowded with Sunday drinkers enjoying a pint or a Sunday lunch totally unaware that Eric Clapton and his band were rehearsing in the back room, or maybe they were aware but were used to seeing him in his local pub. Halfway through the rehearsals Phil Collins casually strolled in clutching a pint of beer, said hello to me, pulled up a chair and sat by me at the sound mixer while he listened to the rehearsals. Nobody took any notice.

After the rehearsals we got ready for the show at Wokingham Leisure Centre, I installed a sound system which consisted of EAW speaker cabinets, I was using my favourite 32-channel Midas XL2 mixer. Kerry Lewis who always did Eric's monitor mix was there and brought his wife and children along for the show. Eric's entire band were involved including Andy Fairweather Lowe on guitar and Chris Stanton on keyboards.

Also along as a guest was Gary Brooker from Procol Harem who did a version of 'Whiter Shade of Pale'. Eric did all his usual best known songs. At midnight at the turn of the New Year he did a version of Wilson Pickett's hit 'In the Midnight Hour' and then his own hit 'After Midnight' written by JJ Cale who also wrote another one of Clapton's songs 'Cocaine'. A good supply of food and non-alcoholic drinks were provided and we had a great time enjoying the party atmosphere, retiring to a nearby hotel in the early hours after stripping down the stage and loading out.

Some bad news almost spoilt the celebrations when word was out that Dave Martin, founder of Martin Audio and a good friend and colleague of mine for many years, was missing, presumed dead. Some blood was found in his garage at home although his body was never found. This was a very sad day for the music industry, one of the pioneers of the modern rock and roll sound system had been murdered, and he will always be remembered as the designer of the Martin PA system.

I will always remember having chats with him over a cup of tea down in his first workshop in a basement in Covent Garden. Asking about his home hi-fi, he'd surprised me when he said he owned a pair of Quad electrostatic speakers rather than his own Martin cabinets, he said it was because he liked to listen to music at low level. After selling his business to the TGI group he'd stayed on as an R&D director, but we all knew he had begun to lose interest in his loud speaker business and was getting involved in a helicopter business with some very dodgy geezers, and had invested a lot of his own money in it. His partner 'allegedly' mislaid £250,000 without any paperwork or receipts.

Even though Dave Martin's body was never found, the police eventually came up with enough forensic evidence to get a conviction and his business partner was arrested, convicted of his murder and went to jail. His business Martin Audio kept going and is now part of the TGI group and has expanded into installing speaker systems into pubs, nightclubs, arenas and stadiums around the world.

ERIC CLAPTON

1993 started off with a series of Eric Clapton concerts at The Royal Albert Hall, Eric now holds the record for the most number of nights performed at this venue by any artiste. Rigging started at midnight for the lighting crew with the sound crew coming in shortly afterwards and it went on all night, I installed twelve EAW speaker cabinets each side of the stage flown in the air, three very small in-fill cabinets on the front of stage for the front row seats, plus two speaker stacks up on the Gallery, on level four next to the follow spot operator, also known as 'the gods' as it's so high up. All this required a lot of cable runs and amplifier racks being taken up in lifts, the main bank of amplifier racks which consisted of eight, each having six 1,000-watt amplifiers in each rack, totalling a possible 48,000-watts, but of course these are never driven at full volume, it would have taken the roof off.

The band consisted of Eric and Andy Fairweather Lowe on guitars, Chuck Leavell on keyboards, Nathan East on bass, Steve Ferrone on drums, Ray Cooper on percussion, Katie Kissoon and Tessa Niles on backing vocals. An impressive band and they sounded really good. Robert Collins who had worked for Eric for some time did the FOH mix.

TWO TRIBES

In March I was asked if I would take on a dual role of tour manager and soundman with an up-and-coming band called Two Tribes. They were a British rock band who played a kind of Funk-Metal Rock with a bit of electronica thrown in. They seemed happy to mix and match their sound that included heavy funk grooves and soul. It was obvious from their album that the four-piece multi-racial band seemed to have an identity problem. The opening track called 'This Ain't Soul II Soul, It's Rock'n'Roll' says it all and the album title 'File under Rock' was a deliberate attempt to make sure the album wasn't placed in the soul section of record stores. Twelve shows over two weeks doing some unusual venues. There were a few I knew, Newcastle Riverside where I spent many nights operating the Nitelites PA system and Rock City Nottingham, some good clubs known for putting on a good selection of rock bands, some of the bands who played there are really famous now.

Mixing sound for them was a challenge some nights as I was having to do my 'make the best of a bad job' situation where the sound system specified in the contract and rider was nowhere near as good as that requested. The contract, which I always carried as my role of tour manager, stipulated that the promoter had to provide a sound system of 4kWatts or more, a 24-channel mixer and some effects units, not a lot to ask but I very rarely got anything like that. Unfortunately I had a disagreement with one of the club owners about his PA system, and when I compared his PA system to his manhood he kicked me out of the club along with my backline roadie and refused to let us back in again. After a couple of diplomatic phone calls from the band's management he let us back in again and I had to use what was no more than a giant hi-fi. I got on really well with the band, a good bunch of lads and when I told them what I'd said to the club owner they thought the whole episode hilarious.

Just because you specify a certain mixing console, mics or other equipment on your rider doesn't mean you'll get it. By the time you get to the gig and realise what you've got is nothing like what you asked for it's too late, but you can't just pull the show because you haven't got your favourite compressor or digital delay. I sometimes feel like a Formula 1 racing driver turning up at Silverstone and being offered a Ford Escort instead of a Formula 1 racing car. But the show goes on and you just have to make the best of it.

HELEN HOFFNER

Another club tour this time with Helen Hoffner. Helen was previously in an all-girl band called The Marines. They had a couple of minor hit singles and supported Kylie Minogue on tour in 1989. Helen then went solo, formed her own band and had just released an album of 12 songs with a track 'Edge of a Dream' featuring Bryan Adams. Helen was quite young and very attractive, she had a great voice and was really thrilled that she actually had her own road crew, a new experience for her and she really appreciated everything we did for her. We did 6 showcase gigs around Europe, three in Germany, one in Norway, one in Sweden and one at the Borderline in London, that's getting to be like a second home to me and I was getting along quite well with one of the waitresses who worked there. Helen was an artiste I really enjoyed doing sound for and I hoped she would do well so I could work with her again. The tour only had two crew members, myself and Steve May from Concert Sound, we took along a small PA system, Steve did the monitor mix and I did FOH, we both helped with the backline for the four piece band. Unfortunately I didn't hear from Helen again.

MARY J BLIGE

A different kind of act in Mary J Blige, an artiste I would put in the Rap, Hip Hop, and R&B category. We did four nights at Hammersmith Odeon and one night at Birmingham's Hummingbird Night Club. Also on the bill for most of the show was H-Town, Father MC, Split Decision and compere Curtis

Walker. Don't ask me to identify who was who as it all seemed like a cluster catastrophe on stage with so many people, I don't think half the people on stage were actually in the band.

Mary J had a set-up of three keyboard players (yes three), a DJ, a drummer, two backing vocals and two dancers, who the others were was a mystery. One disappointing aspect of the show was that she didn't come on stage until 10.05pm and was only on stage for twenty-five minutes, which was a total rip-off and caused the audience to boo her off.

One of the most amusing things I remember about those shows was the American band member who announced Mary J onto stage each night. In London he announced, "Hammersmith-London please welcome Mary J Blige," then in Birmingham he announced, "Birmingham-London please welcome Mary J Blige," (Birmingham-London?) I don't think he understood English geography very well.

It was the first time I'd seen black Americans wearing oversized jeans hanging around their buttocks, their white underpants showing and the crutch hanging down to their knees. I thought what is the point of that? It not only looked ridiculous it was laughable as they had to use one hand to hold their jeans in place. Predictably it wasn't long before youngsters in this country would follow the fashion and walk around the streets with one hand holding their jeans up to stop them slipping down, they must have thought they looked really cool. Maybe that's me just being an old git and out of touch with modern youth fashion, thank goodness it's gone now. A few years later when the fad had gone out of fashion I stopped a young lad in the street and said to him, "Oi mate you need to get a belt on those jeans they're falling down." He looked at me like I was an old codger which I probably was to him. I knew what I was saying but I did it anyway for a joke just to see his reaction.

BRIAN MAY / PEARL JAM

I did a one-off show at Birmingham's NEC with Brian May, the guitarist with Queen, it was a great event and another one of those shows I will always remember.

Four dates with Pearl Jam, two at Brixton Academy and two at the massive Ahoy Arena in Rotterdam, I'm not a fan of Pearl Jam and it was not a very enjoyable few days, in fact it was rather boring, just like their music.

Being crew boss and rigging sound for other people can be a bit frustrating, but three festivals in Germany can make up for all the hassle sometimes. My job here with my crew was to rig several delay towers along massive airfields so that the people at the back could hear the stage without the people at the front being blown away and deafened. The airfields were ex-American NATO bases, now the USAF have pulled out, they have been returned to the German Civilian Authorities.

The set-up meant that the sound from the delay towers had to be synchronised with the main stage sound system. As we all know sound travels much slower than light, so if you're standing 100 metres back from the stage you wouldn't hear the sound from the stage until a few milliseconds later. Installing more speakers further back means the people further away could hear the sound without deafening those at the front, but it creates a problem with a kind of echo or slap-back effect. I rectified this by putting a digital delay line in the signal path before sending it to the amplifiers on the delay towers. It is the slow speed of sound which causes echoes. It's a common occurrence you'd hear in railway stations because there are usually speakers placed in a straight line down the length of a platform, after the sound from the nearest speaker reaches you, the repeats you hear are the sounds arriving from speakers further down the platform.

The speed of sound is approximately 768 mph or 340 metres per second, depending upon temperature and moisture. In practical terms that's about 3 milliseconds of delay for every one metre of distance. I used this basic method to start with by measuring out the length of the field then calculating the distance and sound delay required, but as this method is not 100% accurate I double checked by playing a click-track over the speakers and listening to the time each 'click' reached my ears. If the delay is correct the click from the front speakers on stage and the click from the delay tower should be in sync.

Of course not everyone in the crowd would be standing in the same place, so if you stood slightly off the centre line you will be moving away from the delay tower and the sound sync cannot be 100% accurate for everyone in that field or arena. Nowadays all the hard work is eliminated, sound processors are doing all the calculating for you automatically which greatly improves the phasing of sound in large venues. In 1993 we didn't have that luxury.

The first venue was Wildenrath Airfield, an ex-American NATO airbase near Munchengladbach since abandoned and now derelict. The second was Finthen Airfield at Mainz, another ex-American NATO airbase. The artistes appearing over the two days were Rod Stewart, Tina Turner, Joe Cocker, Foreigner, Prince, Duran Duran, and Ginger Baker, a big line-up. The third venue was a football stadium at Bielefeld with Chris de Burgh.

It was good to see Joe Cocker again, he flew in to just do the two shows. Tina Turner came in with my mate Rory Madden, doing the monitor mix as he had been doing for the last few years since he got dropped into the job, he worked with Tina for many years so he must have been doing alright and I know Tina took a liking to him straight off. Rod Stewart did his usual stomping show.

What made Prince's set different is that he did all the mix himself from on-stage. He didn't have a soundman out front, if he wanted to adjust anything he walked over to the side of the stage and did it himself, he then sent the mixed sound of his band to side-fill monitors on stage and a separate feed to the main PA system for the audience. I don't know if he didn't trust anyone to mix his sound or he is just a perfectionist who prefers to do it himself. Knowing how he records his albums I suspect it's the latter, since he wrote all his own songs and played all the instruments himself, not stopping there he also produced and engineered the final mix.

As you would expect Prince's flight cases backstage were all purple, no surprise there. Similarly Ginger Baker's Gurvitz Army had flight cases all in army camouflage colours, in Ginger's case it seems like a waste of money as it's only the people backstage that ever see the equipment cases and it's not like the band's name will last as long as the cases do.

Michael Ball asked if I'd do the front of house sound for a one-off concert at the Dominion Theatre in London featuring hit songs from the West End and Broadway, another enjoyable show to mix.

ERIC CLAPTON / JOE WALSH / ZZ TOP

Then a charity show featuring Eric Clapton, Joe Walsh from The Eagles, ZZ Top and Joe Cocker. Two shows at Birmingham's NEC and one at Sheffield Arena, these were great shows, seeing Joe Cocker again, ZZ Top were a right bunch of characters doing their own brand of southern rock and Joe Walsh went through a number of Eagles hits and some of his own.

MEAT LOAF

The year ended with Meat Loaf for his 'Everything Louder' tour, we headed out for three days of rehearsals at the International Arena in Cardiff followed by a gig on the fourth day. Eleven more dates in the UK including Wembley Arena. Four trucks for the equipment and three buses for the twenty-two road crew that included catering, riggers and a carpenter.

Meat Loaf put on a brilliant show performing the entire *Bat out of Hell* tracks, the production was faultless and so like the album but then it should be after the years he's been performing it. Over the next three tours in three years Meat Loaf got through as many as three sound engineers, thankfully I was just babysitting their engineer and looking after the system. The FOH guys had such a hard time from Meat Loaf and generally did a good job in my opinion. The soundman on this tour was Carl Gagnon and he did a good job mixing. He introduced me to a Yamaha signal processor which he wanted to use instead of the EAW processor that normally comes with EAW speakers. It made quite a difference to the sound, you could fine tune each crossover band and select where you wanted to crossover, cut and boost each frequency which you couldn't do on an EAW processor. It made the system sound so much cleaner. From then on I always used one myself. Thanks Carl.

Meat (as he was normally called) would walk up to the sound mixer and tell the soundman what he thought he wanted changed. Every show was recorded on a DAT (Digital Audio Tape). Unlike conventional cassette tapes, a DAT cassette played for five hours and recorded in a digital format like a CD, so you didn't get the hiss and hum you got from conventional cassette recorders. Every night he would analyse the show back on his bus or at his hotel, in order to perfect the musicians' performance as much as the stage sound or audience mix, he really was a perfectionist and took the show and the sound seriously which I admire, that's good in a way as some musicians are reluctant to get involved in what they sound like.

I had a massive sound system, as many as 74 EAW speaker cabinets on the truck, 37 a side, I always liked to make sure everyone in the arena got a good sound, and for that you had to point a speaker at them. I've been to arena concerts on some of my days off to see some really big world class acts and was disappointed to find all the sound was directed straight forward. That's OK in an oblong hall but no good for wrap-around seating as you get in arenas. What is wrong with these soundmen? Are they just lazy or don't they have a clue about sound distribution? Don't they realise that people sit on the sides and have paid for a ticket, and more importantly which is something I realised early on, the side seating is where the VIPs and guests always sit and they are the people who have direct access to the artiste, so it makes sense to get it sounding good at the sides as well, not just at the mixing position. Along working with me from Concert Sound was Adrian Fitzpatrick doing monitors and Steve May who looked after the mics and general PA equipment, a good team.

Meatloaf had just completed a major tour of the USA and Canada and had then flown straight over to do Europe. As per normal they brought their own backline equipment and picked up sound and lighting in the continent they were in. Concert Sound provided the sound and Neg Earth provided the lights, four trucks were provided by Edwin Shirley again. One of the easiest venues on this tour was the 11,000-seater Sheffield Arena because its design was based on a typical American sports arena, they are just made for music events, they drove the trucks right inside the venue and unloaded straight onto the stage, and this made life so much easier. Of course there were many arenas in the UK with similar designs but I think Sheffield was the best in 1993.

Even though Meat Loaf put on a brilliant show every night, I've never met a ruder, more ignorant self-important egocentric singer as Meat Loaf. On a personal level I didn't like him.

It's funny how you accumulate a suitcase full of hotel shampoo and soap bottles along with hotel notepads, pens and assorted free gifts during a tour, it's not until you tip the case out you realise how much stuff you pick up along the way. A nice touch at the end of this tour was a request that all those hotel soaps, shampoos and sewing kits that you inadvertently collect as you travel around the hotels be collected and handed in, so they can be distributed to the homeless missions and shelters back in the USA, we all seem to end up with a suitcase full of the stuff.

ERIC CLAPTON

After Christmas I was asked to do another Eric Clapton show mixing his sound again for his Alcoholics Anonymous New Year's Eve party. I didn't mind doing that, the previous year was a good laugh and we were all well fed and watered but not alcoholically of course. It was a real party atmosphere and good fun.

Photo: Tim Boyle
Concert Sound amplifier racks backstage at an Eric Clapton concert.

Photo: Tim Boyle
EAW sound system at the Royal Albert Hall at Eric Clapton concert.

28

END OF THE ROAD

Signs you're an old Soundman:
1. You start your conversation with new roadies, "When I was younger."
2. You're complaining because the music is too loud.
3. Sleeping on the couch hurts your back.
4. You can't sleep without the sound of a bus generator.
5. If you sleep with a Maglite by your bed, it's too late!

RAY CHARLES

The New Year started with a show with Ray Charles at Earl's Court sponsored by Ford Motor Company who were launching their new range of tractors, both from Ford and from New Holland which is owned by Ford, in fact New Holland tractors are just Ford tractors with New Holland badges stuck on the front. After the tractors were revealed with a blitz of smoke, lights and a high volume fanfare the invited audience were treated to a show from the jazz giant Ray Charles. He had a big orchestra and some of the brass section in the band who were backing him were also the Tom Jones brass section, who I knew personally so I gave them an extra monitor speaker which they were grateful for.

Whilst rigging the PA system, I had to run some amplifiers, a few speaker cabinets and cables up to the gallery normally closed off to the public. After I'd done that I tried to make my way back down to the ground floor via a different staircase, but found that it only took me down to a fire escape door out to the street which had a padlock on it. When I tried to return up to the gallery I found that the door was latched from the inside with no handle on the outside; panic started to set in as there was no way I could contact anyone on the crew and it could be hours before they realised I was missing. Banging and kicking all the doors didn't achieve anything and I didn't have a mobile phone in 1994 to call anyone. The only thing that saved me was the fact I had a Swiss army knife and I managed to slide the long blade between the doorframes, forced the latch open and returned to the gallery where I made my back down by the original staircase. From then on I always checked that door handles worked from both sides and I never go anywhere without my Swiss army knife.

MEATLOAF

In March I was back on tour with Meatloaf but with a new soundman at the mixer, Paul Dalen. With six in the band and thirty-six in the crew it was a big production again. Twenty shows around Europe starting off with three days at Wembley Arena, four more in the UK, back to Holland, Denmark, Sweden, Norway, Switzerland and Germany. On this tour I had my old mate Paul (Pab) Boothroyd along as a sound tech helping me rig the system and Steve May from the last tour while I did the babysitting service at the FOH sound mixer. Paul Dalen was a nice guy and did a good job mixing although he had the same problems as the last soundman had working for Meatloaf.

SHIRLEY BASSEY

Another Shirley Bassey tour, always enjoyable to work with her and a thirty-eight-piece orchestra which this time included a twelve-piece string section, eight brass, five woodwind and a five-piece rhythm section of guitar, bass, piano, keyboards and percussion. Twenty-three shows in thirty-three days across twelve venues in the UK including an unusual venue at the 500-year-old Guildhall in London and six nights at the Royal Festival Hall. Unusually we had comedian Adrian Walsh as the warm-up act instead of a musical act.

There were always celebrities in the audience and on one occasion Joan

Collins who was known to be a friend of Shirley Bassey's turned up with her companions, they walked into the audience just minutes before the show started, made their way to their seats in the third row from the front. Joan was wearing a huge fur coat and ballgown, the audience recognised her and for some reason gave her a round of applause which delighted Joan enormously. She turned to the audience, smiled and gave a royal wave back as if she were the Queen, how bizarre, anyone would think she was the star of the show the way she entered the hall.

TOM JONES

Straight after Shirley, we did Tom Jones with the same production and same crew except Tom had an eleven-piece band instead of an orchestra. We set up at John Henry's rehearsal rooms which was a bit cramped because of the small room but Tom Jones eventually walked in with his familiar orange tan with his son Mark who was also his manager. Twenty-four shows around the UK and Dublin. At Birmingham's NEC Arena I couldn't help but notice a brand new Range Rover with new registration plates which Tom arrived in and parked at the back of the stage inside the arena, even after all this time ladies in the audience still threw their knickers onto the stage.

By now I was using the Midas XL3 mixer, the newest mixer from Midas with VCAs (Voltage Controlled Amplifiers). These controlled banks of faders without having to use sub-groups. The precursor to digital desks, as with most new things it took a while to get used to the new format but after playing around with it for a while it soon became second nature.

After the last show in Dublin, Tom flew to Abu Dhabi and Dubai for a couple of exclusive shows which I suspect were very well paid. The UK crew weren't invited along.

MICHAEL BALL

In December I was back doing the front of house sound mix for Michael Ball again. Seventeen shows in thirteen theatres and concert halls, just the kind of venues I like including two final shows at Hammersmith Odeon before Christmas. I had a bit of a problem on this tour in the form of a really heavy cold, my nose was blocked up and running, my throat was sore with a dry cough. I had a high temperature and I generally felt terrible. Worst of all my ears were blocked, the worst thing that could happen to a soundman in the middle of a tour. I had a word with the tour manager Phil Bowdery whom I'd known for years. I remember when Phil was a roadie for the pop band Mud when they had a hit with 'Tiger Feet', I told Phil I thought it best if someone replaced me on the sound mixer as I couldn't guarantee what I was listening to or what the show was sounding like, he reassured me it sounded good and I didn't need to step aside, which was reassuring.

Mike Smith the ex-keyboard player with the Dave Clarke Five was working for Michael as his personal assistant and Michael got him on stage during the show to do a DC5 song, 'Bits and Pieces' or 'Glad All Over'. At the end of the tour Michael Ball gave all the crew a bottle of Michael Ball champagne, in fact it was a bottle of supermarket champagne with a Michael Ball sticker over the top, not complaining though it was a nice touch and a personal present from him as well.

ERIC CLAPTON

New Year's Eve came around again and my third Eric Clapton concert for his charity Alcoholics Anonymous, on my way there I heard on the BBC news that Eric had been awarded an OBE. Gary Brooker from Procol Harem came on and did a couple of songs again including his hit 'A Whiter Shade of Pale'. It was a great night, lavish food was laid on again, plenty of drink but all non-alcoholic of course, I did however find a few discarded empty mini-bottles of spirits under the tables after the show ended as the cleaners were sweeping up. Eric did his usual hit songs and favourites, 'Layla', 'After Midnight', 'Lay Down Sally', 'Knockin' on Heaven's Door', etc. After the load-out we all went back to our hotel, and the following morning I took the equipment back to the warehouse.

After taking the sound system back to the warehouse I collected my toolbox and loaded it into my car. Mick Anderson told me he had another tour he wanted me to start in January, but in my heart I knew that it was the end of the line for me, my heart wasn't in it anymore.

29

HOTEL CALIFORNIA

It finally happened. I realised that I was getting older and I didn't want to spend the rest of my life living out of a suitcase. I had come to the decision that I had done my bit, I'd had enough, I'd stopped enjoying what I was doing and it was time to move on and do something else with my life, I'd done a lot of things in this business and it was now time for a new challenge.

Whilst I felt lucky that I was still healthy and still fit enough to carry a speaker cabinet up two flights of stairs, I thought to myself, do I really want to do this? Whilst most of the crew on the tour bus are a lot younger than me, I realised I was the oldest. When the young guys called me grandad, then you know it's time to quit while you're ahead.

Although age and experience was a bonus over the inexperienced young kids who came into the business years after me it suddenly sinks in when they ask to hear your old road tales. The bands you talk about they've never heard of and they wonder how we ever managed with the primitive equipment we had to work with. Or worse they just simply don't care what it was like in the trenches of the 1960s and 70s.

The lure of the road had lost its appeal and I actually looked forward to sleeping in my own bed each night. Yes, you do get to stay in five-star luxury hotels but it's not five-star hotels every night nor is it five-star on every tour, sometimes it's only one-star.

The physical toll of endless hours on the road, fast food, mind-numbing repetition of soundchecks, the shows, video shoots, after-show parties and all that travelling, both on the road and hanging around airports. It's not always a rock star lifestyle. It was long hours, hard work both physically and mentally and you don't always get the recognition or the thanks you deserve.

I got tired of it all, I've been in the business 30 years and on the road professionally for 25 years. It was the planes, buses, trucks, hotels, seedy clubs, junk food, crap music and some very odd people you have to share a bus or a hotel room with, it wears you down after a while and I was shattered.

I can see now why so many people turned to drink or drugs as a form of escape, both crew members and musicians. I avoided that pitfall but I've seen what it's done to some of my friends, fellow workmates and musicians. Some that I've known very well have died as a result of drug abuse, others who may be a bit luckier have survived but lost their brain cells. Some use drugs, some use alcohol but the effect is the same. I never got into the acid culture or hard drugs, I saw people who did and they suddenly developed different personalities, became different people. I have a low tolerance to things like that whether drink or drugs, a Purple Heart I took one Christmas Eve kept me up all night doing housework, I laughed afterwards the house was so clean. I was so awake and buzzing it was the only one I ever tried.

I enjoyed the Rock 'n' Roll lifestyle for many years, but I couldn't put up with it anymore. The inflated egos even amongst the crew were sometimes worse than those of the musicians, I already missed my children growing up and it cost me my marriage. Driving overnight onto the next town after a show, the people on the tour bus were starting to annoy me.

It wasn't that easy to adjust, once the decision was made not to go back on the road, it did take some time to acclimatise to the idea and to decide what I would do instead. For a while I didn't want to go to any concerts, when I did I couldn't help but analyse the sound and indeed the whole production of the show. I felt disappointed when I did go to a show and felt that I could have done a better job. I would have hung speakers in a different format or mixed the show differently, half the time the soundmen seemed to be asleep on the job whenever I took a look at them or was it just me? They were missing cues or were they just not listening to the music?

I have been asked if I miss being on the road and touring, my answer is mixed, yes I miss the thrill of the live show, the adrenalin and the atmosphere when the house lights go down and the buzz you get mixing those great songs every night even if it is 60 nights in a row. But what I don't miss is the constant travelling, the tantrums from some of the crew members or the egos from some stuck-up artistes and musicians, the airports, the hotels, the venues that can vary so much depending where you are and what country you're in and who you are working with.

The money when your working is good, there's no doubt about that, but when you're not working you're not being paid so what you earn has to last you through the down-time or through the times there is no work around. That means having to choose between a family life and continuously living on the road, despite what many have tried, you can't have both. I know there are married men who work in this business just like those who work in other jobs that take them away from home, leaving home for weeks or months at a time does have an effect on you and your family life. You miss seeing your children growing up, missing important dates like their birthdays, school plays or taking them on days out and of course I don't forget the effect it had on leaving my wife alone for so long. I don't care what others claim, it does have an effect. I've known a few musicians quit the band due to pressure from their wives or girlfriends because they are away from home so much or they quit because the band doesn't bring in enough to pay the rent or feed the family.

The funny thing about the music and sound business is that once it gets into your bones you can't just give it up, going home after a tour, you're restless. I found it hard to sleep without the sound of that bus generator. At home I didn't have that 7.30 pm call when the doors were opened to the public and I put the walk-in music on the PA system. The crew meals backstage after soundcheck are generally good but not as good as home cooking and sometimes you have to make do with a takeaway. I miss that buzz when you get the 5-minute cue waiting for the house lights to go down and I hear the roar of the crowd as the band walks on stage, the adrenalin surge is indescribable, and for a while after the tours you're restless.

I've been doing it for so many years, you still need to adjust to it. When you're at home you do things differently, you need to readjust to not living out of a suitcase, travelling on buses or hanging around airports waiting to fly, on the road it's a routine you get into with a group of people or crew members following the same routine, it could be the same every day. Thank god I gave up whilst I still had my sanity and my hearing (what did you say?).

A sound mixer and effects rack at a typical club gig.

I didn't stop being involved in the music business totally, whilst talking to my barber I discovered he managed a band who did gigs around the pub circuit, he asked if I would come to one of their gigs and help them out with their sound as they were having problems setting up the mixer. Of course I obliged and had a fun evening out, although if felt a bit amateurish using small, low-budget equipment instead of using professional top-of-the-range equipment and of course I didn't have all the equipment I would have liked but I did what I could.

That wasn't the only time, another friend of a friend was in a group and heard about me and asked if I would come down and do the sound for their gig, a bigger band in a slightly bigger hall and they did have a have decent PA system for a small group. They were amazed at the difference I got out of the monitors, using one channel for FOH and one channel for monitors.

Another friend who I was working with also asked me to do their FOH sound in a club venue using an in-house sound system, which took me back to my club tour dates, working on a mixer that didn't have all the channels functioning properly, a multicore cable that didn't have all the lines working. I had to cross-patch wires to get all the mics working, they didn't even have a tech guy on duty to ask at the venue so I just did what I've always done to get it working. The speakers sounded terrible, a low end bass resonance that smothered everything and a high end that was so brittle it hurt your ears, but I did get the best out of the system that it was possible to get. I was told it sounded better than the last time the band performed at that venue which made me feel a little better.

But doing that last gig made me realise why I retired in the first place and it also made me realise that I didn't want to go back on the road and I didn't want to be trying to get a decent sound out of crap sound equipment. Doing that last gig was a chance for me to get the bug out of my system once and for all. I was grateful for having the opportunity to be able to do that.

Looking back I have no regrets. I'd seen Eric Clapton play with the Yardbirds, John Mayall and Cream and eventually did Eric's sound at my last ever gig, which was a good high to end on. I'd seen The Beatles at Hammersmith and Jim Morrison sing with the Doors at the Roundhouse and Pink Floyd perform '*Dark Side of the Moon*'.

Regrets, no, I've had a great life on the road, I've met people I wouldn't have met and been to some places many people wouldn't have even thought about going to. I wasn't the greatest soundman, nor was I the most successful, but I was one of the first and have done more than most have done.

I ask myself have I been successful. Well, I haven't worked in the premier league with The Beatles, Stones or Pink Floyd, but I have worked in the first division with many artistes who have been at the top with top-ten single hits and gold and platinum albums, and with artistes who sold out arena tours and so I consider I have done OK. Of course I could always have done better, but so could a lot of musicians who may only get a top-fifty hit once in their life.

So as I prepared for a graceful retirement, I put my laminated backstage tour passes away in a drawer, my faded tour jackets in a recycling bin and hung up my headphones. I'm now happily retired and living in the country with my wife Janice and I'm happy to pass the honours on to the next generation of soundmen to take the technology forward.

Me enjoying retirement with one of my ducks and my Bengal cat.

A selection of laminated tour passes

LONG LIVE ROCK'N'ROLL

Dedicated to my two children Tamzin and Alex who possibly wondered why Dad kept going off on tour.

To my wife Janice for putting up with me whilst I was writing this book and for the invaluable help and assistance in helping me getting it finished.

Evelyn Daley for proof reading the manuscript prior to publishing.

Andi Banks for helping me on so many tours right from the start.

All the guys at Concert Sound, Robert Collins, Jeff Hooper, Adrian Fitzpatrick, Kerry Lewis, Peter Grainger, Mick Anderson, Paul Boothroyd, Dave Catlin, Rory Madden, Steve May, Dave Dickson, Tim Boyle and the back-up team in the warehouse.

Dennis Locorriere and the Dr Hook band together with Nineyear Wooldridge and the crew for all the Dr Hook tours.

Alan Hull, Ray Jackson, Ray Laidlaw, Rod Clements, Simon Cowe and Marty Craggs for giving me so much pleasure working with Lindisfarne for 12 years.

At Colac, Scott Thompson and Clive Davis for all the work in the early days.

At Midas, Geoff Byers, Chas Brook and Nigel for developing the greatest sound mixing consoles ever and allowing me to work there.

Dave Martin at Martin Audio for all the help and advice and for producing the legendary Martin sound system.

Jim Moore, who now looks after my sound system at Nitelites Sound and Light.

All the bands I worked with along the way too numerous to mention but I have to include Lindisfarne, Dr Hook, Thin Lizzy, Black Sabbath, Renaissance and Vinegar Joe as the bands I spent most time with and all the crew members that went along with them.

For more information about the author go to
Website: http://soundmanwilf.wixsite.com/johnwilford
Email: soundman.wilf@gmail.com

TECHNICAL GLOSSARY

The meaning and an explanation in easy language of what does what, why and how.

ANALOGUE. A device which can transfer an electrical signal into an audio signal and vice versa such as a microphone, loudspeaker, tape recorder, radio, record player or guitar. A device that is not digital.

AUXILIARY MIX. As well as the stereo left and right mix for the PA there are also four or eight Auxiliary mixes on the microphone channel. These can be used to send a mix to an echo, reverb or other effects unit or to the on-stage monitors or a separate mix to a recording device.

COMPRESSOR. This will compress the sound to the maximum level you set it at, no matter how high you turn up the volume it will not go any higher than the level you set, you can also set the attack time, decay time, threshold and compression ratio.

CROSSOVER. This will separate the main mix into separate frequency bands, between two to five bands, this will usually consist of sub-bass, bass, low-mid, high-mid and high. The reason we separate the bands is that each frequency is sent to different speaker cabinets that are designed for that particular frequency. In the early days crossovers were just two-way passive, then came electronic crossovers where each frequency band was separated, two-way crossovers led onto three-way and then to four-way and as technology improved eventually to five-way for a more precise separation of frequencies.

DAT (DIGITAL AUDIO TAPE). A cassette-based tape recorder which records information in digital form like a CD. This allows music to be recorded onto magnetic tape without the old hiss and hum from older analogue cassette tapes. The technology has now been surpassed by mp3 recorders.

DELAY LINE. Used when you want to delay the signal, a short delay will give you a single repeat you could use for double tracking a vocal or guitar, or sending a mix to a delay tower at the back of a field.

DELAY TOWER. A PA system some distance from the main stage PA, so people at the back of festival sites can hear the music without deafening those at the front. The sound is delayed using a delay line so the sound from the stage PA reaches the listener at the same time as delay tower PA.

DI BOX (DIRECT INJECTION BOX). Used to plug your guitar or keyboard directly into the mixer without going through a speaker or a microphone. This has two benefits: one, you get a clean sound direct from the instrument and secondly the microphone doesn't pick up any other noise from the stage. It is also possible to take a signal from the back of the amplifier, thereby getting the distortion that the guitarist creates on his amplifier without the distortion of the speaker.

DIGITAL. Has many definitions but in relation to sound, it is any device that is programmable by computer technology. Displays are shown in numerical form rather than a number on a dial.

ECHO. First used by feeding the recorded sound back into the input to get a repeat of the original sound slightly delayed. By sending the original sound back into a tape recorder a second time you get a second echo and that turns into a third echo and so on. The digital delay devices of today can set your delay or echo times down to the exact milliseconds.

EFFECTS UNIT. Outboard effects for live concerts started to grow in the early 1970s, the front-of-house rack would typically include a graphic equaliser, a Roland space echo and a reverb unit. Now we have compressors, noise gates, harmonisers and anything else to process the sound.

EQ (EQUALISER OR EQUALISATION) Where you control the tone of the sound by adding or subtracting frequencies from bass through to treble.

FEEDBACK. A microphone will pick up the sound it hears and amplify it into a loudspeaker. When a microphone is turned up too loud, the sound coming from the speaker is picked up by the microphone and amplified back into the speaker again creating a continuous loop, which will eventually take off causing a squealing or howling sound.

FOH (FRONT OF HOUSE). That's the position of the sound mixer used for mixing the sound for the audience, usually at the back of a small hall or in the middle of a large hall. FOH can also refer to the area in the foyer of a theatre front of house.

FOLDBACK. First used in recording studios so the control room can talk to those in the studio. In live sound it means the main sound mixer can talk to those on the stage and send a monitor mix or foldback mix to the stage.

GRAPHIC EQUALISER. On your home hi-fi you probably have two tone controls, bass and treble, now extend that to 30 tone controls, each one covering one third of an octave. A graphic equaliser has a spectrum of 10 octaves and these are divided up into 3 frequencies giving you 30 bands of tone control, each one can cut or boost by 12 decibels with a fader. This is where the soundman earns his money, you must be able to pick out a frequency from the 30 faders on the graphic equaliser. It's all a matter of knowing your frequencies and identifying them.

HARMONISER. Sometimes called a Pitch Changer. A device which changes the pitch of the note. If applied to a vocal mic will give the impression of a chorus of backing singers, beware not to overdo it or it will sound false. Also very good on a saxophone to give it a full sound.

IMPEDANCE. This is the AC resistance of an electronic circuit, which is determined by DC resistance, inductance and capacitance. A loudspeaker cabinet will have an impedance of 8 ohms but that is not the same as DC resistance because of components in its circuit.

LIMITER. This is similar to a compressor except it just limits the sound to the maximum you set it to without compressing the sound. The distinction between Compressor and Limiter has been confused in the past, but to me a Limiter will prevent the overall sound from 'overshooting' the desired maximum level, a Compressor will actually 'compress' a signal the more you increase it.

LINE CHECK. Means checking that the microphone and instrument lines (wires) from the stage to the mixer are working correctly.

MICROPHONES (Mics). In brief there are two basic types of microphone.

Condenser microphones, which are sub divided into Dynamic mics and Ribbon mics. They vary between large diaphragm condensers you see in recording studios and cost more than a small car, and small diaphragm condensers you would use on an acoustic guitar or for cymbals.

Dynamic microphones are the second type, which are the backbone of the stage set. The ultimate standard mic that's been used since the year dot is the familiar Shure SM58, and its sister the SM57. If you don't have any other mics to choose from you can do a whole show with just these two types of microphone.

There are specialist mics, for example, clip-on drum mics which look more discreet and are easier to fit; clip-on mics for saxophones so they can move around; head mics for singers who want to dance and have two hands free; radio mics also allow you to roam around without being plugged in by a cable.

MIDI (MUSICAL INSTRUMENT DIGITAL INTERFACE). This is a standard protocol used to connect similar MIDI electronic musical devices and computers together, so they can communicate with each other. It allows one device to be controlled from another, which reduces the amount of different instruments musicians have to carry. All connected together by a standard MIDI cable. A common use would be to connect several keyboards together.

MONITOR MIXER. A sound mixer similar to the front of house mixer except it's designed for eight or more different mixes which are sent to different monitor speakers around the stage for different musicians or to monitors worn in-ear.

MONITOR SPEAKER. Also known as Monitor Wedge. That's the wedge-shaped speaker cabinet usually seen spread across the stage so the musicians can hear more of themselves and select the level of other musicians on stage.

NOISE GATE. As the name implies this is a gate which can open and close a microphone. Typically used on a drum kit, the gate will be closed until the drum is hit, the sound of the drum will open the gate allowing the sound to pass through and will immediately close again. You can set the opening speed and the closing speed, a quick closing speed will sound like a sharp cut-off of the drum, and a slow closing speed will allow the drum sound to decay away naturally before closing shut. It's used to prevent microphones picking up unwanted or stray noises from other instruments.

NOTCH FILTER (or Comb Filter). This is similar to a parametric equaliser but with a much tighter bandwidth, you can literally pinpoint a single frequency instead of a wide bandwidth involving other frequencies and eliminate it, down to one tenth of an octave. There are generally eight filters in a single unit, so eight separate frequencies can be selected and dealt with, good for eliminating annoying bass frequencies and standing waves in large halls without reducing the overall bass punch.

PA (PUBLIC ADDRESS). A device to amplify sound using a microphone, an amplifier and loudspeakers. The term has changed over the years, once used in public areas it was originally used just for speech announcements. PA now refers to any type of sound amplification including live stage sound. Sometimes confused with 'Sound Reinforcement', which generally refers to amplifying vocals and instruments for a live band.

PARAMETRIC EQUALISER. This is the same as the tone controls you have on a microphone channel, it does a similar job to a graphic equaliser except you don't have faders, you have rotary knobs with additional switches for the frequency you want to select and change. You can widen or narrow the bandwidth of a single frequency down to 0.1 octave to affect only that narrow notch. Good for taking out a very narrow bandwidth.

PFL (PRE FADE LISTEN). This switch allows to you listen to the sound before the fader is opened up, you hear it before the audience does so you can make adjustments before committing the sound to the mix. Also allows you to see the signal on a VU meter or LED light bar to set the level of the signal coming in.

PINK NOISE. In audio applications, pink noise is used as a reference tone to check frequency responses and is particularly useful when used with a 1/3 octave spectrum analyser. I use a pink noise generator to check the system is sounding flat in each room that means equal at all frequencies, some rooms are more susceptible to certain frequencies than others. Pink noise is a random signal, with equal energy on each octave and has equal power in all bandwidths. Not to be confused with white noise.

POTENTIOMETERS (POTS). These are rotary controls with a knob similar to a conventional volume control.

REVERB. When the signal is delayed by 0.1 millisecond and repeated. Creates cathedral-type acoustics and gives extra depth to a voice, especially nice on an acoustic guitar or saxophone. Before digital echo and electronic reverb machines were invented record companies would put a microphone in the bathroom to create that live reverberation effect. The reverb chambers at Motown and Hollywood studios were rooms with a loudspeaker at one end and a microphone at the other, the sound coming from the speaker was then mixed with the original sound.

SIGNAL PROCESSOR. Does everything a crossover does with the additional luxury of digital technology. You can select frequencies where you want to crossover each channel, cut, boost and adjust bandwidth and with digital touch control buttons and a digital display you can easily shape the sound you require.

SUB-GROUP. Used to group a few or several channels together so that one sub group can control numerous channels on just one fader. Typically used to control several drum mics onto one group, or all backing singers together.

VCAs (VOLTAGE CONTROLLED AMPLIFIERS). Are used to control a group of faders with just one fader. Similar to a sub-group except a sub-group only affects the level of that fader and not the post-fade mixes. A VCA affects the gain on the whole channel.

WHITE NOISE. Random signals at different frequencies all having the same intensity. Someone once asked me what the difference was between white noise and pink noise. My interpretation is that white noise is a random signal of random frequencies at random levels. Pink noise is where all frequencies are the same level per octave across the spectrum, showing up as flat responses on a spectrum analyser. To the human ear, which processes frequencies logarithmically, pink noise is supposed to sound even across all frequencies, so white noise will sound louder at higher frequencies.

PHOTOGRAPHS

All pictures are taken from the author's private collection except those listed below.

Front Cover	3x	John Wilford
	1x	Lindisfarne Musical Productions
Chapter 5	Soft Machine.	Mark Ellen
Chapter 9	Vinegar Joe	BrianCooke.com
Chapter 12	Cozy Powell's Hammer	RAK Records
Chapter 19	Lindisfarne. NCH	Lindisfarne Musical Productions
	Lindisfarne. NCH	Lindisfarne Musical Productions
Chapter 20	Rock on the Tyne Poster	Barry McKay
	Rock on the Tyne festival	Jonathan Brown
Chapter 23	Lindisfarne band & crew	Lindisfarne Musical Productions
Chapter 27	Concert Sound Amp Racks	Tim Boyle
	Royal Albert Hall	Tim Boyle

The Author

John Wilford, also known as 'Wilf', was born in Palmers Green, North London in 1948. He left school at 14 and started work in a company building lighting equipment where he learnt how to wire circuits and read schematic diagrams. At 16 he started an apprenticeship at an electrical repair shop repairing radios, televisions, record players and tape recorders. He attended Southgate Technical College where he gained City and Guilds certificates in Radio, Television and Electronics Servicing.

In 1965 he joined a semi-pro group as a roadie setting up their equipment. In 1969 he went full-time, professionally working as a sound engineer with British bands touring the UK and Europe.

In 1972 he joined Midas Amplification where he built sound mixing consoles for many famous touring artistes including Pink Floyd's Quadraphonic mixing desk. In 1974 he was offered a job with Colosseum Acoustics, a sound rental company, as a sound engineer where he took large sound systems on tour around Europe with many well-known British and American artistes, eventually setting up his own sound company in Nashville, USA, which he later sold to his partner.

He also worked freelance as a tour manager, production manager and sound engineer with other sound companies including Entec and Concert Sound touring with internationally known artistes on world tours. After a brief venture where he built and ran his own sound company in Newcastle, England, he sold that and returned to Concert Sound where he remained until retiring in 1995.

For more information about the author go to:
Website: http://soundmanwilf.wixsite.com/johnwilford
Email: soundman.wilf@gmail.com